CREATIVE LAND

CREATIVE LAND

Place and procreation on the
Rai Coast of Papua New Guinea

James Leach

Berghahn Books
New York • Oxford

First published in 2003 by

Berghahn Books
www.berghahnbooks.com

© 2003 James Leach

Library of Congress Cataloging-in-Publication Data
Creative land: place and procreation on the Rai Coast of Papua New Guinea
/ James Leach.
    p. cm.
    Includes bibliographical references and index.
    ISBN 1-57181-556-2 (cloth : alk. paper)
        1. Nekgini (Papua New Guinea people)--Kinship. 2. Nekgini (Papua
New Guinea people)--Economic Conditions. 3. Human ecology--Papua
New Guinea—Madang Province. I. Title.

DU740.42. I42 2003
306.83'089'9912--dc21   2002034456

British Library Cataloguing in Publication Data
A catalogue record for this book is available from the British Library.

Printed in the United States on acid-free paper
ISBN 1–57181–556–2 hardback

For Cathie Gibson

In memory of my grandfather T.J. Gibson

Contents

List of Maps, Figures, Tables, and Photographs	ix
Acknowledgements	xi
Notes on the Text	xv
Preface	xvii
Introduction	**1**
The Rai Coast	1
Chapter 1: Process and Kinship	**21**
Kinship, Process, and Creativity	22
Cognation and Flexibility	26
An Alternative to the Genealogical Model	29
The Palem	31
Chapter 2: Residence History and Palem	**33**
Hamlets Past and Present	33
Hamlets as Social Groups	41
The Labours of Lawrence	49
Complexity	52
Chapter 3: Marrying Sisters	**57**
Defining Relationships	57
Myths and Explanations	75
Chapter 4: Gardens, Land, and Growth	**91**
Origin Points	92

Gendered Productivity: The Tambaran 93
Households and Gardens 100
Gardening, not 'Production' 101
Gardens, Land, and Substance 114
Male Continuity, Female Movement 118

Chapter 5: Birth, Emergence, and Exchange 127
The Transactions Between Affinal Kin Focused on Children 128
Mother's Brothers in the Anthropological Literature 143
Affinal Payments and Lineality in Reite 145
Visibility and Recognition 151

Chapter 6: Spirit, Flesh, and Bone 159
The Palem as a Body 159
Performing Places. People and Spirits as Land Made Mobile 177

Chapter 7: Places and Bodies, Landscape and Perception 193
The Concept of Landscape in Anthropology 196
Hearing and Vision as Sensory Modalities 201
Landscape in the Nekgini Lifeworld 206

Chapter 8: Creative Land 211
Land, Place, and Person 211
Simple Principles, Complex Process 215
Creativity 216

Glossary 219
References 221
Index 229

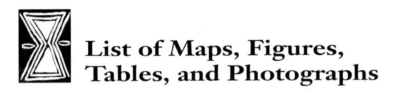

List of Maps, Figures, Tables, and Photographs

Maps

Map 1: Madang and the Rai Coast   2

Map 2: Reite and Neighbouring Hamlets Showing Spirit Places   36

Map 3: Some Previous Palem Sites of Ripia and Reite   37

Figures

Figure 2.1: Kinship in Saruk Hamlet 1994/95   47

Figure 3.1: Nekgini Sibling/Parallel Cousin Terminology   58

Figure 3.2: Nekgini Cross-cousin Terminology   59

Figure 3.3: Three Ways of Reckoning One Relationship   63

Figure 3.4: How P Comes to Have Maternal Uncles   65

Figure 4.1: Divisions within a Garden   107

Figure 6.1: *Turum Maliemung*: The Palem as Body Parts   163

Tables

Table 3.1: Payments Related to Marriage among Nekgini Speakers   67

Table 3.2: Marriages Made by People Still Alive and Resident in
Reite Hamlets (Men) or Born There (Women) [1994]   69

Table 4.1: Numbers of Root and Other Crops Planted in a Garden   110

Table 5.1: Life-cycle Payments Made Prior to Marriage among
          Nekgini Speakers   129

Photographs

1: Looking North over Reite Lands from the Coastal Hills   7

2: The Palem. A Construction of Wood, Wealth, and Garden Food   20

3: The Komiti of Reite, Porer Nombo   35

4: Taro Garden after Four Months Growth   92

5: 'Mother' and 'Child' Taro Tubers   103

6: The *Wating* of a New Taro Garden   105

7: The *Wating* is Tidied Before Harvest   112

8: *Samat Matakaring*. Katak and Taropang Demonstrate the Taro *Patuki*   120

9: A Payment Given Away 'On the Ground', Serieng, 1994   130

10: *Palieng*. Body Decoration and Exchange Valuables   136

11: *Zingsung*. The Payment of *Pununung* to a Mother's Brother   141

12: *Torr* Post Carried in *Sare*   142

13: Sarangama Receive a Palem from Asang, 1999   160

14: Winedum of Sarangama   164

15: Palota Strips the Mast of its Flesh   174

16: Sarangama Dancing Group Lit by a Flaming Torch, 2000   178

Acknowledgements

It is a challenge to write satisfactorily about the help given, and care shown to me, by people in Reite and Sarangama. Words just do not match the actions, or the memory. Naming some people will inevitably leave out others, and I have received friendship, support, gifts, nurture, food and company from hundreds of people on the Rai Coast. Reite people fed me with their best foods, and treated me with great politeness, care, and concern. They showed what others have called 'patience' as informants as well as sympathy as friends. My joy throughout has been that many people there have been happy with the understanding of their *kastom* that we reached together. Whether this work makes sense as an account is my responsibility. What I cannot take credit for, but which gives me more satisfaction, is the consensus that the understanding we reached made sense at the time of our meeting.

My great debt to Porer Nombo is made evident in the text. I thank him most sincerely for intellectual companionship as well as material and emotional support. Pinabin Sisau and I have become brothers. He is a paragon of thoughtfulness, of generosity, and of good humour. I must also mention (in spite of my hesitation above), with love, Yamui, Palota, Gayap, Nangu, Sangumae, Rikrikiang, Karup, Siriman, Winedum, Kambuing, Katak, Hungeme, Poiyong, Salong, and Kumbu. This acknowledgement, however, is to all Reite.

Aiparieng aisimung tapani nam sas, na karmung nana yaan apumo. Na uwie yeye nalokina ya rinunukung. Na po wasireri nete sarikete rop kaka. Na po wasireri kaapu rata tawunerekung. Na alowokutu tapaning yeenung yaning tangawaketemu. Ya rinunuye nukin totungo yewokata nana yapikeina utemo. Na yewokata uwaytung yo api yeng uwaytung.

My time on the Rai Coast, and in the academy, has been made possible by some wonderful people; teachers, colleagues, and friends. Since our first meeting, which I remember vividly in both instances, Tim Ingold, and then Marilyn Strathern, have been truly inspirational teachers. The only drawback to adopting such mentors is one can never equal their achievements. Instead I record my profound sense of gratitude for their brilliance, their industry, and their generosity. Marilyn Strathern has continued to provide close intellectual leadership, and friendship, for which I am most grateful. Jimmy Weiner has also been a great teacher, corresponding with me in a most enlightening manner while I was in the field, and since by discussing this work. In this vein I also thank Mike O'Hanlon, Simon Harrison, Eric Hirsch, Harri Englund, Stuart Kirsch, Peter Gow, Edwardo Viveiros de Castro, and Dick Werbner. Lissant Bolton, Joachim Görlich, James Carrier, Jeanette Edwards, Martin Holbraad, Rebecca Cassidy, and Andrew Moutu have kindly commented on parts of the text.

I have accumulated many happy memories while doing this work. 'A friend in need…', they say, and I have certainly been in need over the years. Lorna Matheson, Robert Storrie and Lissant Bolton were marvellous during the crazy time prior to my initial departure. Ariane and Gilbert Lewis supplied painting materials, contacts, and good advice. I thank Tess Tinker, and Nico Lewis for visiting me in Reite, and Kirsten MacLeod for trying to keep my initial writing about Reite true to my experience. Tancred Dyke-Wells, and more recently Bruce Godfrey, have generously spent hours assisting with the illustrations. I also thank Charles Grey, Peter Livesey, Patrick Eady and David Ellis for their kindness, good sense and friendship.

Fleur and Red Rodgers have supported me throughout my writing. They have also spent time with me in Reite, and we have grown together. Fleur has provided comment, and also helped practically with the text. For this and all the other large and small things, I am enormously grateful.

The book is dedicated to my mother in recognition of all her hard work (as they would say in Reite), of her intellectual and moral guidance, and of her unflagging support. It is to the memory of her father, who also knew and loved New Guinea.

On my initial arrival in Madang, I was taken in by Moses Sihungu Luluaki and his wife Elizabeth. My thanks go to them and their children (Nangwaro, Nigel, and Kilux) for their wonderful hospitality. Siem Yarumbie's house in Madang became my home from home while living in Reite. The generosity and thoughtful care of Siem and his family have been humbling. I also thank Siem for his support of my work in his village.

I was extremely fortunate to meet Peter and Edith Nombo in Saidor. Peter's advice and support have been invaluable over the years. Tom Yangoi was my first friend on the Rai Coast, and I am continually grateful for his and his wife Teres's efforts on my behalf. His younger brother, John Samiti, also became my friend. He and his gentle wife Bernadette (who tragically died while giving birth to their fourth child in 2001) made me comfortable in their house while my own was built. I remember the time with happiness. Tom's other brothers, Steven and Timothy, along with Albert Samaik, assisted me in my travels around the Rai Coast. I also thank Balbal and his wife Anawae (Malalamai) who fed me and let me stay in their house on numerous occasions while I waited for the ship to Madang.

The Economic and Social Research Council of Great Britain funded the research for this book; initially through a Research Studentship, and more recently through fieldwork funds directed through the research project, 'Property, Transactions and Creations: New Economic Relations in the Pacific'. I am grateful to the members of this project for stimulation and assistance, particularly Tony Crook, with whom I spent time in Port Moresby. I am also grateful to The Leverhulme Trust for a Special Research Fellowship which I took up at the University of Cambridge, and during which I prepared the manuscript. I also thank the Cambridge Department of Social Anthropology, and the Isaac Newton Trust for their support.

In Papua New Guinea I have benefited from affiliation to the Cultural Studies Division (now Institute of Papua New Guinea Studies) of the National Research Institute (NRI), and in particular from meeting Don Niles there. More recently I was a Visiting Research Fellow at the NRI, and I thank the Director, Dr Boeha, Colin Filer and all the staff. I am grateful to Madang Provincial Government, and especially the office of Environment and Planning, for allowing me to undertake fieldwork in Madang Province.

Notes on the Text

This book contains words in the Non-Austronesian vernacular language of Reite villagers. This language is called 'Nekgini'. It is indicated by *italics*.

It also contains words in the *lingua franca* of Papua New Guinea, Neo-Melanesian. This language is called Tok Pisin. Tok Pisin words are indicated through italics followed by 'T.P.' I do not Anglicise words in these languages, thus there is no addition of an 's' to indicate a plural.

My orthography for Tok Pisin is based on *The Jacaranda Dictionary and Grammar of Melanesian Pidgin* (1971), by F. Mihalic.

I spell Nekgini words phonetically, following customary English usage for simplicity. For the pronunciation of Nekgini words, the following points may be noted: *ae* at the end of a word is pronounced as is the 'ay' in 'hay'. Apostrophes within words indicate a pause, although of less duration than those between words.

Preface

People of the Rai Coast of Papua New Guinea have been made famous for their innovative interpretations of colonialism. Peter Lawrence's *Road Belong Cargo* (1964) introduced one character in particular who is enduringly associated with what have been known as 'cargo cults', and who embodies for many the contradictory fascinations of those Melanesian phenomena. That character was Yali Singina. Yali's name is still often heard, both on the Rai Coast, and among anthropologists; cargo movements remain staples of anthropological writing and teaching (Lindstrom 1999). What interests us so much about cargo cult?[1] That it is a (critical) perspective on colonialism and globalisation? That it deconstructs Western relationships of production and power? That it makes plain the consequences of interpretations based on cultural suppositions? Most of all, perhaps, we are fascinated by the creative moment apparent in new combinations. One 'culture' meets another, and innovative thinking is the outcome (Leip 2001: 7). The subjects of this book are already known for their creativeness.

While aware of this history, cargo cults were not the focus of my research. There is no linear relationship between this book and the literature on cargo movements, and I do not set out to complete the historical record about such things. Yet there are themes present in both the literature on cargo, and in the present work which have crept up on me. This book takes creative endeavour in the making of people, and the emergence of places, as its theme. On reflection, I realise that I have written about a particular approach to producing persons and things, one which relies upon discussing a version of the creative engagement already apparent in Lawrence's narrative.

The book outlines one instance of a kind of creativity which could be found in many societies. It is not unique to Reite people among whom I lived. That creativity lies in innovation through combination, and recombination. Yet it has a specific, and long-established, salience in the lives of these people which goes beyond the interpretation of colonialism. In general terms, novelty is only apparent with convention as its background; and to distinguish anything from its background, its source, is to make difference (Wagner 1975). As the ethnography presented here shows, this is not a neutral act. Making difference, or encompassing difference to make sameness, has consequences which find their register in the connections between persons, and between persons and things. In terms particular to this ethnography, to claim agency, belonging, or power is predicated on the division of the world into kinds of things; into genders, places, and persons who know one another as different. Thus knowing creativity as combination in Rai Coast terms is also knowing (and manipulating) the separation of things in the world.

The way I make the particularly Rai Coast approach to creativity apparent is through a theoretical focus on process, combined with an ethnographic focus on what people term *kastom* [T.P.]. Reite people incorporate bodies into places and places into persons. They are motivated in doing so by seeking to make effective social forms. In turn, they work to separate these forms into their constituent or potential parts in order to complete new combinations. The work of creation is never complete, and entities appear within the process as moments of reification. Their dissolution is of as much note as their coming into being; and thus power is shown through managing these reifications. Experiencing creativity as generation (the power to reproduce persons) which may incorporate novelty (innovation in social, ritual, and magical form) is described by Reite people as made possible by following kastom.

The translation which these people most consistently gave to express the popular Neo Melanesian (pidgin) term 'kastom' in their vernacular (Nekgini) was *turum maliemung*. Literally translated, this means 'gathering things together [to give away]'. The reference is to the gathering and giving of food and wealth to affinal kinspeople, in exchanges that result from marriage. Kastom in this case appears not as a reification of the past, but as a description of what is known in the present about the process by which (in this instance, affinal) relations are managed; and *turum maliemung* is a description of combination. Reite people approach the world as a whole, as it were, from this position. They are self-consciously 'kastom people'. They articulate their history as one which has produced them as living by kastom, while others have abandoned the practices associated with elaborated ancestral knowledge. This book describes the mechanisms of combination and separation which embody that creativity.

On my arrival, I was informed that Reite people followed kastom, and that I had come to the right place to conduct my research. Having experienced missionisation in the middle years of the last century, they had collectively decided to reject the mission, and live by kastom. Yet it must be pointed out that this 'return' also involved some creative thinking. The kastom advocated by followers of Yali combined Christian, colonial, and local imagery. People sought an effective mode of gaining a measure of control over the world, and were not rigid in experimenting with what might prove effective. As it turned out, cults on the Rai Coast also failed to bring the changes their adherents greatly desired, although it is not unusual to hear the claim that Yali or one of his followers brought about National Independence.

For this and other reasons, the practices-as-kastom Reite people are interested in today are not necessarily the same set of practices-as-kastom which Peter Lawrence encountered. Understandings of kastom and its value have developed over the last forty years. For a major segment of the population of Reite, it has nothing to do with the supernatural generation of wealth. Neither is it a traditionalist revival as is reported by other authors for other parts of Melanesia (e.g. Jolly and Thomas 1992, Keesing and Tonkinson 1982). In other areas, kastom has become a part of a nationalist discourse (see, for example, Van Trease 1987, Bolton 1999). In Reite, it has its own inflection. Generally meaning 'the correct way of doing things', kastom is best glossed for Reite people as 'effective practice (as known in a particular place)'. It is valued as part of what we might call a 'generative approach' to the production of persons, social units, productive difference, knowledge, and so forth. Much of kastom, therefore, has to do with the attraction, generation, growth and incorporation of people. It in no way excludes the outside world, or delimits the interests people have, as a traditionalist revival might be expected to (Keesing 1992).

Historical factors then have influenced how Reite people's own emphasis on combination appears today. In parallel, they have adopted and adapted a language with which to turn this emphasis into claims upon one another. That is the language of kastom. If Reite people's interest in kastom is, in fact, with its power to generate productive relationships, then it can be seen as an approach which has its precedent in the literature, without being the same thing (cargo cult). Thus here I am, two generations on from Lawrence, writing about what was a cargo cult village, and producing a story about an approach to kinship which makes creativity central, and innovation quotidian. Pursuing the value of novel combination also makes sense of another vital aspect of my experience; the interest Nekgini speakers showed in developing a relationship with me.

While I have leaned about kastom, and thus become progressively incorporated in what people do there, my collaborators have shown great interest in learning about the possibilities for bringing elements together, putting things in context, and relating apparently disparate images into a coherent whole. They have, in other words, become interested in the potential of anthropology. My relationships have developed on this basis to a position where anthropological analysis itself plays a part in our conversation. In discussing kastom with certain interested people in Reite, and one in particular, I have presented the analytic insights the anthropological method can bring to Reite practice. Finding 'meaning' (a knowledge of the reasons things appear as they do), is akin to finding 'power' in such practice. It is an acknowledgement of its coherence and thus a confirmation of the validity and effectiveness of a way of living. In argument and collaboration on this basis, Reite people themselves have found interest in the work we have done together. It may be noted here how different this interest is from that reported by Keesing (1992). Achieving codification of laws in emulation of colonial or government categories is not what motivates Reite people's interest in our collaboration.

Contemporary Reite does not have a 'cult' leader, but it does have intelligent and interested leaders who, relying on their assumption of novel combination, were willing to welcome and teach me. Rai Coast people's ability to make me a part of the place, and in doing so develop this innovative form of combination, speaks of the theme of the book. It is their kastom. Of course, none of us had much idea of what would come out of it. Initially their interest was manifest simply in drawing me into the place.

Note

1. Among those who have asked this question recently is Lindstrom (1993).

Introduction

The Rai Coast

In December 1993, I arrived in Madang on the tropical north coast of Papua New Guinea, with the idea of finding a field site somewhere in the group of islands lying off that coast in the Vitiaz Strait. From Madang, the obvious choice was Arop, or 'Long Island', a destination I had picked out while still in England. Arop lies around 40 km from the Rai Coast, and 80 km from Madang town. I was already changing my plans though.

Through introductions made by my new friend Moses (who worked for the town council and thus knew many people)[1] it appeared transport to and from the island was erratic, or expensive, or both. Saidor, situated along the coast and nearer to the island, gave me something to aim for. Perhaps there was transport from there. If not, at least I would not be kicking my heels in this strange mixture of a town, which was unsettling me by its combination of expensive hotels, quiet pretty streets lined with Bougainvillaea and Frangipani, intense heat, and unfathomable mixtures of people. The latter was what I had come for, yet this seemed a frontier town, located between the familiar model of northern Australia, and something inaccessible, embodied by the majority of the people I saw there. The Rai Coast had also been of interest in my pre-field reading, and anxious to achieve something, I made up my mind to visit it.

With Moses' help, I arrived on the right bit of concrete wharf in Madang's extensive and many-bayed harbour to board the MV *Nara* to Saidor. Moses had telephoned the District Administrator (D.A.) in Saidor on my behalf the previous day, and warned him of my arrival. I had no idea of the kind of journey involved, nor of how long it would take. Being unused to the rhythm of such journeys (something that was to change soon enough) I had armed myself only with a bottle of mineral water, a novel, and a sleeping roll. I expected to arrive in Saidor, discuss my proposed research with the D.A., and perhaps even make it back to Madang by light aircraft the same day.

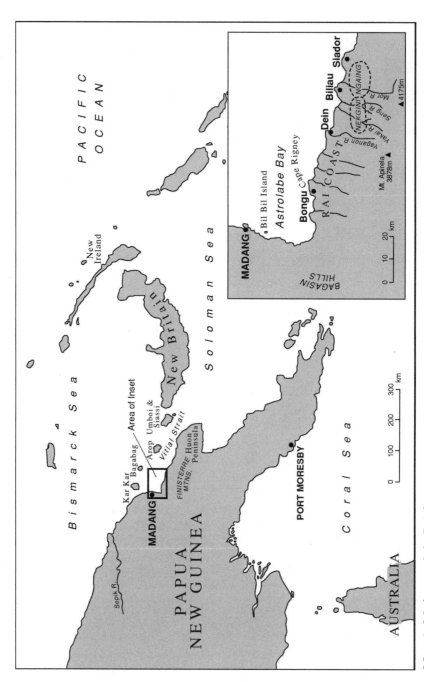

Map 1 *Madang and the Rai Coast*

MV *Nara* was the 15m, steel-hulled diesel launch belonging to Lagap Plantations. It ran (and still did in 2001) between Saidor and Madang carrying copra and passengers to town, and 'store cargo' of rice, tinned meat and fish, biscuits and batteries back to the company store located between the plantation and the outskirts of the station. Other store-keepers from the hinterland around Saidor used the boat for the same purpose: carrying goods from town to stock their businesses. Arriving early in the morning (there being no specified departure time), I sat aboard the boat in anticipation of movement, periodically shifting from one perch to the next as I found myself in the way of loading. I became concerned as the morning passed. Each time I thought we were preparing to depart, that the hold must be full, another truck arrived and hundreds of bails of rice and cartons were loaded. Also, embarrassed at my inactivity in the midst of such labours, I tried to help at times with the loading. I later discovered that this confirmed peoples' suspicions that I was connected in some way to the white man, 'Bill', who ran Lagap plantation. The captain and crew were impressive to watch, the tattooed captain looking like a true sea-dog with a long black beard, and his shirtless crew displaying powerful physiques. The heat and grime of the boat and the long wait were balanced by the excitement of being in the midst of something of which, as I began to realise, I had no understanding. Time (Telban 1998: 43) was my most obvious confusion that day, but my misunderstanding regarding departure pointed to other aspects of the journey which, it belatedly dawned upon me, were not within my control.

Nara left well after midday, the deck, and the roof of the wheelhouse covered with tightly packed passengers; women with babies and small children, old men grasping canvas holdalls and string bags, younger men chewing betel nut and laughing together. We were cramped up, the hull low in the water, as the diesel engine thumped laboriously through the entrance to Madang harbour and out into the open crystal-blue sea. The vista of the Rai Coast mountains, blue and hazy in the distance, opened up as the backdrop to the plodding boat which appeared to stand still in relation to all around.

The Rai Coast is the narrow land which falls from the steep and rugged Finisterre mountains to the sea in Madang Province, on the northern edge of the mainland of Papua New Guinea (see Map 1). It begins at Astrolabe Bay (where the Russian scientist Michlouho-Maclay first landed at the village of Bongu, in 1871), 30 km south of Madang town, and the name is applied to the coast as far as the border of Morobe Province, more than 100 km to the east. The coastal plain is narrow, hemmed in by the mountains which rise steeply to peaks reaching as high as 4000 m, at some points within 25 km of the coast. The terrain is characterised by the fast-flowing rivers which pour from the high mountains, cutting deep channels between sharp forested ridges, as they rush from the heights. This series of parallel ridges, which run roughly south to north towards the coast, make travel in the area difficult everywhere except adjacent to the shore. Even here, for all but the dry season between May and October, the flooding rivers make travel hazardous.

In pre-colonial days, the coastal people of this area were connected to the islands just south of Madang town (Bilbil, Yabob) as ports of call made on sea-going trading expeditions from these islands (Finsch 1996). Thus they were part of the Vitiaz Straits trading system. This system incorporated people as far afield as West New Britain, and the eastern tip of the Huon Peninsular (Harding 1967; 1985), and relied upon large-masted sailing canoes with outriggers, their sides built up with planks. People inhabiting the coastal hinterland and the mountain ridges tended to have 'trade friends' on the coast (Lawrence, 1964: 27), which could be reached by following their respective ridges straight down to the sea and were thus also part of the system that moved shells and clay pots into the mountains, and feathers, dogs' teeth, and wooden bowls to the coast. However, they made little contact with those to the east or west of them, due both to the difficulties of travel and to mutual hostility and fear between small language groups. The coast has a markedly seasonal climate, with north-westerly winds ('Rai' winds as they are known locally) prevailing during the dry season between May and October, and easterly winds (or 'Talio') for the rainy months of November to April.

During 1994/95, the coast (away from Saidor with its airstrip and plantation boat) was serviced irregularly by small boats which collected copra and passengers roughly once a week for the sea voyage to Madang. It was also connected to Madang by a road (the grandly named Saidor-Madang Highway) built along the coast, although this road was only used for a few months of the year. The ferocity of the rivers flowing from the mountains during the wet season each year prevents the construction of lasting bridges, and thus the road could be used only when fording these rivers by motor vehicle was practical.

People seated around me on the MV *Nara* were not unfriendly; but I did not have enough confidence in Tok Pisin[2] at this point to initiate conversation, and they left me to myself as I surveyed the approaching coast with wonder, and watched people around me open and drink green coconut, chew betel, and roll long cigarettes out of newspaper. From mid-afternoon on we tracked along the coast. Close enough to see into the mountainous forested interior, I plucked up courage to ask my fellow passengers if there were people and villages there. 'Oh yes', they replied, 'lots of villages', in a rapid-fire Tok Pisin that despite their obvious willingness to talk, made me even more reticent than before.

By dusk, with no sign of our destination, I began to feel really concerned. Here we were, teetering across the open sea, with the rapidly darkening coast showing no signs that it was going to offer a comfortable haven after what had turned into a marathon day already. By 1993, Papua New Guinea had a reputation for highway robbery and violence. I heard (perhaps half imagined) talk around me of criminal gangs (*raskals* [T.P.]), and looked nervously at the fires that occasionally twinkled across the sea from the coast. I had been in Papua New Guinea only two weeks, and that spent in towns. That morning, thinking a pleasant couple of hours across Astrolabe Bay, on something resembling a pleasure steamer, would bring me to Saidor in time to organise accommodation, I was unprepared for arrival at night. Moses, probably in his characteristic way not wanting to refuse, or to worry me, had given me no idea there might be a problem. I think perhaps, on reflection, he has never been to Saidor. Once I had set my mind to going, there was little he could do without appearing rude. It turns out that there is no way of booking accommodation in Saidor without knowing people there anyway. There is no such thing as a guest-house or hotel. Perhaps Moses felt that pointing these things out would just cause me worries he was unable to solve.

Nara arrived after 9 p.m., in the pitch dark, at a rough concrete jetty in what appeared to be the middle of nowhere. It was in fact the edge of Lagap coconut plantation. Passengers, told they might return and collect their heavy cargo in the morning, began rapidly dispersing and disappearing into the shadowy coconut palms, which stretched away in all directions ahead. Realising belatedly that I was in need of some advice, if not assistance, I began looking for someone I might talk to, and noticed a couple of young men, who enquired politely in a mixture of Tok Pisin and English, where I was going. Having had the outcome that it did, I now think fondly of this adventure; but my friends on the Rai Coast still wince at this tale of stupidity – arriving at night, forty-five minutes walk from Saidor station, in the pitch dark, knowing nobody, and sticking out like a sore, white, thumb. In fact, being in Papua New Guinea came to my rescue on this occasion. It is the place that I have found people to habitually be most considerate in their interest in strangers. My rather reticent and guarded answer to these two, that I was here to see the D.A., and could they direct me to his house, brought an offer of guidance that I still think of gratefully. They led me, asking about where I had come from and what I was doing, through the plantations, along the side of the grass airstrip, and finally through the huts of the dark station itself to a large house on the hill that belonged to the D.A. Savage dogs greeted us there, and a bleary-eyed man emerged at their frenzied barking. He had expected me by plane at a reasonable hour that morning, he said, and not seeing me, had forgotten all about it. He sent me off, with an in-law, Tom Yangoi, to seek out somewhere to stay.

Tom led me back through the station to the Catholic church, and knocked up a very irritable old German priest who wanted to know of Tom why on earth he had not come at a reasonable time. He also spoke rapidly in Tok Pisin, never addressing me. Nevertheless, Tom got from him a key to a concrete-floored room with a bed, where he left me. When morning arrived I found my way, again with the help of one of the young men who had brought me through the plantation the night before, to the office of the D.A. We had a brief and unsatisfactory meeting. He thought getting to Arop was too difficult, that if I wanted to study culture I might do so in any of a couple of villages where they were 'still very backward'. In ten minutes our interview was over. It appeared, probably correctly, that he had no interest in the work I proposed, and made no offers of introductions. At least he knew who I was, and had helped me the night before; but as I left the Nissan hut on stilts that was the District Offices, I was depressingly aware that I had no new leads, and probably would fly back to Madang no nearer my goal of finding a fieldsite.

Outside the office I came across Tom again, who introduced me to his brother Timothy. They showed me how to chew betel nut. They laughed, and said that betel was the most important thing on the Rai Coast. Tom then said that he did not speak good English, but his uncle did, and would I like to come and eat mangoes under his uncle's mango tree? This moment, of spontaneous hospitality and interest in a stranger, was definitive. Tom's uncle, Peter Nombo, welcomed me from where he sat on the gravel in the shade of that mango tree. It stood at the back of the single-story two-roomed brick house that his wife, a nurse at Saidor hospital, rented from the government, and they shared with five children, several in-laws and grandchildren, and endless relatives visiting from their villages. 'Oh yes', Peter said, 'I know about anthropologists. I have met Peter Lawrence and read his book (which was not all accurate, as I told him!) I think it is good that you want to come here and write about our past ways. They are rapidly changing, and much good knowledge is being lost. I will help you.' Brushing aside my desire to explain myself further (the notion I might be doing 'salvage anthropology' worried me), he extended his hospitality and introduced me to the extended family that was always around the house.

That day we went, in a government-owned yellow Toyota Landcruiser, 20 km along the coast back towards Madang, and from there up into the mountains to the village of Maibang, from where Tom came. Peter, as Tom's uncle, was held in high esteem there. I cannot remember the reason for the trip, but was thrilled by the company and scenery. Peter shouted out of the cab window for Tom to point out the village of Sor, where Lawrence had spent much of his time. I felt as if I was in the right place at last. Looking out from the open back of the Landcruiser as we climbed into the foothills, I saw, across a sea flattened by the height from which we were looking, a long flat island with peaks at either end. It was Arop, and in my subsequent three years spent in Madang and on the Rai Coast, indeed to this day, that view from the coastal mountains is all I know of it.

Reite

Over the next three months, I made trips back and forth between Madang and Saidor (although never in this period on board the MV *Nara*), and each time Peter organised for me to 'patrol', seeking villages where I might pursue my research. The first began again in Maibang, from where after a couple of days, Tom sent me on a loop with his younger cousin Albert Samaik, to Reite in the neighbouring language group, (and from where Peter originated) and then down to the coast at Warai. I spent a night in each of these places, talking with old men and leaders about their interest in what they call kastom, and trying to assess them as potential fieldsites. On another trip, I went with a contact of Peter's along the coast to the east this time, and stayed on the white sands of Bonga, a beautiful village on the beach. As seems right in retrospect, it was more the case that a village chose me than the other way around. All expressed interest in my arrival and a desire to

Photograph 1 *Looking North over Reite Lands from the Coastal Hills*

accommodate me, but only in one village did I detect real excitement about the subject of my research. This village was Reite, where an old man, known there as Kiap,[3] showed me with shining eyes and much good-humoured intensity, the paraphernalia of the male cult as proof of their continued knowledge of kastom. He told me if I wanted to come and learn about his kastom, I would have to cook a pig for him, and laughed. I was in no way led to believe from his laughter, however, that he spoke in jest.

The hamlets of Nekgini-speaking people (of which Reite is one cluster) are located in an area between 146°12' and 146°17' east longitude and 5°38' and 5°42' south latitude. They are in the subcoastal foothills of the northern side of the Finisterre range, between 7 km and 11 km inland from the coast, and between 300 m and 800 m above sea level. The hamlets of Reite, in which I subsequently lived, lie between the Seng river to the east and the Yakai river to the west. Hamlets are situated along the tops, and on buttresses formed by, limestone ridges. The terrain is heavily forested with tropical trees and shrubs, and has rich dark soils. The vistas, when available, are of patchwork green hillsides (the legacy of shifting cultivation and rapid regrowth), recent gardens appear lighter and less dense than older gardens. The patches of dark emerald green and deepest shade indicate spirit abodes where the forest is never cut for gardens. In the distance to the north lies the sea, and to the south, the huge and densely forested Finisterre range. From my house in Reite at about 500m above sea level, I could see the 3,700 m peak of Apirella, only 15 km away. Between the steep ridges of Reite lands run many watercourses, which bubble up from many springs, and run away to the two main rivers which drain from higher in the Finisterres. These streams run fast, contained by their narrow beds.

Nekgini is a non-Austronesian language (Wurm 1981) which had a total of around 800 speakers in 1994.[4] This population is divided into four main administrative 'villages' which go by the names, from east to west, of Serieng, Reite, Asang, and Sorang. Local people make much of the differences in dialect between these villages. Each contains roughly one quarter of the Nekgini-speaking population. To the south of Nekgini speakers, separated from them by a steep rise in the mountains, lie the villages of Dau (or N'dau) speakers (Lawrence 1964: 13). This language appears cognate with a large group known as 'Rawa' (Dalton 1992). To the east lie the territories of Ngaing speakers (Lawrence 1964, 1965; Hermann 1992; Kempf 1996).[5] Coastal people adjacent to these territories speak a language related to Nekgini and Ngaing, called 'Neko' by Wurm (1981).

Fieldwork

On account of my initial contacts with Tom Yangoi, I was invited to stay in the Ngaing-speaking village of Maibang to conduct my research. I was unwilling to disappoint those who made the offer. However, I felt I would be better located elsewhere. We made something of a compromise, in that I remained with John Samiti, a younger brother of Tom, in Maibang for a couple of months while my own house was built in Reite. I made the journey between the two villages a couple of times during these months. They are separated by the Seng river, and the trip takes one steeply down for an hour, through gardens and deep forest on a path made wide by the passing of many feet. On the other side of the Seng river, the path ascends steeply again, almost brutally in that hot climate, before tipping over the top of the next ridge and down to where Reite Community School is situated at the place called Ambuling. Maibang children make light of the two hour walk to school each day, although their parents are less easy with the fording of the Seng, which is dangerous in spate. My guide on the first time I made the journey, Albert Samaik, warned repeatedly '*lukaut, ples wel!* [T.P.] ('go carefully, it is slippery'). He was right to do so. The walking tracks in this land are not easily negotiated by a novice. Beyond the cleared school area, and again upon a ridge, lies the cluster of hamlets called Saruk, Ririnbung, and Yapong.

My initial arrival in the hamlets of Reite, along this route, was greeted with interest and even approval. I was told that if I wanted to know about kastom, I had arrived in the right place. They were proud to follow the ways of kastom, and took my arrival as an affirmation of their choice, whereas many of their neighbours (they meant Serieng people, Ngaing speakers, and coastal people) had given up kastom in favour of *misin* (T.P. missionisation) and *bisnis* (T.P. cash-cropping and trade store operation).

Reite people, under the direction of the Local Government Council's committee member in the village (*Komiti* [T.P.]), offered to build a house for me to live in, which I gratefully accepted. The house was a beautiful one, raised on posts with split bamboo covering palm floor-boards, and woven split bamboo for walls. The thatch was of sago leaf, sewn over batons into roof tiles. I had an open veranda to contemplate the view (something Reite people were always a bit dubious about; houses are to be hidden in, not looked out from), a small kitchen with a fire pit on the floor, and a larger room in which I placed my working area (table and chair). There were three other similar dwellings in the hamlet, placed around a plaza of red-brown earth. There was also a house dedicated to the men's cult, and an open meeting-house adjacent to this. From the house one could look down over an intersection of two small valleys, and see the huge rainforest trees that grew around the springs where there were pools used daily for washing and from which to fetch water. As with most things in Nekgini lands, this was reached by a steep path, almost lethally slippery after rain (I learned in the end to go barefoot and stick my big toe in the ground when taking each step), and was a haven of cool, clean, sparkling water, bubbling up and filling pools which then tipped their contents in little waterfalls over rounded boulders and away down a pebbly channel. These springs were one of the many spirit abodes (Holiting on Map 2), and full of magical shadows, bird-song, and the music of the stream.

It is important that I make clear certain aspects of the relationships I established with Reite people at this time. Their incorporation of a disassociated person (myself), managed with such skill on their part, was in part made possible by a negotiated position that began even prior to my arrival in this house. In all my dealings with Reite people at the start, I made it clear that there would be little financial reward for help, other than payment for materials, and that I was present among them as a student who was trained to write about their kastom. This established my work *itself* as something of interest to the community (*komuniti* [T.P.]) as they call themselves. People there, I now realise, were willing to incorporate me on potentially many grounds. This is their interest. I could, in other words, have appeared as someone with cash and consumables to ease my passage into people's favour. Yet this was not what I wanted, nor would it have served for long as a basis on which to make relationships with people. I was encouraged from the very start by leaders there to make our mutual interest in their kastom the basis for our relationship. The Reite *Komiti* was clear that he did not want me there on the basis of payment because of the trouble it would cause him.

I have no doubt that our expectations and understandings of the relationship were different. Webster (1982) discusses the necessary 'fiction' (rather than falsehood) involved in the position of an ethnographer in such a place, where he or she is made to feel like part of a community and therefore share understandings with the members of that community in a way that is rarely possible, while local people almost inevitably expect some access to the advantages the anthropologist patently has at his/her disposal, as a return. Webster describes this as an entry into each other's 'culture', a description I am loath to follow. His point is well made none the less, in that there is a genuine struggle on both sides to make relationships of fundamental inequality into the basis of an exchange. On the Rai Coast, with its history of interpretations of the presence and origin of white people, this kind of misperception on both my part and that of Reite people was, I think, inevitable. I was always shocked when people I thought I knew well implied I knew all about ghosts, or how to procure a book containing the formulae which would bring Western goods, while I think for their part, some Reite people had hopes that my work was going to get them the recognition, and therefore the change in circumstances, they felt was due to them.

I have faced a number of public meetings over the years to respond to rumours and even open accusations that I am stealing knowledge, or making a business out of selling their stories. There has been frustration on the part of some that I have not made a significant change in their lives. The initial principle that I was there to write about kastom, in response to their own wishes, has helped at such times. The brilliance of Reite's *Komiti* in seeing the inevitability of dispute and jealousy if my presence was not continually handled with great sensitivity, has allowed the development of something totally unexpected by either of us. That is a conversation based upon the worth of what I am doing there and mutual interest in the project. While not everyone in Reite has become conversant in the aims and methods of anthropological analysis, the majority of Reite people remained happy with my promise to write a book such as this one, about their kastom, so that it would be available to their descendants and to the wider world.

I may say I also cooked six pigs, with accompanying quantities of rice and tinned fish, as presentations to 'the community' during my time there. These were payments for my house, for their care for my well-being at an important moment when my mother visited, for learning certain items of kastom and for their work on the objects for a collection I made for museums in England and Papua New Guinea. In a place where jealousy over material advantage is dangerous (it causes feuds and can result in deaths), my best recourse as a method of payment for their help and assistance was to present something the whole community could share in. This was fulfilled by mimicking ceremonial food distributions in which many people claimed a part. On the day after the last of these pigs had been cooked and distributed, Kiap came to my house with many other elders and presented me with a gourd lime container and cassowary bone lime spatula.[6] Saying they would not accept any more pigs from me, as to do so would shame them, he outlined that now I could 'carry the mouth' of Reite people and speak for them. I was, in other words, part of the place.

The people in Reite hamlets were, then, extremely welcoming to outsiders. They were also very 'community minded', as were the Ngaing speakers with whom I also spent some time. As a legacy from the years of colonial rule, each community is charged by the local government council with the upkeep of its footpaths and roads, and with other work designated 'community work'. Bush material houses and classrooms for the local Community School at Ambuling are built by community labour, for example, as are pit latrines for old people who cannot manage the work themselves. This work is organised by a representative of the local government council, and takes place regularly every Monday. All members of the community take part. My own house was built by community work, organised by the local government committee member, and on his own initiative my presence was said to be 'between' all the people of the community, not 'belonging' to any one household or group.

My research was enhanced by the enthusiasm of older members of the community, particularly those who had been ridiculed by outsiders during and after the years of Yali's influence, to show their knowledge of, and control over, kastom.

It could be said that there are factions (or at least different interpretations) relating to the importance of kastom. Initially, it was those who had a particular interest in kastom as a part of an authority still remaining from close association with Yali, who were most interested in my arrival. However, kastom has new meanings. There are those who value kastom without subscribing to either the authority, or logic, of Yali's followers. They say that 'real' or 'unbroken' kastom was encouraged by Yali. The distortions of some of his followers has given kastom itself a bad name. In any case, kastom is more worthy and valid for the stability and meaning it gives to community life than anything people have dreamed up on their own, they say.

Once I had been accepted and was settled in the village, I was snowed under by people wanting to tell me important myths, their history, and the practices associated with them. For a time, I abandoned any thought of learning Nekgini itself (as I was by this point fluent in Tok Pisin). I could hardly turn people from my door when they arrived keen to tell me things, on the grounds that I now wanted to learn their language rather than their kastom. My first months were devoted to recording and writing up the stream of stories that was presented to me. Eating local foods, habitually chewing betel nut, and knowing Reite kastom were all taken as evidence that I had become part of the place.

Other factors greatly increased my own sense of gaining understanding.[7] I was included in many activities – gardening, ritual work, the male cult, exchanges, travels to Madang town to sell cash-crops – and also had many long and fascinating discussions with people who became my close friends through our work together. I was funded by the British Museum to make a collection of contemporary artefacts for them, and for the National Museum in Port Moresby, allowing me to witness and record the making of all important objects. I was further assisted in my understanding of musical and spiritual life by the presence of the ethnomusicologist Don Niles (then of the National Research Institute, Papua New Guinea), and his assistant Clement Gima for ten days in June 1995. Together we recorded music tapes, and my understanding of this was greatly enhanced by the intensive involvement with the male cult during that time. In all these activities, the theme of associating people into Reite, and thereby extending the knowledge and influence of that place itself, may be discerned.

In this book, as elsewhere, I refer to people from the villages in which I worked as 'Nekgini-speaking people'. This I mean to stand as short-hand for 'Nekgini-speaking people whom I know, and are happy for me to represent their opinions and perceptions as a coherent body of understanding'. Through working closely, and as mentioned above, comparing understanding and checking analytic moves with certain acknowledged masters of kastom in Reite, I have gained both insight and more importantly given them an interest in the text. Whether this means that the unavoidable impression of some of my prose – that a population full of personality looks rather homogeneous at times – is excusable, remains moot. All I can say is that Reite people themselves defer to certain authority figures. These people gain prominence through age, through oratorical skill, and most of all, through acknowledged completion of life-cycle and ritual practices covered by the term kastom. It is their advice that is solicited in what remain, due to the extraordinary history of Nekgini-speaking villages, the significant shaping practices in their highly valued social form; and it was they that told me to get on and write this down.

Some History: Government, Missions, and War

Although contact with Europeans began in Madang Province in 1871, Nekgini speakers had little knowledge of, or direct contact with, white people until after the Second World War. The early German traders, planters, and missionaries who arrived in Madang and travelled along the Rai Coast appear to have restricted their movements to the coastal plain in this area, although in the vicinity of Astrolabe Bay and south of Madang town, expeditions into the interior were made before the turn of the century and soon after (Lawrence 1964: 35, Reiner 1986: 105–9). Nevertheless, despite the lack of direct contact, it would be wrong to underplay the influence that the advent of steel tools (German axe-heads are still displayed proudly by old men in Reite), and certainly of pacification, on these populations. While steel was at first so scarce as to have little impact on the traditional small swidden gardens made by subcoastal people, its advent did intensify the movements of people for trade and exchange both amongst sub-coastal people (such as Nekgini and Ngaing, and Nekgini and Dau), and between coastal and subcoastal people. Trade brought marriage between these groups, evident today in the relations people maintain with kin across language divides. With the advent of a policy of pacification by the German (1885–1914), and then the Australian administrations (1921–42, 1946–75) on either side of the war, movement became easier, and the kind of fear that meant that hamlets stayed small and were often relocated, subsided.[8] Pacification is referred to by Reite people in Tok Pisin as *gutaim* (good time). As an ongoing influence, steel did have the effect of increasing garden (and therefore family) sizes, which are today having an effect on the size of the population. The beginnings of migrant labour by Reite men during the 1930s also introduced Melanesian pidgin (Tok Pisin) to the area and this, more than anything else (in their accounts), resulted in more congenial relations with neighbouring language groups, particularly those on the coast to the west, with whom Reite people began to intermarry.

It seems that the demands for labour made by missions and planters alike in the early years of the century did not affect Reite people. However in the 1930s, when the gold-mines at Wau and Bulolo in Morobe Province opened, some men left the village to work there. Some of the generation of men who are now, or would have been, great-grandfathers (most of whom died during the 1970's when influenza epidemics ran through the area), worked not only in the mines, but also on ships which plied between Rabaul and Madang. Some also went to work in plantations nearer to home on the Rai Coast. This small-scale, but significant labour migration continues to this day, although now it is centred upon the town of Madang.

Mission influence through the Rhenish (Lutheran) Mission began during the 1930s. In 1923, a Samoan pastor named Jerome expanded the missionary work that had been established in Astrolabe Bay in 1884 onto the Rai Coast with its first notable success. Eight assistant teachers (recruited from Siar and Graged [now named Kranket] islands in Madang harbour) were placed in the coastal villages between Lamtub (near the source of the Yakai river – see Map 2) and Saidor (Reiner 1986: 122–3). In 1932, a mission station was opened at Biliau which remains there to this day (ibid.: 155). By the 1930s mission workers began to appear in Nekgini hamlets according to people there. By all accounts, their arrival caused many changes. Native workers were more willing to use the fear of eternal damnation as a method of winning converts, and to stamp out native 'pagan' ritual, than the first white missionaries had been (Lawrence 1964: 55). Both, however, required local people to expose the ritual paraphernalia of the male cult to women, whereupon the mission workers burned the objects. They also burned other things, including magical charms used in hunting. This fact is frequently remembered with anger by Reite people.

The success of the mission workers in Reite was perhaps based on expectations (whether fostered by their teachers or not) that following Christian ritual would elevate the participants to the material conditions of the whites who, during the immediate pre-war years through patrols, and during the war itself, had impressed their power forcefully on local populations with their destructive technology. Old men in Reite also remember with wonder the arrival of American troops in Saidor during 1944, as some travelled there to work as labourers at this time. The rapid construction of large corrugated-iron warehouses, and the arrival of massive food supplies, were a revelation to those who saw them. Urangari, for example, remembered that they were given access to all the tinned meat they could eat, from a seemingly never diminishing pile.

When the adoption of Christian ways at home in the village did not bring such reward, people began to become resentful, especially since their loss of hunting magic was blamed for any hunger. This dissatisfaction, fuelled by the growing influence of Yali whose position was sanctioned by the Australian administration after the war (see Lawrence 1964 for the detail), encouraged Reite people to 'send the missions away' and reinstate traditional ritual practices. These included the construction of male spirit cult houses and the paraphernalia of the cult during the 1950s. Thus on my arrival, I was informed that Reite people followed kastom.[9]

The male cult (*tambaran* [T.P.]) is today a significant and living part of Reite ceremonial life. For the outsider, its most obvious feature is its exclusivity and the secrecy which surrounds it. Although lacking any form of internal grading or progression, the difference between initiates (adult men) and non-initiates (women and children) is strictly observed. I was thus told repeatedly that although I could partake in the ceremonies of the male cult, I was not under any circumstances to reveal certain aspects of it to women or children. It was impressed upon me that children from Reite were even now at University, and I was therefore not to write about the tambaran in any way other than those forms of speech used in public contexts in Reite, lest Reite women read about it. I have tried to observe this restriction, and thus use the euphemisms common in Reite to talk about tambaran. This will become clear in the sections where tambaran becomes relevant to the argument.

On the administrative side, in 1932 a patrol station was established at Saidor (see Map 2). This became a Government substation in 1936 under the Australian Mandate Administration.[10] From this time, patrols into Nekgini territory were made, giving these people their first view of white people, and their first direct experience of being 'administered'. They were required to relocate into centralised villages by the colonial officials, to bury their dead in a village graveyard instead of exposing them, and to provide labour for the maintenance of footpaths and for the construction and maintenance of a rest house for the patrol officer (a *haus kiap* [T.P.]). However, patrols occurred only annually, and did little to increase knowledge on the part of either side, of the other. They stopped altogether during the Second World War, and were not restarted until 1947.

Japanese troops landed in Madang in 1942 and moved along the Rai Coast seaboard during 1943 (Lawrence 1964: 49). Reite people remember the arrival of the Japanese, and their growing fear of them. Apparently at first the newcomers treated Reite people reasonably well, hiding from the advancing American troops who arrived at Saidor in early 1944. By all accounts, however, as they became more desperate and were cut off from supplies, they began to kill local people's livestock, and to take food from their gardens. Resistance was met with violence. Reite people tell of how they were turned out of their houses, and hid deep in the bush eating only wild roots while the Japanese ate from their gardens and lived in their houses. Patrol reports from the area in 1947 record that almost all seed yams had been consumed by the Japanese, leaving hardship on their departure (Bentinkt 1949/50).

On the other hand, there is an extraordinary tale told in Reite about a Japanese soldier who remained there after the war was over, and who gave his name to a child from Sarangama (Tera). This suggests that there were friendly enough relations between Reite people, and at least some Japanese troops despite their invasion, although this tale does have a tragic twist. Returning home to his house, a Sarangama man, it is told, found Tera eating a marsupial that he had left to dry over his fire, and in a rage over the theft, the Sarangama man took up his bow and shot Tera, who is buried on Sarangama lands.

After the end of hostilities came a time when the administration attempted in earnest to develop the Rai Coast, encouraging agricultural projects such as the growing of ground-nuts to improve soil quality, and of rice cultivation for sale (McAlpine 1953/4). Their efforts were always hampered by the area's inaccessibility, however. After 1954, native local government councils were formed, and a school was opened in Saidor in 1955. These were the years of the rise to prominence of Yali, and the development of the administration was overshadowed in local people's perception by the anticipated developments that various forms of millenarian movement, figure-headed by Yali, were expected to produce. Yali banned the practice of magical killing (*poisin* [T.P.]), which by all accounts had been a more usual method of homicide than open warfare in this area. It is now said that *not* practising sorcery is kastom by some Reite villagers, meaning that it is a law introduced by Yali, of whom some people still speak as a kind of deity.[11]

Yali's influence was positive in many ways. There is a feeling, shared by some in Reite, that he was put in a difficult position not only by the colonial government, but also by some of his followers. It is perhaps some of the latter, particularly unrealistic in their expectations, which brought his eventual downfall. The association with cargo cult has overshadowed the fact that he encouraged his followers to build houses raised on stilts, to separate pigs and other livestock from living quarters, and to dig pit latrines. He also encouraged cleanliness in villages, which to this day are kept beautifully well-swept and have flowers planted around them, as he recommended. Despite being blamed by the administration for much of the millenarian activity at this time, he did much to improve the quality of life in Rai Coast villages such as Reite. The question as to what the expectations of those who followed his recommendations (about village cleanliness and layout) were, must be left open.

In the final colonial patrol report (for 1969/70), Reite appeared as the only village in the area which had no income from coffee or copra production. This may be attributed to the influence of followers of Yali's movement, who held that involvement in business (with its meagre returns) could not possibly be the way that whites had gained their power. The patrol officer for this time wrote that the upcoming 'independence' meant the arrival of cargo in native perceptions (Dyer 1969/70), and stories told about this time by Reite people confirm that millenarian implications were attached to the end of the colonial administration.

Interestingly, real change in Reite people's living conditions, though still not enough to satisfy some expectations[12] did come after the departure of the Australian administration. During the 1980s, by dint of having a Reite man achieve the level of Minister in the provincial government of Madang,[13] they were connected to the Saidor-Madang 'Highway' by a feeder road up into the foothills of the mountains. Reite was chosen as the site for the location of a medical aid post, and also as the site for the establishment of a local Catholic Church-administered 'Community school'.

From the early 1970s, some Reite people also began to plant coffee and cocoa, ignoring what had become a faction in the region which maintained that certain rituals (derived from, or offshoots of, Yali's influence) were the only way to bring development. Thus cash started to arrive in the village at the same time as the development of services on a modest scale.

Cash features in the subsistence regime of all Rai Coast people today. Interestingly, however, cash is still regarded with ambiguity, at least in Reite. It is perhaps too much like garden food, in that it is readily consumed by those possessing it, for people to feel confident that it is really the basis of generative productive relations (Leach n.d.[a]). It is earned through coffee, cocoa, and copra sales, or provided through small remittances from kin living and working in other places as schoolteachers, businessmen, labourers, or politicians. Reite people generally have small plantations of coffee and cocoa, owned by individual households, the produce of which is laboriously carried to the coast, and then on by ship to Madang town where it yields a small cash addition to their subsistence agriculture. Cash is used to purchase rice and tinned fish from small local trade stores, and to buy secondhand clothing, steel tools, and kerosene from Madang town. These items have long been more or less essentials, rather than luxuries, for most Rai Coast people (see Lawrence 1964: 59). Cash is also required for the payment of school fees in the local government or church community schools, which are dotted along the coast and in the mountains behind. Another feature of life on the Rai Coast is the chewing of betel nut, which is almost an obsession with the inhabitants. In the months when betel nut is plentiful (May to September), it is sometimes transported as far as Madang for sale.

When I arrived in Reite in 1994, most households had steel tools, cooking pots and plates, and manufactured clothes. Some occasionally purchased kerosene, tinned fish and rice, while others had luxuries such as radios (and batteries to use them) although these kinds of items were rarely bought from individual income, but were received as gifts from kinsmen in paid employment, or as part of kin-based exchanges. Reite houses at this time were all constructed of local forest material, with floors raised on stilts, walls of platted bamboo, and roofs made from sago thatch. Corrugated-iron roofing material was reserved for the small trade stores which dot the area. Despite the presence of a road, very few vehicles ever attempt to follow it, and because of the rains it is little use for most of the year other than as a footpath to the coast.

Nekgini-speaking people subsist on a mixed swidden system, cultivating yams, indigenous taro varieties, Chinese taro, sweet potato, small quantities of sago, and other (native and introduced) vegetable crops. Coconuts and areca palm (betel nut) grow at these altitudes, although the former only slowly. There are, however, many coconut palms along the coast, the majority planted during the years of colonial administration when native, mission, and company plantations were all established there. Most of these plantations were in the care of local people in 1993, although there are some (Lagap and Nom plantations near Saidor government station, for example) which are still run by expatriate workers and owned by large corporations. Coastal people are able to care for many more pigs than the people who live in the mountains, feeding their livestock on the flesh of dry coconuts.

Around Reite, pigs (both domestic and wild) are scarce, but marsupials and birds exist in the densely forested hills, and these are hunted to supplement the mainly vegetable diet. Nekgini speakers make regular trips to the coast to collect coconuts, often received in exchange for garden food, as coconuts are valued for their oil and flavour in cooking. Reite people also collect eels and crustaceans from the streams and rivers.

Above Reite lands, the first rise of the mountains proper is so steep that it is uninhabited. However higher still, at altitudes above 1,200 m, the mountains tend to level out again into a series of steep valleys and ridges with inhabitable land along them. At these altitudes, a number of ecological zones exist, rising from lower mid-montane forest, to grassland near the summits of the mountains (Kocher Schmidt 1991). People here practise mixed swidden agriculture and pig husbandry. They have no access to coconut, such an important item in the diet of the other Rai Coast dwellers, and cultivate temperate rather than tropical vegetables.

In terms of literature, the Rai Coast lies in between seaboard areas which have been the subject of intense ethnographic interest. These are the New Guinea Islands, and the Sepik river. It is the literature from these areas that I use most often for comparison and support in this book. Drawing selectively on ethnographies provides support for interpretation, and also throws Rai Coast ethnography into relief through contrast. I do draw on other work from further afield in Papua New Guinea where it seems appropriate theoretically or because of material similarities. Nowhere do I wish to imply however that there is some kind of culture area wherein interpretations from one place can be automatically transposed onto another. Similarities or differences of data and interpretation at times seem worth noting.

People

Reite people have a great interest in outsiders. This perhaps explains their willingness to accommodate the Japanese soldier, Tera. However, as with that tale, attracting and accommodating people does not mean one suspends judgement about what sort of people they are, or whether they behave in a manner appropriate to the kind of relationship one wants. There is nothing sentimental about this desire to accommodate others. Here, alongside some background information, I have told a story about my own transition from disassociated outsider arriving on a boat, to a person associated with a particular place and set of people. I have chosen to introduce the book in this way because one of the main concerns of the Rai Coast people whom I know lies in the appearance of wealth and power that a large population gives. Creating new persons is the object of their gardening, exchange, and spiritual activities. An apparently unattached person, such as Tera, or indeed myself, is therefore welcomed as a kind of addition to the wealth of the hamlet or village in which they are (in local perception) enticed to reside.

I was always struck when Reite people used to question me as to the status of what they termed *trango man* [T.P.] (vagrants or dispossessed people). Having heard (from somewhere) that there were tramps, or people without land and family in other countries, they suggested that if this were really the case, could I not bring them over to Papua New Guinea, where they would be looked after (in the sense of given land, kin, and work)? I believe this 'charitable' offer came from their amazement that there were 'free' people somewhere, and the idea that if so, they could be incorporated into Reite to swell the population and therefore increase their prestige and appearance of wealth. My own welcome and acceptance may well have been based in part on a variation on this idea (and especially that white people might have relationships or knowledge of a powerful kind), and therefore should be snapped up if they appear wandering through one's lands with no other connections. Fred Damon writes of Massim societies in similar vein:

> For all Massim societies the production of children is a principal activity, and the establishment of conditions to reproduce them is an important outcome of mortuary rites (1989: 7).

The theme of this book is how social life here is geared to the creation, and innovative incorporation, of people. In the next chapter I outline how this may be understood utilising recent anthropological work on kinship.

Notes

1. Luckily, I had been put in contact with Moses by mutual friends in England. He was my only contact in Madang at that stage.
2. Tok Pisin is the lingua franca of Papua New Guinea, and its second official language. I indicate Tok Pisin terms in the text by 'T.P.' after an italicised word.
3. 'Kiap' is a Tok Pisin word derived from the German 'kapitan'. It was used to refer to the colonial patrol officers. Siriman (Reite's Kiap) was given this name (by himself I suspect) as a vociferous local orator and prominent leader. He often declaims that he is *lokal kiap* (local government/official) because of his knowledge of kastom, and prominence in exchange; and also because he was prosecuted by the colonial government for involvement in the millenarian (cargo) movements which took Yali as their figurehead. Escaping unpunished, Kiap bases much of his authority on this apparent acceptance of his control over and use of kastom. Even Yali went to prison, as Kiap reminds people. How powerful must he be then, to have escaped?
4. The Nekgini-speaking population in 2001 is well over 1,000.
5. Yali came from the Ngaing-speaking village of Sor.
6. *Koro*. An accessory usually restricted to people who have done much for their hamlet group.
7. And see Gow (2001). Reite people probably felt that I had been told enough once I had publicly and obviously recorded their stories (*patuki*).
8. It is told by old people in Reite that before pacification, hamlets did not advertise their presence by planting coconuts and betel nut in large stands anywhere near dwellings for fear of attracting sorcerers and other hostile agents.

9. Although the population of one Reite hamlet, Marpungae, counted themselves as (Catholic) Christians and had a small church in their hamlet during the time of my stay in Reite. Reite people now generally agree that both kastom and church 'have a basis [in truth]' (*misin igat as, kastom igat as* [T.P.]).

10. For a fuller history, see Lawrence (1964: 34–61).

11. Other changes, and perhaps even the development of the significance of the term kastom as a whole may also be attributed to the influence of Yali, and his followers. Kastom whether traditional practice or innovative ritual, was said to be the power which would bring significant change to local circumstances (*kago* [T.P.]). Hence the short-hand definition of *kastom* already employed: 'correct practice'. It is a term which potentially covers *both* new and old, because of this emphasis on effect, through precedent.

12. There are those in Reite who today claim to be still awaiting 'full independence'.

13. Peter Atat Nombo.

Photograph 2 *The Palem. A Construction of Wood, Wealth, and Garden Food*

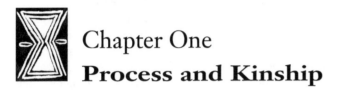

Chapter One
Process and Kinship

As the major element of marriage payments made amongst Nekgini-speaking people, the bride's group receive wealth from a wooden construction.[1] This construction, called a *palem*, has two elements. Wood and bamboo form the base, while garden produce and wealth items are piled upon them. The former are called the 'bones' of the palem, the latter its 'flesh'. Once stripped of wealth at the end of the exchange, the 'bones' are left for the donors to reanimate with new 'flesh', in order to make future affinal payments. In Nekgini understanding, there is a dry, stable, fixity to bones, while flesh (or rather bodies animated by it) move fluidly through the landscape. One such movement is that made by women in marriage. Their relocation is a quintessential act, gendering the person who moves by changing the relations in which she is engaged daily.

A woman's transformation from sister, to bride, is instigated by her removal from her natal hamlet. In turn, a brother's feelings of loss at his sister's removal precipitates his expectation of recompense for those who claim to have an interest in the girl. This recompense comes in the form of a palem: a body of wealth. In receiving it, he develops his own position as a man (Leach 2002). By making a wider group's interests apparent, he takes responsibility for bringing them together in one place. The moment of fixity created in this action similarly develops his gendered identity.

Fundamental changes in a person's identity and familial position are generated through physical movements across the landscape, as well as by residence. In the light of this, all Nekgini-speaking people avow that a woman will *never* marry a man unless she is forced to do so by love-magic (*maesea yaending/marila* [T.P.]). Love-magic moves women, not only to emotion, but also physically from a known place of security (their natal hamlet) to a new and unknown place of marital obligation. In placing her as a gendered person, rather than a person defined through siblingship, it precipitates unprecedented changes in her life.

Among Nekgini speakers the appropriate response to an act of love-magic, explicitly seen as the extraction of a person from their natal residence, is anger. This results in violent actions on the part of her siblings. Their anger is directed towards her lover and is, in part, due to a disruptive definition imposed from elsewhere. Negotiated distance based on difference is the appropriate position of in-laws on the Rai Coast. Love-magic and the violent response it calls for develop both physical and conceptual separation between the parties involved. The fights following love-magic ensure that affines do not reside in the same place. They also concentrate people's minds onto which side they feel most connection, and whether they support the man in his extraction, or feel the need for recompense for a loss to themselves. Either way, a moment of definition has come upon them. Young men should not take the practice of love-magic upon themselves. Their own elders, as well as their victim's siblings, may resent the position it forces them into.

Nekgini-speaking people's ability to extract people, and transform them into brides through love-magic, rests on the power of places. Places gain power from the bones of the ancestors, which are kept and tended. On marriage, women are fully incorporated into their marital hamlet. They become 'siblings' to the other residents. This incorporation is complete upon the payment of bridewealth (appearing in the form of a palem). A consequence of this payment is that a woman's bones remain with her marital kin on her death. Her bones add to the power of the place at this point. While women in the Western Highlands of Papua New Guinea famously maintain their otherness (M. Strathern 1972; Stürtzenhofecker 1998), here there is a different dynamic altogether.

The centrality of movement is arresting. How can removal, or placement, bring about what have conventionally been viewed as the 'givens' of kinship (gender identity, lineage affiliation)? The difficulties of describing kinship in this area without reference to place begs the question, 'how can we see placement and mobility as part of kinship?'

Kinship, Process, and Creativity

It is the actual enfolding (Wagner 2001) of person and land within a process of becoming for both that poses the descriptive and theoretical challenge for this book. This is as much an ethnographic as a theoretical concern, and following from this, I look to find a solution within the understandings with which Reite people themselves work. By doing so, I am following recent work in social anthropology which has reinvigorated the study of kinship (Edwards 2000; Holy 1996; Parkin 1997; Peletz 1995; Schweitzer 2000). These scholars, through a focus on indigenous models of persons and social relations, make modes of 'relatedness' (Carsten 2000) the basis for comparison, and thus avoid the well-worn dichotomy between biological and social aspects of kinship (unless, of course, these concepts figure in the thinking of the people discussed).

Within this move comes a relocation of emphasis in another sense. To paraphrase some current arguments, whereas in the past one might have looked for the structure of society in kinship categories, now it is the life-cycle, and particularly the ascription of identity and relatedness through activities, which takes narrative prominence (Carsten 1995, 1997; Astuti 1995). One way of understanding this move is to say, '[T]he phenomena of kinship and relatedness are to be viewed as processes' (Böck and Rao 2000: 29); and this is because the agentive, creative aspect of people's interactions seemed to be missing from earlier understandings of kinship.

It may be that it was in fact impossible for kinship analysts working in the classic paradigms to see anything creative in kinship *itself*. Creativity instead lay elsewhere (intellect for Morgan, society for Durkheim, culture for many later theorists; or perhaps even in the dialectic of nature and culture which originated human society itself, and of which kinship systems were a fundamental part [Lévi-Strauss 1969]). The conceptual separation of terminology and role from biological positioning in a genealogical network allowed differences between systems to be established against the common denominator of biogenetic genealogy. In turn each instance could be approached as a system of ordering another, more fundamental, reality. This ordering was viewed as 'creative' of social form. It also allowed for the analysis of function within systems *as* systems, and of life-cycle transformations to be analysed as matters of symbolic manipulation. However the myriad separations of both functionalism and structuralism (which include the study of kinship itself as an object) and which stem from the initial dichotomy between mind and matter (Ingold 2000), or the social and the biological, have been seen by some to have created an impasse from which the topic would never recover (Carsten 2000: 2).

The classical formalist approach institutionalised the separation between biological reality and social or cultural reality as universal in at least two different constructions. We might characterise these as, firstly, 'objective universality': the idea that biological kinship is objectively distinct from social kinship, whatever particular peoples may think about 'kinship'; and, alternately, 'subjective universality': the idea that all people on earth distinguish and value differently biological kinship (whatever may pass locally for 'biology' which may include feeding and other body-constituting practices) from social kinship (whatever is deemed social, locally: adoption, choice, friendship etc.). Although both are problematic, they are distinct; the first being a sociological-biological thesis, the second a cognitive-psychological one. Schneider (1984) made much of the problems inherent in these dichotomies, as have many others. They allow a confusing mix between notions of 'real' biological connection, 'perceived' biological connection, terminology and role (Wagner 1972), fictive kinship based on metaphors of biological connection, fictive kinship based on other kinds of connection (and so forth) in a series that wends its way back to Morgan's distinction of classificatory from natural description (Morgan 1970). These are not only problems of epistemology (what basis is there upon which to compare kinship systems), but also of agency and individual experience. Humans may create ideas about biology, or relations modelled on biology, but sociological and cognitive theses alike leave actual creation in the realm of the biological. As Carsten puts it 'formalist approaches omitted not only some of the crucial experiential dimensions of kinship, including its emotional aspects but also its creative and dynamic potential' (Carsten 2000: 14).[2] How social creations relate to biological generation remains a problem, however much we acknowledge the creative and dynamic potential of society or cognition.

If we are to pursue an interest in the creative and dynamic potential of people's activities it will be necessary to put all these separated entities back together. I infer from the evidence presented in this book that Nekgini people know as well as recent kinship theorists that entities exist as moments in processes which are also the dissolution of those entities. My argument here, in following Nekgini understandings, is that we do not look at kinship or subsistence economics or religion, but at the very process of realisation and becoming from which entities (persons, spirits, places, garden food, songs) catentate.

Yet being able to do so is dependent upon the understanding of process with which we arm ourselves. If we are to leave conceptual room for developing an understanding of creativity, process must indeed be a coming-into-being, rather than a revelation of what is already there, or an animation of entities somehow pre-specified. There is a danger in using the notion of process as a corrective. Its introduction to the study of kinship appears in an attempt to represent flexibility among the entities otherwise defined, and constrained, by genealogical position. This may be appropriate to some ethnographic contexts (see Stafford 2000). It is also seen as particularly useful in analysing 'cognatic kinship'. Yet it does not mark the radical departure necessary to describe Reite people's creativity. While process appears to threaten the notion of structure altogether, employing process as anti-structure may serve only to reinforce the analytic necessity of describing what flexibility can be judged against. Hence the static appearance of kinship as a structure will be maintained. The results of people's choices appear against the system, while constructed kinship itself appears against the background of biological givens, as it were.

In my focus on creativity in this book, I develop the use of process in a way appropriate to Rai Coast understandings of personhood. To this end, I start with processes, and look to discover the significant outcomes of them for Nekgini speakers. That these outcomes take the form of persons makes it possible for this to be a book 'about' kinship; but it demands a re-formulation of the place process assumes in description and analysis. 'Kinship' in this context cannot be separated from other creative endeavour. The processes whereby persons and places come into being through work *elicit* specific relationships, just as they invoke specific places. Such production is also the dissolution of other reifications, of other structures and entities, including persons and previous definitions of them. Persons, *along with* other outcomes of the processes of generation, such as song and design complexes, or garden produce, are alternative and commensurate reifications. The 'bringing things together' (*turum maliemung*)[3] which a presentation of bridewealth in the form of a palem amounts to, and the dissolution of the body so produced, is the working of this creative process in microcosm. It is creative not just of 'a body', but of songs and designs, of relationships in a new order, and of new definitions of the persons and places involved. It is a 'process' in this sense which I describe.

Another issue in the understanding of process is that it can be invoked as the medium through which what is pre-specified, outside process, is revealed. I think of this as follows. Classical kinship studies relied upon process; that is, kinship structures and their political implications were made apparent in the actions of living people. In their associations and activities, structures were revealed to the observer. They were 'performed'; but this does not make them 'performative' (Austin 1976). Performance in this instance is a process of revelation, not of constitution. People's lives revealed or performed the structures which would not have been maintained without the 'process' of life.

In other words, there is a kind of process which shows forth innate differentiation. Matrilineal and patrilineal rules can be found in the activities whereby kinship is made apparent. Yet people living their lives also reveal the malleability of such rules. Hence in some cases, the designation 'cognatic'. Cognation in fact *assumes*, of course, that there is a genealogical or biogenetic connection to both mother and father. Actions thus 'reveal' a bias in one or other direction, depending upon context. What is revealed by the process is a deeper structure. This understanding of process allows for flexibility, and some degree of individual choice to enter the analysis, but the constitution of 'structure' remains beyond its scope. This observation is fundamental to my desire to find an alternative.

Hence I take a slightly different route, and begin by co-opting a definition of process with a positive slant. The philosophy of A.N. Whitehead describes process as a fundamental aspect of life. Process for him can refer to structures coming into being just as effectively as entities coming into being. Process here refers to a different order of life than the (conceptual) struggle between structure and agency, or structure and particular experience. It is the order of how things, including structures, come to emerge, and how they dissolve. Creation is apparent in process itself, because process is historical and cumulative. Process is not opposed to structure, it is the enabling and dissolving condition. 'How an actual entity *becomes* constitutes *what* that actual entity *is*; so that the two descriptions of an actual entity are not independent. Its "being" is constituted by its "becoming". This is the "principle of process". (Whitehead 1929: 34f./23 original emphasis.) We need, in other words, to look for the description of the entity in the process of its becoming, and not look to animate already existing entities (persons, kin categories) by making them 'processual'. The latter amounts to making static things, which have an intrinsic and separate identity or essence, 'perform' this essence in order for it to be recognised. Whitehead's philosophy, in assuming process, works in a different way. It encourages a description which captures the becoming of entities and structures, which describes their uniqueness by describing the history of their emergence. Inspired by Whitehead and others, this is the route I chose to take. I find this position an appropriate parallel, or perhaps approximate translation of some of the things Reite people say, and certainly of their social theory as it is visible (to me) in their practices. But that does not mean that these philosophies or explanations would work everywhere. Anthropology is based on ethnographic work because it is here that the answers and explanations must ultimately be generated. Attention to context is vital (Englund and Leach 2000).

When women on the Rai Coast complain that they have been forced into marriage through love-magic, and that without this technique, no woman would marry a man, they acknowledge, in their throw-away wisdom, things that we look hard to establish in social anthropology: that gender is constructed dialectically and depends on the recognition of others, how the self-generating meaning systems that inform and guide human existence come about through action and practice, and that one's knowledge of oneself and of one's world come into being as the same process. It is just this kind of process that I describe, as a representation of Nekgini-speaker's practice, in this book.

Cognation and Flexibility

The major ethnographer of the Rai Coast was Peter Lawrence. He worked both there and in an area south of Madang town known as the Bagasin Hills (see Map 2). His work on cargo cults (*Road Belong Cargo* 1964) was based on fieldwork undertaken with the cult leader Yali between 1949 and 1958 in the Ngaing-speaking village of Sor, on fieldwork among the Garia of the Bagasin Hills, and on detailed historical research. It has become a classic of Melanesian anthropology, as it sets out with great clarity the history of interaction between 'natives', planters, settlers, colonial officials, and missionaries. The burden of the work is to explain the colonial presence from the point of view of the native people, and thus the rationality, in their own terms, of both their dissatisfaction with their experience of white people, and of their ideas about how their situation could be improved (the millenarian movements) despite the administration's and mission's apparent hostility to their cause (see Lawrence 1964, *passim*).

On the other hand, Lawrence's ethnographic accounts of social organisation in the region were received with less enthusiasm (Lawrence 1984: 1–2). As became clear soon after he returned from his fieldwork in Madang, the kind of data he had collected on kinship and social organisation appeared anomalous in the context of other areas of Melanesia, and did not fit with the theories that, at the time, were fashionable in social anthropology. One reviewer of his first published work, on the land tenure system of the Garia of the Bagasin Hills, so disliked the ethnography he presented that he accused Lawrence (or his informants) of falsification. At best, it was supposed that Lawrence had got his facts wrong (Leach 1956). As Meyer Fortes wrote many years later, in a preface to the monograph Lawrence finally published on the basis of his earlier fieldwork:

What later came to be designated the African segmentary descent group model was still a novelty and to many of us full of promise. Melanesia meant, above all, the Trobriands, Dobu, Manus, the Solomon Islands, and descent groups resembling those of the African Model seemed to occur in all of them. The Garia were conspicuously different... they seemed to have a structure without boundaries.... Coupled with the absence of leadership offices corresponding to chieftainship or headmanship, this fluidity of structure posed the problem of how any sort of social continuity or cohesion could be maintained in Garia society. (Fortes 1984: ix)

It was this kind of reaction that prevented Lawrence from publishing his ethnographic material immediately. Instead, as he implies in his introduction to the Garia monograph (1984), he concentrated on a less controversial topic, that of cargo cult. He left aside the ethnographic materials on kinship and social organisation from his field site on the Rai Coast (about which, an ethnography, although planned [1984: 1], never appeared). Published material on the Ngaing exists only as a brief introduction to 'the native cosmic order' in *Road Belong Cargo*, and an article on traditional Ngaing religion (Lawrence 1965).

It was, in part, the kind of difficulty Lawrence faced in analysing and presenting his data on social organisation that got me interested in Madang in the first place. I do not mean the difficulty that he experienced with his colleagues; nor do I mean to resurrect his structural functional modelling of society through a reinterpretation of his data. Marilyn Strathern has shown how his assumptions about the role of society hindered his understanding of Garia personhood (Strathern 1992b). Rather, the ethnographic content of his work suggested an interesting relationship between land and kinship, or people and their environment.

Lawrence attempted to find the structuring principles of the cognatic system he found among the Garia by looking for them in associations based on land use and landholding (1955). He was right to look to land, and the associations people make with respect to it, in order to understand Garia social organisation; but I will suggest that instead of looking for corporate and enduring groups based on the shared ownership of land (which he did not find), he might have looked to how people gain identity directly from the land on which they produce themselves as social entities. This is different from looking for the basis of 'society', as a set of structural relations, made visible in land ownership.

In an article entitled 'Parts and Wholes', Strathern shows how Lawrence, in modelling Garia social organisation on the individual, was led to formulate his idea of 'ego centred networks of interpersonal relationships ... call[ed] security circle[s]' (Lawrence 1984: 5). It appeared that each individual was able to align him or herself freely with kin on the side of either of their parents, or to make alliances through shared land – or what Lawrence called 'bush god domains'. This resulted in a picture of 'a society based ... not on unilineal descent groups but on ramifying cognatic kinship relations' (Fortes 1984: ix, also quoted in Strathern 1992b: 78). Strathern identifies this as posing a double problem for the social anthropology of the 1950s: first, 'how to conceptualise a society that was not composed of groups, and second, [how to conceptualise] the relationship of parts to wholes' (79).

The Unilineal Descent Group model was being newly defended at that time (Fortes 1953). It was the fresh and powerful paradigm which had excited people with its explanatory power. The model worked on the assumption that persons belonged to groups, and that membership of these groups gave individuals membership of a society constituted by the amalgam of these politico-jural entities. This in turn rested on the notion of a division between politico-jural and domestic domains. Society, recruiting from the domestic domain of biologically complete individuals, made them socially complete, and in turn was made up of the domains in which these socialised individuals gained their (social) identities. However, it seemed that Garia persons mixed freely their domestic (i.e., kinship) connections and their 'social' connections (bush god domains, shared land holdings etc.) to form their own, ego-centred circles of 'secure' kinsmen with whom to operate. Individual persons appeared responsible for their own positions and affiliations, not society.

Strathern stresses, however, that Lawrence's analysis of pragmatism by individual Garia persons should not lead to an analysis of individualism. She argues that relations are not conceptualised by Garia as 'external' to the person, as a structural functional model would have it – with its notion of social relations being added on to biologically complete individuals – but rather social relations were understood to be already *within* persons, as part of their substantial composition. There was no biological/social divide in Garia personhood, thus the search for 'society' as the medium for relating individuals already formed (biologically) without the aid of social relations was fruitless. In short, Lawrence's problem was that society, in its role of structuring relations, was not apparent; that is, coherent institutions to govern and structure a person's relations, were elusive. Instead, Strathern suggests, there were relations (that is people's possible positions *vis-à-vis* one another) already existent, waiting to be acted upon by the persons who embodied them:

> the singularity of the Garia person is conceptualised as a (dividual) figure that encompasses a plurality. If in the Garia view there are no relationships that are not submitted to the person's definition of them, then what the person contains is an apprehension of those relations that he or she activates without. If they pre-exist, it is as internal differences within his or her composite body. (1992b: 82)

Society did not add a structure of relations to existent bodies, and thus make persons. Rather the constitution of a person's body was also the constitution of the social relations they would eventually be able to act upon. What they are, to paraphrase for my own purpose, could be described in their becoming. Taking Strathern's position as a starting-point, I want to pursue her assertion that Garia, or other Madang persons, embody an apprehension of the relationships they may activate. In a place where land and residence appear to be the most enduring and stable principles around which people associate, I have been stimulated to investigate what kind of relations people have with, or to, the land itself. In other words, what is it about land and its produce in these places that makes it possible for its inclusion within, rather than existing as a backdrop to, the most profound of human relations, those of procreation and kinship?

An Alternative to the Genealogical Model

Thus the ethnographic component of this book centres around a presentation of the processes of 'production', modelled on procreation. As will be seen, the crossover between these 'domains' of analysis in Nekgini understanding provides a framework for an integrated theoretical analysis of kinship, land, and place-ment. Whereas kinship studies in this area in the past have run into difficulties because they assume that land is a substrate *upon which* the important relations of society work to order people's activities and associations, Reite ethnography shows us that the incorporation of land and places into a history of social relations is where life exists. Persons are not created by society moulding biologically pre-specified individuals. Rather persons (offspring) are seen as emerging from a set of relations between other persons. They are not 'performing' the relations they have within them but actively taking up, and developing, aspects of the process whereby in each moment, they have their existence. There is then no need for analysis to focus upon how individuals become related through structures beyond the processes which constitute them. People apprehend and act upon the relations which they see as making them up. I summarise the theoretical implications of this focus upon process in understanding Nekgini personhood below.[4]

The challenge, highlighted by the difficulties faced by Lawrence, is to split apart the connection between the sharing of substance (which Reite people do describe), and genealogical connection that lies at the heart of conventional kinship theory. Even an innocent looking kinship diagram has built into it the assumption that the essence of a person is received by transmission at the point of conception. Each line in the diagram depicts a channel for the transmission of this essence, or more strictly, one component of it. It follows from this assumption that a person's essence is given ahead of his or her growth in an environment. Of course, in conventional kinship theory, it is not denied that children grow; what is denied is that they *are grown*. That is to say, growth is conceived of as an autonomous development which serves merely to 'express' or 'bring out' what is already present (the received essence). This is precisely in line with the structure of modern biological theory (whose roots also lie in the genealogical model), with its genotype/phenotype distinction. It is assumed that what is 'passed on', through genealogical lines of transmission, is a context independent specification of the organism-to-be.

The crux of the ethnographic presentation here is that human beings are grown, and that in their growth, they draw substance from the land, just as plants do. People share substance, and are therefore kin, because they have grown in the same land. This growth does not take place in isolation, but in what might be called a field of nurture (comprised by relationships to other humans and the environment) which is constituted in the work of other people. This work is the work of growing people. Such a perspective is fundamentally contrary to the genealogical model. To draw a line from father to son (in a kinship diagram), and to say that this is a kinship connection is meaningless. For the role of the former is not to pass on some component of substance to the latter, but – through his work – to establish the conditions for the latter's growth on the land. Growth here is not merely expressive, it is generative. Thus notions of ancestry, descent and the transmission of substance should be replaced by the notion of *regeneration*.

All this has implications for the way we use metaphors of containment, and for the way we view land and placed-ness. In the genealogical model, the land – indeed the entire environment – may be viewed as a kind of container in (or on) which life goes on. It holds life, but is in no way constitutive of it. Life itself is equated with what is inside, with the transmitted essence received at the point of conception. Thus the land, being external to life, is inanimate – it is dead. The genealogical model describes the succession of animate beings on an inanimate, ever-present substrate.

In the model I work with here, to the contrary, the land is very much alive, and enters directly into the constitution (generation) of persons. The relation between land and person is not one of containment, with the land outside and the essence of the person inside, but of integration. The person enfolds, within his or her being, his/her relations with the environment, including those social others who provide the work of growing that person. Conversely, these relations unfold in purposive action. It is in action that persons reveal themselves as fully constituted agents, revealing their connections to others and places by the effects they can have. Agency is integral to the constitution of persons. If there is a container here, it is the woman, in whose body a child is initially grown. A woman must be brought onto the land so that a child can be grown within her. Maternal kinsmen provide another sort of containment – that of social recognition – and thus they provide nurture for the name and identity of the growing child. By contrast – in the genealogical model – the land is a kind of container to which a woman must be brought so that the child can be grown *from* her. It is true that in both models the metaphor of the womb as a container is apt, but in the genealogical model the growth is supposed to come not from the land but from some kind of 'seed' that has been planted in the womb.

Apropos placedness, in the genealogical model the place is simply occupied. It is where a person happens to be. Each place is like a kind of slot, as on a peg-board, into which a particular descent line can be inserted. Kinship relations themselves, since they are defined by the transmission of context-independent components of essence, can be fully specified without reference to place at all. In the ethnography presented here, by contrast, places enter directly into the generation of persons, while persons – through their work – engender places. Persons, constituted by kinship relations of shared substance, are not joined to places constituted by geographical relations of spatial propinquity. Rather the constitution of persons and of places are mutually entailed aspects of the same process. In this sense kinship is geography, or landscape.[5]

Finally, this undermines the conventional dichotomy between the study of kinship (as an aspect of social organisation) and of work on the land (as an aspect of subsistence economics). Thus the logic of my argument points to the conclusion that kinship is not about descent through genealogy but is an outcome of the relations between land and people.

The Palem

Central to my description of the growth of persons, and the emergence of social groups and places among Nekgini speakers is an elaboration and description of the indigenous notion of the *palem*. In the chapters that follow, I unpack how this term is applied *both* to the structure upon which bride and body payments are displayed, mentioned at the beginning of this chapter, *and* to the group of people who in important ways *become* close kin through working together to produce the structure and payment. This group of people becomes a coherent entity in making such a payment, an entity which is given the same name as the land upon which the structure is built. They, in fact, over time become *a* palem. Thus people in Reite say, for example, 'I am of Yawaspiring palem' – Yawaspiring being the name of the place where these people make their affinal payments. The notion of the palem then describes not only a body, made of wealth, to be given away in transactions with affines. It also describes the social body who, in the process of making such a body of wealth, come together as an entity. Person, place, and identity are bound together in the same process of becoming. The next chapter looks at the history of formation, duration, and dissolution of the social units (palem) in Reite. This is my entry into the specific ethnographic demonstration of processes which produce persons, social groups, landscape, and thus ultimately, what we call kinship.

Notes

1. Contemporary Nekgini practice, with historical precedent.
2. Although it might fairly be said that the formalist approach never intended to capture such aspects.
3. See Preface.
4. I am grateful to Tim Ingold for clarifying the ideas contained in this condensed summary. And see Ingold (2000, Chapter 8).
5. Gow (1991) concludes that for Piro people of Western Amazonia, 'kinship *is* history' (2001: 7, original emphasis). The emergence of a lived landscape that I describe here is, of course, also historical. The historical process of generating persons produces a 'lived world' (in Gow's phrase).

Chapter Two
Residence History and Palem

Why should the materials of Iatmul culture drive the abstracting scientist to greater com-
plexities of exposition than are demanded by, for example, the culture of the Arapesh? Is the
complexity of exposition the reflection of a real complexity in the culture, or is it only an acci-
dental product resulting perhaps from a disparity between the language and culture of the
ethnographer and those of the community he is describing? (Bateson 1958 [1936]: 219)

Looking at the history of palem formation and dissolution is my starting-point in
understanding social organisation among Nekgini speakers. I begin by laying out
as clearly as possible the situation as I found it on arrival in 1994. Lawrence's
struggles with such a description lead me to examine further the assumptions of
the genealogical model. The apparent 'complexity' of rendering the Nekgini situation from an outside perspective is discussed in a digression at the end of this
chapter. As well as some history, in what follows I give the reader an entry into the
nature of Nekgini speakers' relations to places, and to one another.

Hamlets Past and Present

The name 'Reite' is used to refer to a number of different things. These are:
firstly; an administrative district, defined at the lowest level within the structure of
local government of the modern state of Papua New Guinea. Secondly: a centralised village, no longer existent, formally established by the colonial
administration. Thirdly: a collection of six separate hamlets; their distinct names
being based on recent residence in certain named areas of land, and which
together make the administrative district mentioned above. And finally: the name
of an overarching social grouping from which residents of two of the above hamlets claim to have originated. I discuss these senses of the name in what follows.

As an administrative district, defined at the lowest level within the structure of local government of the modern state of Papua New Guinea, Reite is represented by its own committee member on the local government council. The primary functions of this committee member (*Komiti*, a titular role in modern village organisation) cover dispute settlement, the organisation of community work (which occurs regularly and includes most of the residents of the six hamlets every Monday[1]), and other organisational roles pertaining to government projects. He (for the Komiti is invariably a man) is also thought to be responsible for the accommodation of, and gathering an audience for, other visitors who come to the area in an official capacity such as schoolteachers prior to the construction of their own accommodation, staff of the government coffee boards outreach schemes, and so forth. Today it is the responsibility of this man (the present Komiti has held the post since the early 1980s) to bring together residents of the six hamlets most obviously included in the area defined as 'Reite' by the local population. His role includes keeping the peace.

As an administrative area Reite includes the hamlets of Sarangama, Reite Yasing, Reite Yapong, Saruk, Ririnbung, and Marpungae (see Map 2). Each of these hamlets has its own particular history and status, as I touch upon below.

* * *

Reite[2] was the name of a centralised village, established by the colonial administration, which no longer exists today. During my fieldwork in 1994/95, Reite was a collection of dispersed hamlets rather than a single village. However, the name at one time referred to an administrative district established under the colonial government of Australia – based on a centralised village. It appears that under colonial government, people from the *palem* of Reite,[3] another palem called Ripia, and the palems making up the village (*yating*) of their near neighbours to the south (Sarangama), were encouraged to leave their traditional scattered hamlets[4] and join together in larger units for census and administrative purposes.[5]

Reite – the centralised village established by the colonial administration – included people who moved from Ripia yating and Sarangama yating. It is from this confederation that the present administrative area has taken its name. The colonial village was situated at the site known now as Reite Yasing. One must be aware of local people's own interest at the time to associate in such a settlement pattern. Lawrence (1964: 142–50) discusses the millenarian implications resettlement had for the Rai Coast populations, and argues that their participation in them during the post-war years was motivated mainly by the desire to catalyse the supernatural generation of wealth.

However, there are other reasons to be considered as well. In the case of the hamlet of Marpungae, where depopulation threatened,[6] they came under the protection of, and then became a part of, Reite during the middle years of this century. It can be seen from examples such as this that in his emphasis on millenarianism, Lawrence

Photograph 3 *The Komiti of Reite, Porer Nombo*

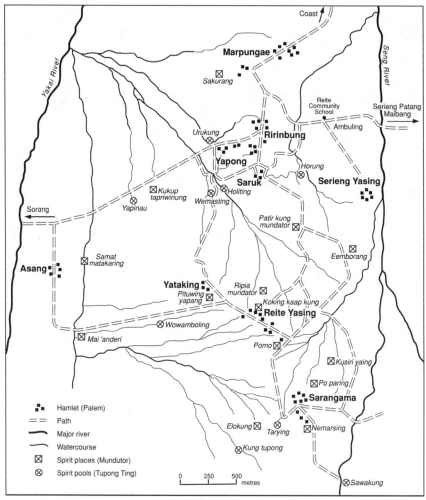

Map 2 *Reite and Neighbouring Hamlets Showing Spirit Places*

may have underplayed the indigenously changeable nature of hamlet formation and confederation. To be fair, however, he does note something similar in his monograph on the Garia of the Bagasin Hills: 'the northern Garia, while preferring their traditional system of small settlement local organisation, did not resent the new one imposed by the Australian administration' (1984: 103). Whatever the reasons for this interest, it was confined to the years of the administration's influence, and in fact long before National Independence in 1975, the village of Reite had fragmented into small groups based on landholding, ease of access to owned garden land, and proximity to either water or ritual/mythic sites. In short, by the time of my arrival, scattered hamlets based around single palem[7] were once more the norm.

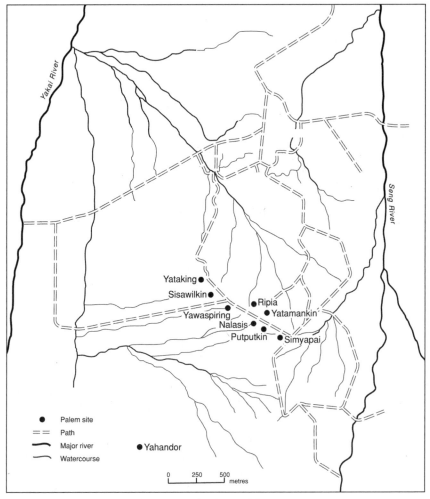

Map 3 *Some Previous Palem Sites of Ripia and Reite*

Even when obliged by the administration to live together as neighbours in one village, the hamlets making up the Reite administrative village chose to come together at the borders of their respective landholdings, and build their houses on named land owned by each group. This is in significant contrast to the trajectory of the neighbouring village of Maibang which I discuss below, and is testimony to the alternative interpretations of the colonial presence made in these two places.[8]

Map 2 shows present settlements within Reite. Map 3 shows the distribution of land names referring to past settlements. Changes in settlement location are significant in terms of the kin groups to which the land of a settlement gives its name. Thus changes in settlements highlight important changes in the history of

Reite groups. Recently, the most significant of these changes has been the move away from the original sites of the two settlements of Reite and Ripia, and the return of the bilingual Sarangama hamlet[9] to a central position on its own land, once the threat of warfare, and the colonial pressure on it to stay in the large Reite 'Yasing' village at the place known as Simyapai, had been lifted.

The move by some Reite people to Yapong, or the 'new camp', occurred in the early 1970s. The reason for this move was always stated as proximity to the most reliable water supply. One could, however, read more into it than this – as it was a return by the members of one palem to the centre of their landholding. The people of Ripia Yatamanikin palem were the first to move, and they moved onto their own land. Following them, again, people moved not to a single village site, but to areas of their own land, in reasonably close proximity, but nevertheless not banded together in a single settlement. The movement away from the original Yapong site, and the establishment of hamlets at Ririnbung, and then Saruk, occurred as the original settlers moved away from newcomers and more firmly onto their land. Saruk, with its *palem* and *passae* (see note 3), represents the culmination of this movement by those considered to come from Ripia Yatamanikin to their own settlement in the centre of their landholding. The completion of Saruk as a new hamlet site occurred during my residence there in 1994, when the *passae* (spirit/cult house) was opened. Thenceforth it became a place from which hospitality has been given, and named as 'a palem'.

* * *

Today Reite is a collection of six separately named hamlets, plus associated land-holdings and local social groupings based in name on recent residence in certain named areas of land.

In statements people make about the past, they assert that there must at one time have been a single palem called Reite, which having generated a number of named locations, with a palem situated on each, became known as a yating (or village), rather than being identified with a single palem. If this is a generative model for places or kin groups, not only is it phrased in terms of parentage by Nekgini speakers, it also involves the active separation of one place/kin group from another, based on separate residence. Yating ('ya' – house, 'ting' – shoot, extension, eye;[10] i.e., cleared plaza at the front of houses) refers to something like an extended family, to continue the Nekgini metaphor. Within it are separate dwellings that may have names of their own (i.e., they are palem), but are not defined as such by their separation *from their originating palem*. Definition has come instead through exchange with other, distant palem beyond the yating, prototypically in marriage. While nominally named, they still come under the authority and encompassing name of their originating palem, as do those palem that join others in a yating for their protection. The relation between palem in a yating is discussed further below.

Today, as Map 2 shows, there are six Reite hamlets, namely: Reite Yasing, Reite Yapong, Ririnbung, Saruk, Sarangama, and Marpungae. (I do not include Yataking for reasons given below). These are under the authority of the Reite Komiti. Serieng Yasing and Asang are conceptually and administratively distinct.

Map 3 shows the sites of some of the no longer existent hamlets (palem) which people in these current hamlets claim as their origins. The names of these previous hamlet sites are the source both of their connections (through living together in them), and their differentiation (they are separate named places within Reite). The significant names of these hamlet sites are as follows. From the old single hamlet of Reite were generated *Yawaspiring, Sisawilkin, Yawaspiring Simbiomb, Yataking,* and *Yahandor.* From the hamlet at Ripia came the hamlets of *Nalasis, Yatamanikin,* and *Putputkin.* At the time of my arrival, only *Sisawilkin, Yahandor* and *Yawaspiring* were represented by people who claimed the palem Reite as their origin. It is in collective reference to these people that the name Reite is used in the last of the four senses enumerated at the beginning of the chapter. Those claiming Ripia as their source and connection to one another were included in people from *Nalasis, Yatamanikin,* and *Putputkin.*

Thus people claim previous hamlet/palem association as their source of difference from one another within the broader designations of 'Reite' people or 'Ripia' people. Nevertheless, they may all claim to be 'Reite' as members of the administrative district, and as having lived together at Reite Yasing under the colonial administration. In terms of current residence, the people claiming connection through being Reite *Yawaspiring, Sisawilkin,* and *Yahandor* are all dispersed and differentiated. For example, one of the *Sisawilkin* brothers has a palem shared with the only surviving *Yawaspiring* child, and their new palem is known as *Yapong.* Yet they are all still 'Reite' because of a yet more temporally distant common place of origin: Reite palem.

The processes which produce named entities such as palem and yating are by nature ongoing. Nekgini speakers appear to make use of their named residence histories in ways that make sense for current ambitions, political considerations, and convenience. The move into a central administrative village was thus not resisted. Its form has influenced subsequent connections. Yet it has not been maintained, although it is one factor in the current organisation of processes of production and reproduction centred on residence and exchange. It also gives a coherence to the current perception of the six hamlets as a '*komuniti*' [T.P.].

In this area memory and tradition influence residence patterns. This influence is balanced by a marked absence of any prescriptive rule on settlement (i.e., one sanctioned in some law or power structure within the social groupings, other than the power of landowners to grant permission). In effect, people could construct their houses wherever they wished, and associate with one another – at varying degrees of relatedness – more or less at will. Thus the location and composition of hamlets was always changeable. As Lawrence puts it for the Garia:

The internal structure does not emphasise group formation. The inhabitants of a settlement never coincide with a particular unilineal group. Indeed, social structure is based ultimately on chains of interpersonal relationships between a man and various classes of people who, while they have no corporate existence in themselves, collectively represent what may be called his security circle. (1967 [1955]: 101)

Even so, people remember the places where their predecessors built their settlements, for they are cognisant of their connections through the places in which their ancestors made themselves significant, by providing hospitality and/or wealth from these places (from their palem) for affines or trade partners. Such connections are often apparent in shared myths or rituals associated with those places. Some gravitate towards these when planning their residence. At times, this tendency appears to the outsider to be inexpedient, as the older hamlet sites are without exception further from water than the newer, colonially influenced ones.

The settlements at the site of Reite Yasing were specifically said to be places where Reite people had always lived. They are named in the myths through which people there identify their claim to the land and their knowledge of how to make it productive (and see the density of spirit places around the Reite Yasing site on Map 2). Although residents of *Yasing* (*ya* house/place; *sing* egg, testicle, fruit; *yasing* 'old place or seed house/place') recognised the difficulty they made for themselves by living at a remove from water for much of the year, they often said their choice was made for the more significant reason of complying with and following customary ways (*behainim kastom* [T.P.]).[11]

It is interesting to note in this context that over the period for which I have been able to gather data, the residence patterns for neighbouring peoples have differed from that of Reite people. As might be expected from people who think of themselves as reciprocally implicated in the emergence and naming of places in their lands, these differences in the local interpretation of residence patterning, and the subsequent history of variety in response to the demands of the colonial government, are understandable at many levels.

The large Ngaing-speaking village of Maibang, 5 km to the east of the area of Reite hamlets and garden land, has remained along a ridge, uninhabited before colonial rule, to which people were moved by the administration in the years following the Second World War. There have been no moves on the part of Maibang villagers to return to the scattered hamlet pattern of the past, and they have consolidated a drawn-out settlement consisting of members of four or five *clans* (T.P.) around an area presently known by the name *Haus kiap* (T.P.: government rest house), after the house built for the region's colonial patrol officer on this spot. The original name of this place, a significant site (and for those who have knowledge of its history, a powerful one) in local Ngaing myth, has been superseded by this modern name in young people's usage. This is consistent with the acknowledged status of Maibang, at the present time, as a modernising village. Awareness of the outside world and orientation towards possible future change through the naming of sites in terms of contact history, rather than *patuki* (mythic enactments which produced the world in its stable form), is significant.

There is another possible reason for the change of name of this site, as it was known for the deposit of an object powerful to those performing sorcery. The replacement of the original name with the modern one may have been part of the drive to suppress the practice of sorcery (or at least maintain an appearance of having abandoned the knowledge) in what is now a Catholic village. The implication of each possible explanation of the name change is similar, and there is no basis on which to choose between them.[12]

Hamlets as Social Groups

I now turn to a more detailed analysis of social grouping and hamlet formation. I begin by describing the appearance of the hamlet, with its constituent buildings. I go on to a further explanation of the indigenous term 'palem', which leads to a discussion of the nature of hamlets as social groups, i.e., what it takes for a palem or place to be recognised and viable as a unit for social action, and for palem to associate in a yating (or village). Finally I examine the relation between the notions of clan and palem, focusing on the (anthropological) issue of lineality versus residence.

The Hamlet

The hamlets that make up the district of Reite are small affairs located on the ridges between the Seng and Yakai rivers. In its mature state a hamlet consists of the following buildings: a *passae* (a spirit or cult house),[13] a *palem* (a meeting house and bed from which food can be distributed to visitors), a number of dwelling houses for married couples and their female and younger male offspring, a boys' house (*haus boi* [T.P.]) for unmarried men, and possibly a building associated with the cash economy – a chicken-shed or a small trade store. I say in its mature state, as this is an ideal form for a hamlet to take. Of the hamlets that made up Reite, four were in this condition during 1994/95. When a hamlet is established in a new area, ritual work must be completed in order that the passae can be opened. Hamlets as places, and as groups of people, are generally only recognised by name after this has occurred.

It was often asserted that in the past, young men and married men frequently slept in the passae. During 1994/95 it was normal for there to be a separate dwelling for unmarried young men and boys, located somewhere in a hamlet. The institution of separate dwellings for young men removed from the spirit house was, I was told, a recent introduction. This would appear plausible, as when the mission workers who entered the area in the late 1930s suppressed practices openly associated with the spirits from everyday life, they also destroyed the furniture of the practices. These were most obviously the central spirit houses and their content (Reiner 1986: 172). Today one sees married men living in single dwellings with their wives, daughters and younger sons. Young men live in separate dwellings, and no one lives in the passae other than occasionally when men stay there during ritual activity. Modelling settlements on a Christian idea of conjugal relations, husbands and wives were encouraged to reside together when the passae were destroyed. Yet the problem of what to do with young men remained. All of the early mission workers who actually entered the area of Reite were native converts, recruited from areas close to the mission stations. They came from backgrounds where the separation of young men and women was thought desirable for the well-being of both, and their policy was, in secular affairs, to disrupt local practices as little as possible (Lawrence 1964: 55). It is unsurprising, then, that the practice of a separate dwelling for unmarried young men was retained, but after the destruction of the passae, this took place in a 'boy's house', built specifically for the purpose. This practice persists today, both in adjacent areas which consider themselves Christian, as well as those such as Reite which have turned away from the missions.

While it is interesting to consider why men have not returned to dwelling in the passae as the direct influence of Christianity has waned, it is possible that simple changes in dwellings themselves, and more to the point, in the ease of building houses, is the cause. Young men are able to build and occupy comfortable single-sex dwellings removed from the passae (which are 'traditional' in design, and, being on the ground, far less comfortable). Larger houses for married couples allow the physical separation thought necessary for the well-being of both husbands and wives.

The variation of buildings within hamlets, even within the administrative area of Reite, is worth noting. In 1995, one hamlet had a small Catholic church (Marpungae), three had a trade store each (Marpungae, Ririnbung, Sarangama), one a chicken-shed (Saruk), one a cocoa fermentary (Ririnbung), and two (Yasing and Yapong) had no buildings relating to the cash economy.

The make up of each of these hamlets, however, is centred upon the existence of the palem and passae (hereafter called just palem)[14] from which the people of the hamlet take their name, and which in turn takes its name from the land on which the palem is situated. As it is men who own land, palem tend to be made up of a group of related men and their unmarried sisters, their wives and their daughters. However, to be more specific than this would be misleading. A palem does not mean a group of men who are related a priori as certain kinsmen.

More about the Palem and Social Groups

Nekgini hamlets (*ya* – house/hamlet), are named after the land on which they are located. All land (and most land forms) are named in Nekgini discursive practice. Often the name of a site or an area commemorates a significant episode in a myth, or in the remembered ancestral history of the people whose land it is. Often the land is named with reference to a physical characteristic or feature. These are one and the same, as physical features attest to the actions of ancestors or mythical beings. People who established a hamlet in the viscinity of the small place called Reite became known as Reite.

A palem is the name for a platform or bed on which food is piled in an affinal exchange. Standing as it does next to the hamlet cult house (passae), the term is also used by extension to refer to the covered sitting area where people are welcomed, accommodated, and fed, on visits to the hamlet; the significant feature of this construction is the bed on which people sit or lie, and from which cooked food can be distributed. While not all hamlets in Reite while I lived there had staged an affinal presentation, all had a palem in the sense of somewhere to accommodate and provide hospitality for visitors.[15] Palem is also the term given to a group of people who have shared the use of one of these buildings ('at their door') to become significant persons, 'persons with a name', in the eyes of those who receive wealth and food from this structure. The extension of the term from the structure on which affinal presentations are made, to the place where hospitality is given, is understood as an extension of the same function – that of accommodating outsiders 'at one's door'.

People from the hamlet established at Reite came to be known, through sharing the palem there, as Reite people. Those visiting such a hamlet are ushered into the palem, and will refer to the residents of this place as if they were a single entity – having one door. Through their identification with the land upon which their hamlet is located, people come to have a certain kind of identity through time, and their descendants remember that they are part of the group once located at, and thus known as, Reite.

A collection of linked hamlets make up what we might call villages, known by the indigenous term *yating*. Yating take the name of the original palem site, although other house sites in a yating may in time become named palem of their own (i.e., become known by the name of the land on which they are situated and thus gain a name through recognition of their social presence in their own right). Yating formed in one of two ways. The prototypical emergence of a yating is generative; that is, a single palem gives birth to offspring. When a man has more than one son, it is likely that the male children of these men will wish to make camps of their own once they marry. As we will see below, one must make ceremonial presentations at one's own 'door'; that is, one must make a palem in one's own residential camp to distribute food and wealth in affinal presentations. Thus one palem may spawn several palem over the generations. Significantly in local people's explanations, these palem by default come under the authority of the senior man in the originating palem. As offspring of the same palem, people in them are siblings. The eldest sibling ideally has authority over his juniors. The group of palem generated in this way are called a yating. They are distinct houses, but join facing one plaza. However, internal disputes, particularly over marriages within the yating, will cause fission and the establishment of new palem geographically and politically removed from their originating palem. Yating then describe conceptual communities based on previous co-residence in the form of multi-palem settlements. I have heard the present six hamlets of Reite community described as a yating, coming as they do, under the authority of a single leader. Yating is both the plaza between palem and houses, and the conceptual connection between those who recognise one authority, making them, in part, siblings.

This appears to contrast with the Manambu of Avatip in the middle Sepik of whom Harrison writes. For the Manambu, small residential wards of patrilineal subclans were part of wider political organisations; large villages with 'politically equal descent groups' (Harrison 1990: 28, 29) and hierarchies built out of ritual control. For Nekgini speakers (who, it should be remembered, were and remain a much smaller population with less dense and less permanent settlements), it appears that palem were (as they are now) not fractions, or parts of a wider coherent whole that was somehow disrupted and fragmented by colonial influence. Palem themselves embody the principles of generation and differentiation which are fundamental to Nekgini social life, thus yating were always inherently unstable.

Yating, as physical and/or conceptually unified entities often appear to contain a division of labour between what we would term 'ritual' offices. Porer Nombo explained this in 2001 as follows:

> The first man or the first born should have authority over the others. A sensible man, a man with good thoughts who remembers to look after his younger siblings will have authority of this kind. He will be a leader. Before we called these leaders *luhi ai* (or 'gorogor man' in Tok Pisin). Such a man would tell people when to do what according to kastom. Warriors (*salap ai* 'bowmen') and sorcerers (*mernung ai* 'poison men') would arise as follows. In initiation, boys would be tested for their suitability for sorcery, or magically transformed into warriors. The *luhu ai* would know who these people were. Others would not (for their protection). They were underneath his authority, and when he said 'stop' they would stop. Another word for this man is *topi*, the man who leads in all things. If one of his people was threatening other people, these others would appeal to the *luhi ai* to stop them. Any who disobeyed his authority would be banished by his other followers.
>
> When a family gets large, there are certain ways that a palem such as this might be broken apart. One route is anger and fighting within the family. In this case, some of the group will decamp and make their houses elsewhere. When they want to marry, they will make a bed for food (palem) of their own there [in their new place]. Another reason would be marriage with a sister, and the fights following from this. Some would go and make another palem elsewhere, and become enemies (*birua* [T.P.]). Making a new palem occurs when something has occurred to make people angry with one another. It makes you a different lot of people.

The division of labour in a palem is often seen reflected in the division of labour between palem in a yating, whether physically present, or conceptually important as knowledge of past siblingship and co-operation. As the model is generative, it seems to have been the case that a man who learnt sorcery would find among his sons one suitable to learn it from him. But this was not rigid. Knowledge is not necessarily transferred from father to son, as land usually is, but rather is given, as power, to those who show aptitude and wish to control that power. They were and are exclusive, however; a man who could nullify the effects of *mernung* could not practice it. Ritual offices then could become associated with palem, without this being a defining feature of their difference. As all palem needed such knowledge, the confederation of palem into a larger entity (yating) was not a necessary element of social organisation.

I was told that at some time in the past, Reite and Ripia had a palem and a passae each. The descendants of each of these two palem separated and made palem of their own, leaving, in the case of Ripia, a settlement on the original named site. New hamlets took on the names of their new sites. Thus new palems at Nalasis, Yatamanikin, and Putputkin were added to that of Ripia. The palem of Yataking, Yawaspiring, Sisawilkin, and Yahandor replaced that of Reite. From the proximity of the appropriate named places in this area, it is apparent that the significance of movement lay not in the quantity of physical distance, but rather in the quality of movement. This was embodied by the construction of a palem which, in each case, although spawned by Ripia or Reite, was distinct within each yating. Each hamlet thus became a named palem, and a unit of social action in itself.

However, here things become more complex. The make-up of such a hamlet is not prescribed by kinship. People are relatively free to move and make a new hamlet on their own land, or with another's permission on another's land, as they see fit. They are also free to join an established hamlet if they are accepted by its members. Some authority is exercised by elders of each place (each hamlet site) as to where its inhabitants might move, but their words carry little sanction other than disapproval. This freedom would have been circumscribed in the past by the need for safety. Though people were free to move residence, considerations of warfare and sorcery significantly affected hamlet location prior to the influence of the Australian administration from the late 1930s.

The 'Clan' and the Palem: The Problem of Lineality versus Residence

To summarise, groups of a certain kind are significant in the settlement patterns of this area. These are to some degree land- and residence-based. Men are considered landowners and stay on the land of their fathers. Residence is generally patrilocal. Hamlets thus are usually established by a man and his brothers, or a man and his sons, on his own land. Women move to the hamlets of their husbands on marriage. The groups so formed are called palem after a ritual structure, and are named after the site of the structure, the mediatory role of which is to make persons and groups of persons appear as agents in the eyes of specific others. Marriage both enables, and compels, the emergence of palem. Yet the composition of these palem, in terms of personnel, is variable. What form do these variations take?

Nekgini-speaking people living in the hamlets that make up the contemporary designation 'Reite' sometimes speak of themselves as belonging to *clans*, a term introduced through the lingua franca Tok Pisin.[16] Nekgini speakers translate palem into *clan* for outsiders. I intend here to establish, through the examination of two contemporary examples of hamlet formation, how the palem is made up, and what relevance – if any – can be attached to the way that people who share an affiliation to the same palem speak of themselves as members of 'clans'.

When newly arrived in the field in 1994, I assumed that the term 'clan' accurately described what I saw as groups of male landowners who handed land on to their sons and brothers' sons. I imagined that the term referred to a group of agnatically related persons, a segment of a patrilineage. In the context of a professed ideology of male landholding, I assumed I was looking at a system of patrilineal descent. By making genealogies of all the hamlets in the area, I thought I would end up with a neat set of residential groups based on subdivisions of the overall clans of Ripia and Reite.[17] My first doubts about this arose when I came to look at the kinship links between the members of the very hamlet in which I was resident.

In what follows, I use the terms familiar from our genealogical modelling of relatedness. In many ways, this is unsatisfactory. My argument so far has been that assumptions which lie behind, or are invoked through using this terminology, are inappropriate to this case. At first, one might forgive the use of them. As I mention, my use of the genealogical method to gather data on the 'kinship' of people around me was my first clue as to the difficulties which that modelling of relatedness presents in this case. However, as my argument progresses, the use of the term 'sibling' or 'cross-cousin' makes less and less sense as a conventional referent to a genealogically defined position. Thus I take the evidence I present about Nekgini residence, marriage and exchange, their perception of relatedness, as a cumulative re-definition of terms such as 'siblingship' and 'cross-cousin' as I go along. Even where the term may be appropriate to genealogically based referents (i.e., that siblings are siblings because of sharing the same father and mother) I ask the reader to remember that siblingship is a specific Nekgini relationship, and that my description works towards a translation of the referents 'siblingship' has for Nekgini speakers. To paraphrase Viveiros de Castro (2001), it is not who is a brother (in our sense), but what is a 'brother' (as the chosen translation of an indigenous term) which I work to establish. Siblingship, in other words, does not rely on a perception of shared biogenetic substance.

Another strategy might have been to use only the Nekgini terms. However, whether rightly or wrongly, I judge that this would be unwieldy and complicated. Chapter 3 describes the complexities of translating the Nekgini term *upaning* in terms of genealogical referents, for example. My description in these chapters *amounts to* the translation of Nekgini kin terms. Thus I ask that the reader modifies their understanding of 'cross-cousin' or 'sibling' to one of '*upaning*' or '*paap/wanik*' as we proceed. As with the translation of *asurung* ('blood') which I come onto, I intend to both use, and highlight, the problematic nature of the use of terms we are familiar with.

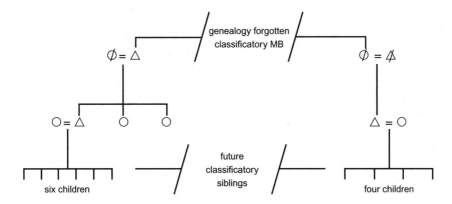

Figure 2.1 *Kinship in Saruk Hamlet 1994/95*

In the hamlet of Saruk lived an old man and his two unmarried children, a girl and a boy, his married son, and this son's wife and children. They had built a palem adjacent to their houses, and an unopened *passae* on ground raised a little from this. There was another man in this hamlet (apart from myself), however, with his wife and children who was, to the elder man, a classificatory sister's son, and thus to his son, a cross-cousin (*sumei*) practising name avoidance. This cross-cousin had brothers living at a small remove in an adjacent hamlet (Ririnbung), but had chosen to locate his house with his mother's brother (the connection is more like father's mother's brother's son). In doing so, he removed himself from the hamlet his brothers had on their land. More significantly, he and his wife became known as part of *Saruk* palem, in which he was henceforth obliged to make ceremonial food presentations. The first time this palem was used, he helped purchase the pig which was cooked at the opening of the passae, and in distributing part of this pig to a man who had helped with the previous year's planting, he became known as a member of the palem in the named area of Saruk. Even were a palem as a social entity to turn out to be merely a residential group, and to have nothing to do with inheritance, my idea of clans and lineages as the basis for residence at least looked questionable.

Reite people say that it is unacceptable for a man to make a presentation away from his own house (it must be 'at his door'). Thus in moving to Saruk palem, this man committed himself to being known as *Saruk* rather than of the palem of his brothers. More significantly from the point of view of my investigations, I discovered that his children will be known as *Saruk*, and will be 'of' the same palem as the children of his mother's brother's son (MBS), in the same way as this man was himself originally 'Nalasis' – a palem name shared by his brothers who lived at Ririnbung. The children of these cross-cousins living at Saruk are considered to be 'siblings' rather than 'cross-cousins'. It is this kind of entity that was being called a *clan* in Tok Pisin, as the word was used in direct translation of the term *palem*. What is more, there appeared to be no other significant principle of social organisation. That is, many reasons were given for association in palem, but there was nothing beyond the association in palem that was cited as explanation for association. *Clan*, as a way of describing association through previous palem, was being used as a kind of descent construct, but not one based exclusively on lineality. Men passed their previous palem affiliations on to their children, but this did not appear to constrain these children in their subsequent residential alignments. There is thus no guarantee of continuity across three generations, from grandparent to grandchild, which is the minimal condition for lineality in the conventional sense. Men and women descended from the same palem referred to each other as brothers and sisters, with the retroactive logic that they were 'siblings' precisely because they were of the same palem.

I soon began to come across other difficulties in following the logic of the kinship connections I was being presented with – many people told me with great emphasis that they were 'brothers' to one another, yet could not find any common connection other than a link through a palem site which each of their ancestors had inhabited. Ripia as a *clan* was turning out to be Ripia as a historically distant residence site (a yating). The link people made through this connection appeared to be one of kinship, yet it seemed to be based on common origin in terms of place, not of biogenetic ancestry.

The hamlet of Saruk turned out to be a typically 'irregular' example. In some cases, hamlets were not apparently so complex. The hamlet of Yataking consisted of a man and his two unmarried daughters, his three unmarried sons in a separate dwelling, and a palem and an unopened passae. However, as a hamlet (opposed to a piece of land) it was never referred to by its name. Thus those who lived there did not go by this name. This was partly because the actual site – *Yataking* – was occupied by a man who came from the now physically absent palem of *Sisawilkin*. In wealth distributions I witnessed he was called 'Sisawilkin' rather than 'Yataking' because of his origin in the sibling set of the *Sisawilkin* palem. In other words, since he was not descended from the old palem of Yataking, it was not yet relevant to describe him and his sons as this new and separate palem. His sons would have to make the palem their own, and be recognised as active persons in their own right by wealth distribution from there, before they could be named as a palem, and thus take on the name Yataking. Until then recognition was due to their father, not to them or their new place of residence.

People referred to the hamlet at Yataking by the father's use name rather than with reference to the name of the land (it was referred to as 'Aisir's compound' – Aisir being the use name his affines and cross-cousins applied to him).[18] The future recognition of the palem, for the purpose of giving a separate identity to the sons of this man, would depend on the active appearance of these men through acts of exchange from this position. This case, just as the previous one, illustrates the numerous possible referents to which people appeal to define their connections with others.

From the two brief examples presented above, we may conclude that the palem is patently not a division of a patrilineage. There are, in fact, as many examples of divergence from a simple descent-based residence pattern, or from socially visible groupings based on patrilineal connection, as there are hamlets in Reite. Although palem may well, and often do, consist of groups of brothers, they also often consist of cross-cousins or even more distantly related people whose descendants come to call each other 'sibling' because they live together and aid each other's enterprises.

The Labours of Lawrence

The situation is reminiscent of one Lawrence found along the coast. He writes, 'Garia society is cognatic or bilateral, there are no stable local units' (1967: xii) – or, we might say, no principles of association that he could discern that provided stable and corporate groups – the 'building blocks' of society. My analysis begins with residential groups and places because kin groups of a kind (and they are the most visible and stable kind of grouping in Nekgini social life) appear to be based on residence and landholding. Lawrence too focused on land, but he was concerned with how the ownership of this resource revealed extra-genealogical factors which *along with* biological connection, would provide a basis for modelling society. Lawrence writes:

> The potential social relationships which can be deduced from titles to land are of great theoretical importance. They represent an interlocking system of rights and obligations which can reinforce purely biological relationships (those of kinship and descent) within the security circle. (1967 [1955]: 114)

He looked to society to designate land rights, and then to how groups formed around these jural and political divisions. In other words, society, if it was anywhere, appeared in the divisions of land, and in the groups made apparent by these divisions. (I come to the issue from a different direction. If Reite people say that land produces people (see Chapters 4, 5, and 6), then for them, people are related because of sharing land, not the other way around.)

Lawrence found himself dealing with a situation similar to the one I have outlined above not only in writing about the Garia of the Bagasin Hills area south of Madang town, but also in his ethnography of the Ngaing – immediate neighbours of the Nekgini to the west (see Map 2). The problem is limited neither to his analysis, nor to this specific area. Harrison, for example, writing much more recently, reports that for Avatip (Middle Sepik): 'the problem from the point of view of these societies was not simply how to establish and maintain ties between political groups but, more basically, how to create discrete groups out of these webs of interconnections in the first place' (Harrison 1993: 64).

In what I have so far reported of Reite residential organisation, we can find parallels with Lawrence's portrayal of the Garia. As Strathern notes, Lawrence found that the source of his problem in re-presenting Garia organisation as a structure, in codifying its norms and patterns, lay in the complexity of apparently individual choice as their basis for living together (Strathern 1992b). As Harrison observes

(1993: 64), the problem appears to be one whereby groups are intrinsically unstable because of the strength of their member's 'external' ties. Lawrence writes:

> local organisation is not a function of any single feature of the social system, such as common land rights in a particular bush god domain or membership in a particular descent group. Populations of most settlements are irregular and unstable. They are aggregations of persons who are interrelated according to no set pattern – in some cases not interrelated at all – but who have come together because, at least for the time being, they have common economic interests.... (Lawrence 1984: 33)

At times, according to Lawrence, these aggregations are based on biological kinship, at times on economic self-interest. Lawrence's book on Garia social organisation (1984) is testimony to his dedicated attempt to follow Garia interconnections, and to produce a model of describing them. This model is highly complex, and develops the notion of a 'security circle' (1955, 1967, 1984). Each individual or 'cognatic stock' (sibling set) is at the centre of a set of relations based on kinship, landholding, trade, and friendship. Lawrence divides this circle of kinsmen and associates into a 'close grade' and a 'distant grade', based on whether or not ego may marry them, eat their produce, and rely on them in warfare/sorcery.

> The close grade of the kindred is essentially the core of ego's security circle. Apart from the biological relationships involved, strict rules of behaviour are imposed. These prevent ego from marrying within the close grade and eating any pig, dog or fowl raised by its members. (Lawrence 1967 [1955]: 102)

Although based, in his account, on the pre-given connections of biological kinship ('patrilineal and matrilineal kin… each with an agnatic core…', [Lawrence and Hogbin 1967: xiii]), within this close grade are included what Lawrence describes as 'bush brothers' – that is, those who share landholdings and garden plots in the same area as ego. The connections to these persons are stated explicitly in kinship terms: 'As bush brothers are considered the equivalent of kinsmen of the close grade on the grounds that "one bush is the same as one blood", they are included… within the security circle' (Lawrence 1967 [1955]: 125). External ties must be given as much weight as 'internal' (biological/genealogical) ones. Yet despite this inclusion of non-agnatically related persons into the close grade of a person's kin, Lawrence insists on maintaining the importance of patrilineal and patrilateral connections, as biologically given, in his account of the make-up of the security circle:

> The fact that non-agnatic cognates can hold personal cultivation rights on plots bearing its name means that they are linked to its members by economic as well as biological ties. This results in a complex network of relationships between patrilineages on the basis of interlocking land rights. (Lawrence 1967: xiii)

* * *

In his work on the Ngaing, Lawrence finds things slightly easier, in that he can discern more significant lineages – in fact he characterises Ngaing society as 'double unilineal' rather than 'cognatic' (although in some of his writings, these terms appear indistinguishable or interchangeable). Lawrence describes the Ngaing hamlet 'as a pseudo patriclan' (Lawrence 1965: 200); that is, he assumes that because these groups of men, whose offspring call one another sibling, live together, there must be a genealogical rationale for their association. As Carsten has recently described, 'while it may be easy to find resemblances between what anthropologists call social and biological aspects of kinship and certain indigenous notions, such resemblances may be misleading' (Carsten 2000: 27). As with Nekgini hamlets, it appears that agnatically related men (siblings or parallel cousins) form the basis of residential groups. We have come around again to my premature assumption concerning the meaning of the lingua franca term *clan*. As Meyer Fortes wrote, in commenting upon Lawrence's Garia monograph, 'in some…New Guinea cognatic systems, there is, however, a patrilineal and patrilateral bias in that the most important land rights are vested in patrilineages' (Fortes 1984: xi).

It seems that in Lawrence's desire to find the groups which made up Garia society, he was willing to call groups of men resident in a hamlet 'patrilineages' even if they were not based on descent as it is usually understood. In Durkheimian mode, Lawrence looked for superorganic entities which made society present, and which provided a jural and political framework. These appeared to be provided, despite the complex pattern of external ties (i.e., those beyond co-resident groups to 'bush brothers', 'matrilineage', 'trade friends' and so forth), in landholding groups based on descent through the male line. Where this was not the case, he was forced to resort to statements about 'fictitious' kinship and 'pseudo' clans. The problem lay not in Garia or Ngaing organisation (they manage okay), but in Lawrence's conception of the principles governing association. Where anomalies to the patrilineal principle intruded into his analysis, he accommodated them with talk of 'individual choice' (1967 [1955]: 102), 'flexible' society, and 'manipulation' (1984: 2).

In the context of a discussion of the place of land and produce in kinship, Andrew Strathern charts the possible courses that anthropologists of what he terms the 'pro-genealogy' school and the 'anti-genealogy' school might take, in dealing with the collapse of the African segmentary lineage model when applied in the New Guinea Highlands (Barnes 1962). This moment was a decisive one in the anthropological understanding of kinship and social organisation there. He writes that:

> The model began to break down on all three fronts of definition: it was not clear in all cases whether groups were corporate; their modes of segmentation and political recombination did not appear to follow the patterns established for Africa; and, worse, it was unclear whether Highlands groups could be called lineages at all. (A. Strathern 1973: 24)

Strathern concludes that the essence of the problem lay in the tension between society and biology, or between social relationships and genealogical relationships (in anthropological accounts). In the case of Lawrence's account, this tension is clear in his need to relate association based on land to that based on lineage affiliation. Let me return to his assertion that connections based on land 'represent an interlocking system of rights and obligations which can reinforce purely biological relationships (those of kinship and descent)...' (1967 [1955]: 114). In assuming a duality of society and nature, Lawrence was left unable to reconcile two incommensurate logics – those of 'real' (biological) relationship, and of 'fictitious' (social) ones. There are plenty of social relationships (principles of association, cross-cutting ties) in his account; but no 'society' as a system of corporate groups. Thus he is left arguing that 'common residence may lead to friendships which he [a native] expresses by means of kinship fiction' (Lawrence 1967 [1955]: 133), as if it were biological kinship which was to provide the model for all relations of identification.

I discern two sides to Lawrence's problem here. The first arises from the assumption that real kinship implies genealogical connection. This forces him into making the untenable distinction between real and fictitious kinship, which is mapped onto the even more problematic distinction between the biological and the social. The second problem arises from the assumption that for there to be social relationships there must be 'society', conceived as a system of corporate groups. But Lawrence simply could not extract such a system out of the maze of cross-cutting links and 'fictitious' (social rather than biological) kinship relations that he claimed were so important among the Garia.

As Marilyn Strathern has argued (Strathern 1992b), it is the assumption that 'social' implies groups that leads us to view cognatic kinship (classically defined as a web of genealogical connections) as not social but residually biological, constitutive of the individual in opposition to society. One could argue, then, that the assumption that underlies the second of Lawrence's problems (that society implies groups) has a consequence (the identification of genealogical kinship with biology), which then dictates the terms in which a solution to the first problem is attempted (by distinguishing 'fictitious' kinship as non-biological and therefore social). However the result of all this reasoning is plainly contradictory, since 'fictitious' kinship turns out to be just as web-like as 'real kinship', and lacks the character of corporateness by which the social was supposed to be distinguished in the first place.

Complexity

Complexity appears when our explanatory apparatus fails us, making the object of analysis seem incomprehensible – hence 'complex'. The modelling of Garia and Ngaing social structure that Lawrence gives us is nothing if not complex. The exceptions to his principles of group formation are, 'ramifying' and, in the end, overwhelming. Codification is not the source of the problem, nor does it lie necessarily in the language of rules, which in these kinds of instances follows statistical analysis to reveal trends and regularities. It is the imperative of translation itself that binds us to certain forms.

Marilyn Strathern has discussed the way 'complication' arises where there are 'always more things to take into account'. She cites a background, 'a cultural milieu', to this, which is committed to notions of pluralism and multiplication.

> A cultural account of Western pluralism would address the way a sense of both diversity and of an increase in the complexity of phenomena is produced by changing the scale of observation (Strathern 1992a). By changing scale I mean switching from one perspective on a phenomenon to another, as anthropologists routinely do in organising their materials. It is made possible by a modelling of nature that regards the world as naturally composed of entities – a multiplicity of individuals or classes or relationships – whose characteristics are in turn regarded as only partially described by analytic schema (Strathern 1991: xiv, emphasis removed).

And this pluralism (modelled as a complex structure) is exactly what we see in Lawrence's account of the Garia. Individuals multiply their reasons for associations along ramifying principles. Whether he focuses on the individuals, the principles, or the organisations, explanation is only partial. Entities multiply, while the modelling of their relations becomes complex.

If our analytic disposition both distances us from, and makes ramifying complexity out of, the object of study, how might we go about an alternative: describing persons and their actions and motivations as they make themselves appear? If we could look to how Reite people produce palem, names, produce, and affines, we might find principles that underlie their work. Such an investigation will provide us with an alternative notion of personhood to one predicated, as Lawrence's patently was, on the socialising and stabilising influence of society on biologically related individuals. An alternative notion of personhood, and of human/environmental relations, would in fact amount to an alternative social theory. I replace the complexities of group formation around 'flexible', 'individualistic' (Lawrence 1984) rules, with a translation of the real complexity of Nekgini understandings and concerns which centre on the issue of how one produces persons.

Whereas Lawrence asserts that 'social structure and local organisation cannot be described simultaneously' (Lawrence 1984: 33), I argue to the contrary that social structure and local organisation are simultaneously presented in the creation of palem. This is possible because Reite people do not distinguish between a real and a fictitious genealogy, and regard substantial connections as created in shared land and production, not in genealogical descent. This has consequences for kin terminology, and marriage. Or rather, marriage is one aspect of the generative process whereby persons are defined. I turn to this in the next chapter, and begin to outline the generation of persons and places.

Notes

1. *wok Mande* (T.P.).
2. Lawrence (1964), Wurm (1981); or Reiti (Bentinkt 1949/50).
3. *Palem* is an indigenous term by which social and residential groupings are described. Although as I discuss below, it is translated by Reite people as *clan* in the lingua franca Tok Pisin, I refrain from using the anthropological term 'clan' here. Rather, a palem is in fact the platform from which food is distributed in affinal payments. It stands beside the cult house (*passae*) of each hamlet, and by extension, the word palem also refers to the open meeting-house of each hamlet: the place from which food is distributed, and in which visitors to the hamlet are given hospitality. People are connected through this activity, and thus become conceptually linked with the structure itself. They 'are' a palem. This is clarified and explained at length below. Where I use the Tok Pisin term *clan* in the text, I report directly from the speech of informants, and use italics to highlight this.
4. Although in the case of Sarangama, two palem were resident in one place (yating) for the protection of the smaller.
5. Compare Lawrence (1955: 40–1; 1964: 143).
6. Perhaps caused by a smallpox epidemic which is reported to have passed along the Rai Coast seaboard between 1893 and 1896 (Burton 1998: 19). Marpungae at this time were settled on the banks of the Yakai river, close to the coast. The Sarangama palem of Kumundung also suffered almost terminal depopulation three or four generations B.P. It is worth noting that these historical events were put down to aggression by others, and achieved through *mernung* (spirit poisoning). Large loss of life in the 1970s, however, was always said to be because of influenza.
7. Hamlets are viewed as buildings grouped around this bed/meeting/cult house.
8. Briefly, while Nekgini speakers of Reite tended to rely on kastom (traditional religion and exchange forms) to bring modernisation, Maibang residents have gone the other way, expecting change to come from following the ways of the mission and commerce.
9. Sarangama people speak 'Dau' (Lawrence 1964, 1965, N'dau) as well as Nekgini, presumably because they have migrated from higher into the Finisterres and retain their old language despite their inclusion in Reite as an administrative (now) or protective (past) group.
10. And see Chapter 4 for more on the translation of 'ting'.
11. Whether Nekgini hamlets were on ridges for defensive reasons, for comfort in the rainy season, or for more esoteric reasons (proximity to the 'dry, hot' places where ancestral bones are kept), or all of these combined, is unclear to me.
12. In Reite no such Tok Pisin names are given to any sites, yet the suppression of *mernung* has been just as vigorously pursued.
13. Called a *haus tambaran* in Tok Pisin.
14. *Passae* and *palem* are necessarily a pair. The platform (*palem*) on which an affinal payment is constructed requires ritual work to complete. A *passae* is necessary to house the spirits during this ritual work. Thus the *palem* as a significant structure does not exist without a *passae*. However, it is the presence of a *palem* which gives a hamlet a name and a certain permanence as a social grouping. Both the material constructions, and the social grouping (the people who live around the two) are called *palem*. Hence I use the Nekgini term for a hamlet and its residents (*palem*) in what follows.
15. Importantly they were not named palem in the sense of a social group (as yet), however. For that to be the case, they would have had to complete significant hospitality, i.e., an affinal exchange, from this bed. And see below.
16. As do Ngaing speakers, hence my use of the word in the previous section.
17. One might think that my pre-field reading, especially of Lawrence (to whom I shall come below), would have made me wary of such assumptions. However, as Roy Wagner describes so well in *The*

Invention of Culture (1975), arriving in the field tends to encourage theoretical amnesia, and a desire to organise what one sees and hears into a recognisable system as quickly as possible.

18. Name avoidance is required between many categories of kin in Nekgini speakers' practice. These include affines, cross-cousins, and the parents of cross-cousins. Use names sometimes replace true names in these cases, and are based on accomplishments, failures, or physical attributes.

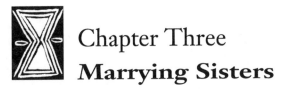

Chapter Three
Marrying Sisters

This chapter is divided into two parts. The first part (Defining Relationships) introduces Nekgini kin terminology in relation to siblingship, gender, and marriage. I report on the recent history of Reite marriages, and on a surprising prevalence of what they term 'wrong marriage'. The first part concludes by discussing 'wrong marriage' in relation to aspects of the anthropological literature on incest prohibition. The second part (Myths and Explanations) introduces Nekgini understandings of productive separation. I outline a myth in which the mechanisms and consequences of marriage are given a peculiarly Nekgini shape. It is this that makes sense of the material presented in the first part. The productive separation described in the myth is also central to the 'generative' nature of Nekgini social organisation. I conclude with a theoretical digression on the consequences of arguing, as I do here, that persons are defined by their placement in a field of generative relations.

Defining Relationships

Nekgini kin terms could be included in those systems called 'Iroquois' (Murdock 1949), where cross-cousins are distinguished from parallel cousins. Terms for cross-cousins recognise opposite-sex difference in the parental generation, but parallel cousins are classified with siblings. Cross-cousins are called by a term which differs significantly from the term for siblings, as the latter takes no account of relative sex. The terms for cross-cousin take account of the relative sex of the speaker and referent.[1]

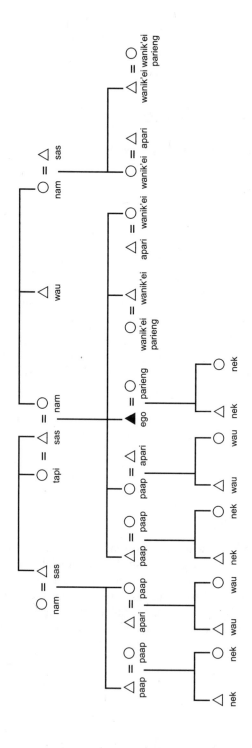

Figure 3.1 *Nekgini Sibling/Parallel Cousin Terminology*

FOR MALE SPEAKER

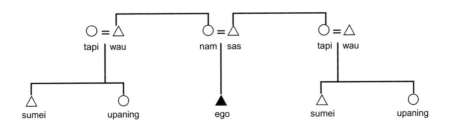

FOR FEMALE SPEAKER

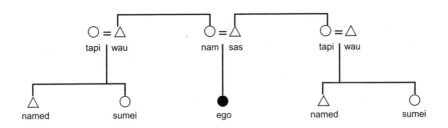

Figure 3.2 *Nekgini Cross-cousin Terminology*

Sibling Sets and Hamlet Groups

Nekgini terminology differentiates between elder and younger siblings. There is no obligation of name avoidance among siblings. Spouses of siblings are also called sibling, unless there is an opposite-sex relationship between the speaker and the sibling who is espoused. In this case, although the speaker will continue to call that sibling 'elder/younger sibling' or by name, her spouse is referred to with a term that appears to mean 'married to sibling' (*apari*) and name avoidance is required.

The word for elder sibling is *paap*. The word for younger sibling is *wanik'ei*. It is possible to distinguish male from female siblings with the addition of the word *parieng* to the term, so an elder female sibling may be called formally *paap parieng*, and a younger *wanik'ei parieng*. In practice however, the word *parieng* is unheard. It does not amount to a primary term of reference.

In contemporary Reite, Tok Pisin is often used in referring to kin, and the translation of both *paap* and *wanik'ei* is '*brata*'. The term *susa* is generally used to mean opposite-sex cross-cousin. Although there is no hierarchy built into this terminology, differences of seniority within the category *brata* are in practice both relevant and asserted.

In these hamlets, children grow up with their sibling set. They are surrounded by parallel cousins who are undifferentiated terminologically from what we would term true brothers and sisters. They call all their parental generation in the hamlet (palem) mother (*nam*) or father (*sas*), and all above this *asi*.[2] There is emphasis on hierarchy and authority, as we saw in the previous chapter, within the palem. This is replaced by an emphasis on gender between palem (in that cross-cousins are referred to in primary terms which take account of sex, not birth order). What does this mean for gender relations within sibling sets?

On reading discussions of gender as it has recently been presented in ethnographic analyses of Melanesian societies (Strathern 1988), people I know in Britain are likely to object to the claim that, in a sense, sibling/children may be ungendered (as the terminology here implies). 'Come on!', they are likely to say, 'Melanesians cannot be that stupid. They must recognise the difference between girl and boy children'. Recently Lambert (2000) has made this point in a scholarly fashion, arguing that however much the associations in others' kinship systems differ from European cultural conceptions, kinship is nevertheless 'fastened in bodily sexual difference, with all that this implies about the embodied, material nature of one's relation to the world' (123).

Of course people in Reite recognise physical difference, and they allocate tasks and the company of children accordingly. Girl children spend time with their mothers to a later age than boy children, they learn to carry net-bags of food, firewood, and water on their heads rather than on their shoulders. They learn to cook in a pot before boy children do. What is not clear to some observers is that by these apparent gender roles, people are not confirmed in their *essential nature* as gendered. The significant, or visible acts of a gendered person are not these 'roles', which are in fact interchangeable (and are interchanged regularly), but rather the major gendering conditions of child-bearing and feeding for a woman, and gardening and hunting for a man. These attributes must be *elicited*; and thus gendering is something people do with one another. I am not presenting a novel argument (Strathern 1988, and see Lambert 2000: 125, fn. 2) in asserting that for Nekgini speakers, these are the *significant* moments in gendering the person.

Comparative ethnographic support from a geographically proximate region of Papua New Guinea can be found in Goodale's study of the Kaulong of West New Britain to which I refer throughout this chapter. She writes, 'Kaulong are not as concerned with maintaining a cultural distinction between men and women as they are in distinguishing between the sexually active and the celibate' (Goodale 1981: 277). Siblings in a hamlet group are *by definition* not sexually active together, thus their sex is recognised without this being the recognition of gender.

In a hamlet, then, children grow up together as, if you will, male and female people, but their possible productivity as sexual and therefore gendered persons is not an aspect of the exogamous hamlet. A productivity of a kind is present, there are girls doing female tasks with their mothers, and boys learning (in no structured sense) to hunt, shoot, fish, and so forth. There is the time of puberty, when initiation for both sexes occurs, and a time of separation at this point. After initiation, both male and female siblings continue to share the hamlet,[3] and become more involved in the daily tasks in which their complementarity is apparent. As ageing parents leave more to them, this asexual complementarity is strengthened.

I was struck by the depth of feeling, the admiration, and joy with which grown-up opposite sex siblings treated one another during my time in Reite. Young women whom I had known for months and had never seen as more than polite and industrious became animated, laughing and conversing when their male siblings came to visit them where they were staying in town. The freedom for young women that is possible with a sibling is unparalleled elsewhere in their lives. In a return, as it were, to the freedom of childhood, in being able to joke without sexual connotations, to talk openly and animatedly with persons of the opposite sex who are not ambiguous and threatening (as are potential affines), people appeared to me to relax and come out of themselves as personalities. If I am right in my perception that marriage is an onerous idea for both young men and young women,[4] it is only with those whom one is unable to marry – one's siblings – that one is able to relax. With anyone else there is the danger of attracting their attention, and possibly more than this, encourage them to use love-magic.

The other side of this affection and ease between siblings is the anger and occasionally hatred (men especially) have for their in-laws. I recall a respected and powerful man, married for many years and with grown and married daughters of his own, sitting swearing viciously about the man who married his youngest sister within the last few years. She had been staying with her brothers in her natal hamlet, seeking a cure from them for her sick baby, and her husband's only current fault was his immanent arrival to collect them after their stay. There was no open hostility between the husband and the brothers, he often visited, and sat late into the night talking and laughing. However, the memory of his arrival to take his wife away from her brothers caused this mature man to curse violently. In doing so, he was exhibiting an anger which was commonplace. Women I was close to, women who had grown-up children, would still look thunderous and become sulky when reminded of the moment they first felt attraction to their future husbands. I began to realise that there was resentment between even long-married couples when recalling the separations enforced by marriage. Love-magic complicates the issue, but Herdt writes for Sambia people, 'What woman would willingly leave hearth and home and loved ones to take up squatters rights with a stranger in a hostile hamlet' (1999: 48).

Cross-Cousins

Cross-cousins are called by terms which denote gender relative to the speaker. A mother's brother (MB) is called *wau*, and a father's sister (FZ) called *tapi*. The children of one's *wau* and *tapi* are called *sumei* if they are the same sex as the speaker. A man calls his female cross-cousins *upaning*. A woman may call the names of her male cross-cousins. It is correct to practise name avoidance with one's same sex cross-cousins, and it is expected there will be a humorous or hostile tension between these people. Cross-cousins prototypically belong to a different palem from one's own. Virilocal marriage suggests that the cross-sex relation in the parental generation equates to physical separation between cross-cousins. A man is supposed to marry a woman he calls 'upaning'.

The terminology is more interesting than this, however. One calls the children of *sumei* (same-sex cross-cousin), 'child'. In return they call you *sas/nam* (father/mother). One calls the children of opposite-sex cross-cousins 'child' also; but in return they call their MB or FZ *wau* and *tapi* respectively. Thus the children of same-sex cross-cousins become default siblings, despite their parents' status as something other than siblings. In a parallel to this, cross-cousins are not all automatically marriageable. In fact, the designation *upaning* from a man's point of view may denote a person who is said to be 'too close' to marry. Time and generational distance are factors in terminological use. One's fathers' sister's and mothers' brother's female children are cross-cousins, denoted through the terms *sumei* and *upaning* depending upon the sex of the speaker. Yet their children and the speaker's children are thought of as siblings, thus the sons of two *sumei* will call one another 'elder/younger sibling' (*paap/wanik*), not *sumei*. Being in another palem, the male children of two *sumei* will call the female children of the other 'parent' (children of people who call one another *sumei* call their parent's cross-cousin 'parent'), *upaning*. Being in a different palem, they are siblings of another kind. This is made clearer in the Tok Pisin translation of these terms. Parallel cousins within a hamlet call one another *brata* whether male or female. Cross-cousins (resident in another hamlet) of the same sex call one another *kandere*, and cross-cousins of the opposite sex call one another *susa*. All *upaning*, by extension, are called *susa* in Tok Pisin. Susa is a reciprocal term used by opposite sex cross-cousins.

Making principles into rules is one way of making sense of statistical analysis to reveal trends and regularities. Following through the data at hand, and looking to produce rules for behaviour which follow terminology and work consistently on the basis of genealogical connection, however, brings one to a dead end. I give a brief example to illustrate this, quoting directly (in translation).

U and Z are brothers of P's mother from another palem. This is the case because her father and their father called one another 'brother'. They did not originate in the same palem, but they spent a lot of time together and aided each other. Thus P calls both U

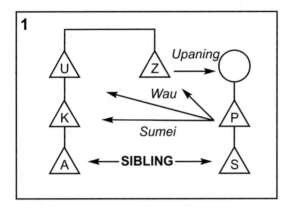

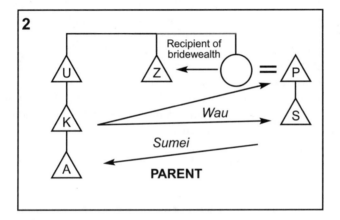

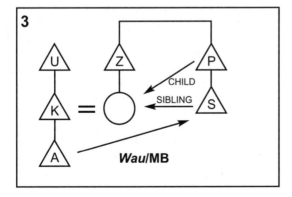

Figure 3.3 *'Three Ways of Reckoning One Relationship'*

and Z 'wau' [MB], and calls U's son (K), 'sumei'. P's son should call A, who is U's son's son 'paap/wanik' [sibling].

However, U and Z call P's wife and her siblings 'sibling', thus U's son also calls P 'wau' [MB, i.e., married to his FZ], and so P's son should call K's son (A), [who in the previous explanation P's son called 'sibling'], 'child'.

But this does exhaust the issue. In fact, it is U's son's son (A) who calls P's son 'wau' [MB]. This comes about because A's mother is a daughter to a brother of P. Thus she is also P's daughter, and thus 'upaning' to P's son who received pay (bridewealth) for her. For this reason, A *in fact* calls P's son 'wau'. It is 'eating' pay for the mother that makes P's son 'wau' [MB] to A. They think of the pay, and call each other accordingly.

In a muddle reminiscent of the apparently multiple possibilities in the formation of palem, and reckoning connection though them seen in the previous chapter, we see here how looking for principles based in genealogical connection as the foundation of terminological practice presents multiple and contradictory possibilities for each person. What is clear is that due to these multiple referents, there is always some 'choice' in the way one calls people at the margins of one's own family or residence group. Overriding this 'choice' (which so exercised Lawrence) in Nekgini speakers' explanations and practices, however, is the element that appears at the end of this translation. People there will always refer to who has eaten with whom, and who has helped whom in making affinal payments. It is not individual choice that is decisive; rather, proximity and connection is judged on who has helped whom in making affinal payments, and who has been separated from whom by eating these payments.

Thus the man (P) who outlined these three possible referents for his son and his MB's son went on to explain that:

> U and Z were brothers of my mother, but their fathers and their grandfathers were not the same. They were of different palem. However, my maternal grandfather and U and Z's grandfather used to call each other 'brother'. Thus Z calls my mother, 'sister'. Now when we grew up, we did not have a close maternal uncle, my maternal grandfather did not have any male children within his palem. For this reason, we not only called U and Z *wau*, but they were the ones who initiated me. We make our *kastom* with these two. If we had not done so, then we would indeed think of them as distant maternal uncles. Yet we made payments to them for initiation, and now we may not marry their children (our upaning). Why? Because they have worked hard to teach us *kastom* and we have worked hard to make payments to them. They have become our close maternal uncles. Once we have made something [a presentation] and made them our close MB's, why would we then turn back on ourselves and marry with them all again? They support us in making us grown men, and in our endeavours which include marriage.
>
> We say *behainim blut* [T.P.] ('follow blood'). With the work they did for us, and the payments we made in return, we have become one blood. If you start by thinking of whom you help and who helps you to make *kastom* payments, then you will find the right people to marry.

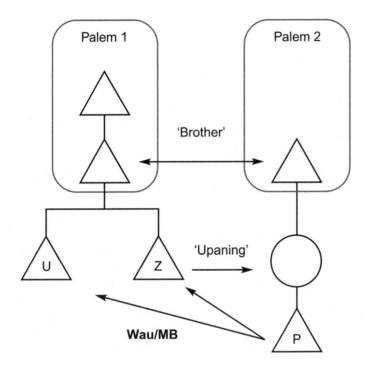

Figure 3.4 *How P Comes to Have Maternal Uncles*

The term *upaning* then means cross-sex sibling in another palem. As such, it denotes someone who may be marriageable. Although they may indeed not be. What is clear though is that, as Nekgini people say, one must look for ones marriage partners 'in the middle' of one's maternal uncles and paternal aunts. In other words, in another palem.

Why is this so? Lawrence notes for Ngaing speakers, neighbours of the Nekgini language group, that:

> A man had to marry a cross-cousin – the daughter of a true or classificatory mother's brother or father's sister. Outside marriage, he could indulge in casual liaisons with all his other female cross-cousins without incurring enmity provided he compensated their husbands with gifts of clay pots and food. Liaisons with other female relatives were condemned as incest. (Lawrence 1964: 15)

Lawrence's findings do not describe Nekgini speakers' marriage rules or sexual mores. He brings up the term incest here, to which I shall return. In fact, although all women a man should marry are *upaning*, not all *upaning* are marriageable. It appears that the question of who is marriageable is more complex than Lawrence states because being 'cross-cousin' does not automatically make the necessary separation between persons. That is, although their terms of reference take account of the sex of each speaker, they are not necessarily in, or suitable for being in, a gendered relationship. The idiom to describe such people is one of physical closeness. One says of one's close mother's brother's son/daughter (MBS/D) or father's sister's son/daughter (FZS/D) – *sumei/upaning tewung* – that they are a 'nose cousin' or one 'at the face'. The speaker quoted above said that he would *not* be able to marry his MB's daughters. They were now too close (*upaning tewung*). Thus despite a relation based on separation in the parental generation (between a brother and a sister), they are ambiguous. Being too close to marry makes them like siblings, and like siblings their proximity is expressed in physical terms. His son, like palem siblings, eats their bride payments.

Reite people speculated that it is the prerogative of 'big men' (*ai sakwing; ai topi* – leaders/elders) to determine whether two people are marriageable. As a young man, one knows all opposite sex cross-cousins as *upaning* ('sister') only. When I questioned this, it was said that this encourages respect for all women, and discourages young men from thinking too much about sex before they are ready for marriage. Indeed, at initiation a young man has 'the tail of his loincloth tied tightly' to prevent him wasting the power for his own growth and development on sexual liaisons.

For this reason perhaps, *upaning* who are distant enough in generational terms to be marriageable are not in a straightforward position either. Although they are of another palem, they are related. As cross-cousins their relationship is the outcome of a cross-sex relation made explicit through marriage and the removal of a female sibling in ancestral generations. Thus men demand compensation in bridewealth not only for their parallel cousins, whom Nekgini kin referents term siblings (with no reference to their sex until marriage), but also for their *upaning*. All such persons, marriageable or not, are classed as having come from one or the other sides of the same *maal-naie*, that is, of a bark loin cloth and of a string skirt that were once joined (siblings). Judging who to receive a share of bridewealth from and who to aid in gathering bridewealth depends upon previous exchanges. People judge their position, proximity, and ultimately identity by reference to the history of their own constitution.

Finally, the relative sex of female siblings is terminologically irrelevant until they bear children – or we could say they are not recognised as gendered in operational or significant ways until they are desired by and return the desire for a man other than their siblings. Siblings start to call their married female siblings 'mother of', rather than 'sibling' or by name, after they have borne their first child. This kind of change in ways of referring to a person when they enter a relationship which genders them productively is reported from elsewhere. Goodale tells us that sibling terms change when the referent marries and becomes engaged in sexual activity (1981: 279).

How does it come about that two people are seen as marriageable? Or indeed, how is a young man to know who is marriageable? This was a complaint I heard often from men in Reite. Until they were married, it appeared to them that there were no suitable marriage partners. The role of elders in determining marriages seemed reliant on the fact they could *find* reasons for marriage where young and less knowledgeable people could not. Everyone seems to be related to everyone else. There is then a problem in finding someone different enough to marry, although in theory, one marries *upaning*.

Marriages

Historical factors have resulted in a situation where marriages arranged by parents, either on, or before, the birth of their children, have declined dramatically since the middle of the last century. I see this a major factor in the conundrums faced by those who can apparently find no one suitable to marry, and thus resort to love-magic in an aggressive and creative (Rapport 2000) (that is, unexpected) attempt to extract a bride *and oneself* from existing relations providing definition. I come onto this below. Arranged marriages on the other hand would have meant that for years prior to a union, the parents, already separated geographically (and thus by palem affiliation), would have been developing that separation into one appropriate between affines through exchanges providing on-going definition to their respective positions. The exchanges between affines prior to the birth of children are set out in Table 3.1.

In the last sixty years, people have become mobile. They cannot be relied upon as future village residents. In addition to this, the powerful authority of elders (*ai topi*) reinforced by their control over sorcery and warfare, has progressively dimin-

Table 3.1 *Payments Related to Marriage among Nekgini Speakers*

Sendang	'[Blocking] the path'. Wealth (*Palieng*) and pig meat to M and F of the girl from the M and F of the future husband.
Si'sorung	'Footfalls'. Family of the man gives palieng and meat to M and F of the girl so he and his future wife can come and go to her M and F's house without shame or comment.
Parieng huli	Completion of marriage. Woman is decorated and brought to her husband's hamlet. Accompanied by MBS carrying banana plant, FFZSS carrying flowering tree, e/yB/Z carrying *gorogor* (T.P.).[5] Each given wealth. Also line of B/Z to receive payment individually. Pig given without a rope (*rawirawi*)[6] attached to be divided among the recipients.
Matopo	'Insides'. Husband and wife together give *palieng* and pig with *rawirawi* to family of wife. For keeping her bones on husband's land at her death.

ished. Thus, now many people chose their own partners (*marit long laik* [T.P.]). Many still defer to the advice and elicit help from elders, but they do so as grown men. In the past, *topi* could define marriage partners long in the future, knowing the separation would be *made real* before the children were mature, through transfers of wealth and food to a set of people *made* different through receiving it (Wagner 1967). Now definition must happen quickly, and love-magic performs this admirably.

What is fascinating about this change, and the consequential high proportion of marriages that are now taking place 'too close' is that it *does not matter*. How can this be the case? To answer this, I must elaborate further my alternative to a genealogical model which defines the person. This is to be in keeping with the above statement by P that 'eating together' is definitional (and see Weiner 1988: 82).

In all but the most serious discussions of potential sexual and marriage partners, men speak generally of those with whom one might possibly become involved not as 'distant cross-cousins', but as *birua* [T.P.]/*munsing*. These words, literally translated, mean 'something dangerous'. To meet a *birua* on the road means to have an accident – to fall prey to an unfortunate or painful occurrence. Someone being aggressive will be described as *birua*[7] to whomsoever their aggression is directed.

While all cross-cousins at a distance may be described as birua, one might say that in fact all women to whom a man is not in the relation of sibling, child or father, are birua. *Upaning* are birua (except those too close to marry). Complete strangers are birua, as are genealogically distant cross-cousin women and those with whom specific kinship links have been forgotten. Thus, if pressed, or if trying to think of whether two people might marry, birua – more closely defined as distant cross-cousin (i.e., someone from another place separated in a cross-sex link in a preceding generation) – was stated as the proper marriage to be made. Men laughing together about a planned trip to a neighbouring village would giggle at the thought of lots of 'birua women' there to be joked with, without considering anything other than the fact they were from other palem. People deciding if a marriage was advisable might go further and work out whether the couple being proposed were in the right relationship (*munsing mito rauoka, enei* – 'a munsing/birua wants them, give them [to them]') through considering generational distance and previous exchange. In many discussions that I heard among younger men, this appeared to preclude the marriage. Connections were almost always found. The alternative, which is now a genuine possibility, of marrying a woman from another region, while attractive to some, was denigrated by most. To not have affines in close proximity, and therefore avoid the continual obligations of affinity (compelling the emergence of palem) was seen as ultimately unproductive. '*Mmn, em marit longwe*' [T.P.] (Humph, he married far-off) was used dismissively about men who knew little of kastom and therefore had never proved their knowledge or abilities.

The startling fact, and one it took me some time to accept, was that one third of marriages I recorded were not to women classified as birua (see Table 3.2). This was

Table 3.2 *Marriages Made by People Still Alive and Resident in Reite Hamlets (Men) or Born There (Women) [1994]*

	Permissible marriages		Marriages to sibling, parent or child		
	Stranger /distant	Sumei/ Upaning	Upaning too close	Child/ Parent	Sibling
Men	7	12	3	8	2
Women	12	10	1	6	0

Totals as percentages of all marriages

Permissible marriages	'Wrong' marriages
67%	33%

more than merely an occasional case of prohibited sexual relations as defined there (sexual relations with anyone not birua), but a systematic breaking of an 'exogamic principle' as defined both in the terminology and in people's statements about what was possible and what was *ne naki epi rara' kata'ka* (marriage/taking oneself/us) – marriage to oneself – and 'wrong'. (*Rong marit,* or *marit kranki* in Tok Pisin.)

People would often say to me 'I married mistakenly', or 'I took my sibling/mother/child' (as appropriate to their case). I noticed in these statements no shame. Men gave me sly looks, and laughed about shortages of women. 'What was one supposed to do under such circumstances?' I discuss below some cases in which there was recognised to be a problem.

Now why should people have a marriage prohibition, a rule about whom one can and cannot marry, if it is only sporadically followed, and there is no apparent difficulty in breaking it? Why did those men most interested in kastom see no inconsistency between their revelations about their own marriages and the dictates of kastom (one marries upaning), which they also outlined as *the only* way to behave? These are distinct questions, although the answers seem linked. It is apparent that the activities described as love-magic – where difference is empha- sised between cross-cousins – are also practised on, and work upon, persons in relation to whom sex does not appear as a significant factor in their terms of ref- erence (siblings, children). In other words, my surprise was linked to my assumption that terminology referred to an underlying system of biological relat- edness, that it referred to connections that are immutable.

Also, if marriage rules are the Nekgini form of incest prohibition (they have no other), how might we understand their disregard by so many people? Although it may be sensible in some contexts to distinguish incest prohibition from marriage rules for purposes of analysis, I believe their conflation is appropriate in the Nekgini case. As I explain below, Reite understandings of gender and personhood themselves conflate potential spouses with potential sexual partners because the very possibility of sexuality in a cross-sex relation depends upon the gendering of the partners, and the mechanisms of this gendering imply separation. Marriage to a sibling, and incest, are the same thing in their social recognition. Sexual relations of any sort imply the recognition of gender.[8] I turn then to an aspect of Reite kastom which people themselves emphasise. That is the use of love-magic.

Love-Magic

Both men and women in contemporary Reite assert that no woman would ever marry a man unless she is coerced to do so through love-magic. The whole discussion of who is and who is not marriageable must take this factor into account. We have seen already that terminology follows sharing, co-operation and separation generated in palem and inter-palem (affinal) relations. The acceptance that love-magic is necessary for marriage to occur, and the figures which show that marriage consistently takes place between people 'too close' to marry, highlights the generative logic of these practices. People perform love-magic on each other whatever their relationship. The number of marriages between siblings, and parents and children, bear testimony to this.

Love-magic itself is a secret known only to a few older men in Reite. It is said that indeed women have their own form of love-magic, and that it is powerful, yet women are highly secretive about it. I know of no man who does not think that he (and his supporters) was the agent in his own marriage. Love-magic turns a woman's mind, it is said; it moves her to emotion for a man. It inexorably precipitates her move from her natal hamlet to the hamlet of her lover in marriage. Women's response to such feelings is irritation and even anger (cf. Harrison 1993: 122). In feeling an emotional pull to a man who is not her brother or father, a woman knows herself to have been the object of someone else's extractive attentions.

We are looking at an explicit form of coercion here, of the use of power. Yet such use of power, and the apparent removal of subjectivity it results in, are acknowledged as absolutely central to what continue to be the most important set of relationships in Nekgini sociality – those made to affines through marriage. Thus women and men are ambiguous about love-magic. They complain when it is directed against them or their own, but delight in the notion of using it on others.

Meetings over the expressed desires of women to marry a certain man almost inevitably result in violence in my experience, and in people's narratives. The male kin of the women were furious at the perceived attack made against their sibling or sister. This is the case whether the two are in a cross-cousin relationship or not. The logic of the practice of love-magic and sibling relations ensures that there can be no mistaking who is responsible. The fact that a woman expresses desire for a man incriminates him and his supporters beyond argument. There is a crucial extension to this, however. Far from making the marriage impossible, it is this violent response that in fact *guarantees* the marriage will take place. Kastom dictates that any women who has been fought over by her brothers must be given in marriage to the person to whom they have caused damage.

Harrison (1993) is one of many who discuss the coercive potential of aesthetic forms in Melanesia (see also Hirsch 1995a for example), and the ambiguous nature of emotion caused by another's actions or performance. In a description that could be of Reite women's reactions to the thought of having love-magic performed on them, he writes that Avatip '[w]omen are outraged if they believe themselves to be bespelled, and view it as a dangerous injury' (122). The only time that love-magic does not result in violence in Reite is when, in a long arranged marriage, it is performed after a wife has taken up residence with her husband (after *huli*). In such cases the separation and definition has *already* been dramatised through the presentation of a bride payment.

You could say that when people act, they do so only because of what another person recognises them to be; even in gender there is no essential nature, only what others see you as, and this is only apparent in the way they are treating you. As Roy Wagner writes, behaviour with regard to, and terminological definitions of persons, 'elicit some form of response, and the way the kinsman responds – appropriately or inappropriately, as the case may be – serves to realise or create the relationship itself' (Wagner 1986a: xv). It is this ability to generate position, gender, substance, identity – all those things the genealogical model assumes are given – that makes processes of generation, including love-magic, such a potent element in creating affinal relations among Nekgini speakers. The fact that a full third of all marriages are between those who are not cross-cousins or birua is indicative of understandings of substance and relatedness as part of the ongoing process which brings persons (and places) into being. It is not predicated upon them.

In his 1972 article 'Incest and Identity', Wagner makes a telling critique of the separation of role (as the function) and terminology (as the structure) in structural functionalist analyses. He argues that it produces a problematic contrast between 'real genealogies' as we recognise them, and apparent indigenous reworkings of biological connections, in terms of an ordered structure of roles which are governed by a person's position in a genealogy. While incest is seen to relate to a 'real' genealogy, kin terms are seen as a structure constructed in response to the functional needs of the society. Wagner asserts, however, that kin relationships cannot meaningfully be separated from kin categories.

Anthropology and Incest

This relates to an issue in which anthropologists have long been interested; namely the question of why incest should be prohibited, and what the effects of that prohibition are. I summarise some of the anthropological debate which seems relevant to my critique of assumptions within the genealogical model. My critique of the literature on incest is linked to the argument presented in the previous chapter concerning the assumptions built into Lawrence's work; that is, about the relationship of individuals to society. Here I focus on where kin differentiation is thought to arise, and its relation to terminology and genealogy.

Lévi-Strauss (1969) explains the prohibition of sexual relations with close kin as marking the essential distinction between humanity and animality, between culture and nature. His argument assumes that culture and society are basically rule-governed entities, and the first and most fundamental rule in human social life is that one may not marry one's sister. This forces people into relationships with one another whereby women are exchanged between men. The relationships of a man, his sister, his sister's husband and their child, together constitute the 'atom of kinship', the elementary building block of society. This set of relationships is necessitated by the incest prohibition. Incest prohibition is a universal fact of all human cultures, and being universal is therefore somehow 'natural'. Nevertheless, being the original rule, in following it humans (universally) become fully cultural.

Lévi-Strauss has been criticised for conflating the prohibition of incest with rules for marriage (Fox 1967). As I am making a similar conflation (although for a different purpose) I do not take issue with him on this point. I do wish, however, to highlight something else about his theoretical position. Analysts such as Lévi-Strauss appear interested in the specifics of each incest prohibition, each marriage rule, at a level beyond the particular contexts in which they are found. His is an analysis at a remove from the logic in which the specific instances of the prohibition appear, 'exogamy and the prohibition of incest have a permanent functional value, co-extensive with all social groups...' (Lévi-Strauss 1969: 482).

In this Lévi-Strauss is akin to other theorists of the incest prohibition both within and beyond anthropology because the analyses they present may explain the universal phenomenon of 'incest prohibition', but at a remove from the meanings and interpretations of exogamy or prohibition that appear in actual situations. Meaning is seen as social and specific while biology/nature is universal. This is the standard position. It highlights human cultural difference against the background of human biological similarity. There is nothing wrong with this. However, one consequence of the position is that terminology, language and culture appear arbitrary in relation to the underlying reality of genealogical relatedness. The danger then is that universal assumptions organise data on 'kinship'.

Those who posit a biological rationale for the universality of the prohibition on incest, those who see it as explained by society's need to harmonise the socialising family unit by excluding antagonistic sexual relations from it, and those who think familiarity within the family breeds sexual contempt, all have to assume that the rule prohibiting incest amounts to an a priori imposition which perhaps facilitates the emergence or functioning of the social structure and its associated cultural meanings. As an a priori rule, the prohibition is universal and generative of society and culture, or of a healthy gene pool, or whatever, but is on a different ontological level from that of meaning and motivation in the lives of people themselves.

This split between the level of the 'human' and the 'beyond-the-human', is pointed out by Mimica (1991). Mimica argues that our (bourgeois) fear of incest, and our understanding of it as a universally prohibited phenomenon, come from a mythically structured consciousness governed by an angry and law-giving deity (50). In cosmological terms, universalising the prohibition on incest is a projection of our own moral and mythic consciousness. It 'makes the world' in the image of that consciousness (mythopoeia). For in all theories purporting to explain the prohibition, its source is assumed to lie at a level beyond the human, whether with a deity, as a law of nature, or of society; wherever, in fact, the author happens to situate his or her (Judaeo-Christian) belief in a transcendental entity.

Wagner (1972) makes the same point in a different way when he writes of the idea that rules lie at the basis of society, and therefore human-ness. He points to Rousseau's notion of a social contract in which there is an a priori need for discipline to guarantee the existence of society. Both Wagner and Mimica insist that we should look at the myths and motivations by which the consciousness of those whom we wish to understand is formed, rather than assuming that our own mythic consciousness is universally relevant (even in this most fundamental matter).[9] In other words, contra Lévi-Strauss, Radcliffe-Brown, Robin Fox, and many others, they argue that in order to understand specific instances of the incest prohibition, or the relation of exogamy to the definition of persons, we must stop thinking of incest as a 'real thing' (because in doing so we think of biological kinship as a real thing) and look instead to how people are constituted *as* persons within their own lifeworld, their own cosmology. What part does a prohibition on certain sexual relations play in this constitution?

Moreover there is a suggestion in those writers taken to task[10] that incest is a desire innate in humans – otherwise the rule forbidding it would be unnecessary. There is also a contradiction in that the desire, although natural (i.e., innate), is 'unnatural' in effect, producing dangerously close combinations from a limited gene pool. Mimica reminds us that such certainties amount to a form of supernatural sanction. In breaking rules, impelled by a desire arising from the natural or animal side of the human organism, we open ourselves to a punishment. Freud, of course, linked the desire for incest to the desire to regain one-ness with the mother, and developed his theory of the unconscious as an explanation for what happens when animal desire – the libido – is suppressed by human/cultural forms. His is a universalist theory for the human psyche, positing the same conditions of emergence, and the same suppression of the libido, in all societies. There is a commitment in classic anthropological writings on incest to the notion of prohibition, that is to the notion of a rule.

There is another a priori assumption involved as I mentioned: that of the differentiation between kin. I believe what we find, in Reite marriage data and terminological use, is evidence of the active and purposeful differentiation of kinds of person. Wagner, in his argument for an analysis of kinship which takes the 'analogic' nature of relations in such places as Reite into account, and which avoids 'homological' assumptions about the potential for comparison between kinship systems, criticises Lévi-Strauss for making just this a priori assumption. 'The existence of a "given" kin differentiation, however abstracted, preserves the essentially homological character of this model' (Wagner 1977a: 626) and positions on incest which appeal to the sovereignty of the rule, are 'ultimately contingent upon the validity of the idea of natural kin differentiation' (ibid.).

Now, we have seen that although Reite people do have ideas about whom it is appropriate to marry, they imagine no supernatural sanction as the consequence of breaking this recommendation. As with the Iqwaye people about whom Mimica writes, Reite people do not share a Judaeo-Christian tradition of thought which has at its base a deity ready to wreak punishment on all who break His commands. Therefore they do not have laws handed down that have to be observed to avoid supernatural sanction in the form of deformed or handicapped offspring. These laws and sanctions, Mimica argues, are the products of cosmological speculation in the mode of Western mythopoeia. Thus, while Mimica says that the Iqwaye have a passion for incest, Reite people regularly practise what they would call prohibited sexual relations (*ne naki* 'ourselves' marriage) and break the ideal of marriage to someone 'other'. The difficulties they experience in doing so are cosmological in terms of their own history and mythopoeia and not in terms of Western psychoanalysis, sociology, or cosmology. I discuss one such difficulty below.

A man complaining to me that he had married his sister because it had been recommended by his elders to keep landholding together, said '*mi rabisim skin bilong mi yet*' [T.P.], i.e., that he had 'made his own skin rubbish', had shot himself in the foot as it were. In marrying his classificatory sister (sibling), he said, he had lost out on eating (the term used to describe receiving wealth for a sibling in bride payments) all those other sisters who became birua to him through his transactions with the girl's other brothers (previously his brothers). These were transactions appropriate between them as in-laws. Now, when they ate a sister, or received wealth for a sister's child, he was not one of them, having separated himself from them in the act of exchange which married him to their sister. In other words, although there were ways of *making* his spouse birua to him, producing her as *upaning* and therefore marriageable after the event; the flows of wealth and knowledge that he would have been expected to participate and become visible in had been radically curtailed when he literally changed his own definition in relation to certain kin. He had not anticipated the number of relationships out of which he was effectively painting himself. Nor had he anticipated his invisibility, and therefore irrelevance, to exchanges of wealth between certain people in the future. 'Wrong marriage' in this sense shortened his 'kinship', circumscribed his relationships and thus left him less fully present in the social world. He was less fully visible than he would otherwise have been.[11] This was what was 'wrong' about it. Complaining that his elder brother still ate pigs for certain women and he did not, he regretted that he had been advised to make this unproductive self-closure.

Marriage to 'prohibited' kin, apparently so prevalent, seems to have little to do with a rule or a prohibition, and everything to do with the practicalities of making oneself central to exchange relations and thus of fulfilling the 'autopoetic' potential of the quintessential productive relation – marriage. Mimica's use of autopoesis, which I follow here, is explained thus:

> What has to be grasped here as a general characteristic of human self-transcendence is that, being the synthesis of temporality – its past present and future – human organismic existence is the origin and end of its own projection into the world, that is, its engagement through praxis. In this sense the primary task of human praxis is self-creation for no other reason than the reasons of it own existence. That is, since humans exist in the world, being in the world is their primary existential project – their sole *raison d'être*. Thus the primary ontological project of humanness is the realisation of its own mode of being-in-the-world. It is self-creating (autopoetical). Human cultural activities (praxis) then, are constellated by the vital structures of humanness – not as universal facts to be dealt with by human biology and physiology, or ecology, but as activities which have to be understood anthropologically. Since they themselves are at the core of humanness, seen as its own ontological project... any existence is always and only about existence; the structures of being in the world are about that particular being-in-the-world. (1991: 35–6)

Nekgini kin terms, when looked at in the context of marriage and gender, appear not to refer to fixed roles or identities in a social structure, or to have reference to a genealogy as we understand it in terms of biological relatedness or 'given' differentiation (Wagner 1977a). That 'incest' does not appear as a problem of this kind, despite the number of 'wrong marriages', suggests that their perception and naming of connection and disconnection has a different basis.

Myths and Explanations

The conventional focus upon incest implies that sexual distinctions are given universally from the start as biological properties of individuals irrespective of social distance. This makes possible the idea of sex between people who are (too) close. But this logic will not work if the processes of social separation and sexual differentiation are one and the same. All Nekgini marriages involve separation. The problem that comes from marrying oneself (*ne naki*), rather than someone who has been made other to some degree already (in previous generations) as a cross-cousin (and through exchanges between the parents of the partners based on this distinction), is that not all relationships can easily be refigured. Palem fission, as we saw in Chapter 2, is a consequence of the violent separation marriages classed as *ne naki* may necessitate. This is the source of the marriage preference.

My intention in writing about anthropological views on incest has been to point out how certain assumptions lie behind the concept of incest prohibition, and thus how these have been built into anthropological theorising on the nature of society. I now make this into a specific ethnographic critique, filling in one of the fundamentally 'autopoetic' principles of Reite cosmology.

Here I outline a view of myth which emerges as an alternative to the way the myths of this area have often been interpreted. While my primary intention is to highlight the mechanisms of differentiation between kin as aspects of relationships, not genealogy as conventionally understood, I must come slightly circuitously to the myths themselves. As readers are aware, the Rai Coast is famous in the ethnographic literature for what have been known as cargo cults (e.g. Worsley 1957). As one of the myths that Reite people say is central to their lives has previously been talked of in relation to 'ethnohistory' (Kempf 1992), mythic history (Pomponio 1994) or most powerfully, loss of cargo (Lawrence 1964), I diverge slightly from the theme of this chapter to examine how we might understand this emphasis.

The notion I have in mind when reading this myth is that within the imagery may be found moments of differentiation and transformation that take the action forward. This affords an insight into how, in Reite, significant actions occur, and what must proceed from them if they are to be recognised as significant. One can see the intermeshing of myth and practice in processes which produce kin as marriageable, and thus result in separations between places and persons. This may be rendered as a self-generating system, the mode of self creation that has been called mythopoeisis (Mimica 1988). Mimica writes, 'there is no possibility of the human mode of being-in-the-world without the work of the imagination which is the main source of human cultural praxis...' (1991: 36); and he cites myth as a central element in this 'imaginal' (after Corbin 1969). People make their world through practice informed by myth. What we describe for them is thus best termed not as a culture or society, but a 'lived world' (Gow 2001: 26). In turn, Weiner (1995) suggests that we do not take myths as templates for lives lived, but think of them as revealing the lineaments of human existence. Myth provides one outline of the limits of language to evoke meaning in any given community. Rather than providing certainty, order, and coherence, speech itself is a source of contingency according to Weiner. Myths then might be said to provide possibilities for the elicitation and recognition of meaningful experience in relation to social others.

The multiple referents of the Nekgini term *patuki* are relevant here, as they suggest that the Nekgini understanding of 'myth' is indeed vital knowledge of the world by which people generate the conditions for their own existence. 'Patuki' is both the narrative of a myth, *and* the characters which appear therein. For Nekgini speakers, all revelation of knowledge about how to do things in the world comes through the actions of such beings; and there are commonly used idioms in speech which make it clear that mythic characters are not disconnected, but very much present in quotidian life, just as their mnemonic markers populate the contemporary landscape. One example of this is the admonition used to prevent people making up their own rules of behaviour: *patuki reinung'keni taparet iko ma keweyung iko masau sirai, o, iko rombom sirai.* 'Hey, patuki did that, but saw it was useless and planted a cordyline. Forget it.' Invoking such authority is backed up with tangible coercion. If the person carries on, they will be charged to cook pig for disregarding the law of kastom. Patuki then do provide reference points in validating or denigrating types of behaviour.

Patuki is 'story', as in the English noun: to tell a...; it is also *stori*, a Tok Pisin verb describing what one does when one tells a tale, or even holds a conversation; it is today glossed by people there as equivalent to the 'God' that they hear about from missions. It is also a gloss for knowledge. What people do in the evenings when they discuss things and pool understanding is patuki. Finally, patuki is a kinship term for ancestor, above the fifth generation, the point at which Nekgini speakers I know give up tracing descent, and refer instead to the forms in the landscape – the characters of myth – 'patuki'. Myths which are common knowledge and in fact direct people's everyday perception of events hold a crucial place in people's imaginative and interactive constitution of their world. They trace the outline of a cosmological world which allows people their own generative and creative acts.

Knowledge that comes to have effect *is* patuki. People live at once with the power of patuki for self-creation and revelation, while generating their lives as human and quotidian. Citing the myth of Pomo (see below) in marriage transactions, and making evident knowledge of the myth in copying the palem that those patuki built, people validate action though indisputable reference to primordial power. Yet they also make themselves fully human: fulfilling the self-creation (autopoesis) that exists as human possibility within the recognisable contours of the mythic.

Manup and Kilibob in Reite

It is reported (Pomponio 1992: 29; Lawrence 1964: 21–24; Harding et al. 1994) that the myth of Manup and Kilibob is shared by many of the people native to Madang (and parts of Morobe and West New Britain) provinces. It has been interpreted as the indigenous explanation for the loss of Western goods (Lawrence 1964; McSwain 1977).[12] Other commentators have seen it as an Odyssey, the legendary charting of the journey of a culture hero explaining distributions of populations and of wealth (Pomponio 1994). The idea behind both these kinds of commentary is the same, that this myth allows a *post facto* rationalisation for the division of productive capabilities in either trading communities, or communities faced by the need to explain colonial power.[13] In this tradition, Pomponio (1992) has argued that the version of the Manup and Kilibob myth she heard from Mandok Islanders in the Siassi group does not amount to an origin myth as such, as people are already assumed to exist at the start of the myth. Rather it is a myth of how the world came to be shaped as it is. The culture hero,

> develop[ed] a distinctive culture... [t]he premise that Kilibob did not create the human race may also indicate the relative recency of Austronesian settlement in the Vitiaz and Dampier Straits. What requires explanation is not 'how humans got created' but 'how they got here'. (34)

In this vein, Lawrence (1964 and followers) see it as a 'template', or a 'part of people's intellectual life' (Harding et al. 1994: 5), whereby they make sense of the changes that overtake them. It is because of Lawrence's ability to trace the ways that this particular myth was used by Madang peoples in trying to make sense of, and gain control over, white people and their deity that *Road Belong Cargo* succeeds in persuading us of the rationality of the thinking behind what he terms 'cargo movements'. It is this reading that I wish to move away from, not in order to rein-state a 'sociological view of myth' (Harding et al. 1994: 6), with the 'patronising' subtext that natives are intellectually lacking and cannot respond to colonialism rationally, but for two reasons of my own.

The first is that I find the intellectualist position on myth put forward by Lawrence, Pomponio, and others to need extension if we are to understand the myth's centrality to Reite people. Their approach imagines Madang people searching around within their limited set of cultural and intellectual possibilities to explain innovation, change, and something as radical as the arrival of whites, as if they were having change imposed upon them. The logic runs something like this: 'it was not their choice to be left out of the modern world, or to be presented with it by colonisers, but they made strenuous and *intellectually* satisfying efforts to understand the changes they were being forced to acknowledge and thus to estab-lish after the fact reasons for the said exclusion'. It seems to me that such an analysis comes from a genuine sympathy and liking for the people amongst whom the anthropologist has lived, but nevertheless from the standpoint that these are people who inevitably know less than their colonisers. We marvel at their intel-lectual athletics and creativity, but cannot help smiling (or weeping) in sympathy as we see how the inevitable limitations of the elements they have to organise into a mythic structure cannot do justice to the real powers of Western capitalism and colonialism. In other words, by building up their intellectual ability, the limited horizons of their possible symbolic schemes becomes apparent. The world their myth describes is fundamentally the same as our own.

The second point is that this is a view of myth as stories, as elements of intel-lectual life, and thus as explanatory, but not as part of the constitutive process whereby persons and their orientation in the world come into being. These myths are seen as pseudo-history: a cultural explanation of where people found them-selves. As with genealogy, it appears they are working with a flawed or incomplete understanding of something of which western science, or western history, has a complete description.[14]

> As Peter Lawrence recognised... the episodes in the legend of Kilibob-Manup-Mala-Ambogim-Namor are not random tales. They employ metaphors that have great cultural importance in laying forth values important to Mandok history and culture. (Pomponio 1994 : 87–8)

Another reading of this myth is possible, one which demonstrates the relevance of mythic consciousness to everyday life, not as an explanation, but as constitutive imagination in the constructive relationships between persons. As Weiner has written for Foi speakers of the Lake Kutubu area, 'the many images of Foi domestic, social, and ceremonial life depicted in myth are no less accurate a rendering of Foi "everyday life" than an observer's narration of daily activity' (Weiner 1988: 16). For Reite people, far from being a *post facto* explanation for the appearance of white people and the loss of cargo, the version of Manup and Kilibob with which I have been made familiar is an elaboration of personhood in which loss always occurs, a projection of the agency persons must evince in order to create themselves and their counterpart viewers in the world. In finding another reading of this myth, I do not discredit those who see it as a myth 'about' cargo or the distribution of people in the world, but show how it can *only be* these things for Nekgini people if the imaginative and practical engagement within the world which it projects, is in fact autopoetic.

Pomo: A Myth of Creation

I must admit to a sense of disappointment on my arrival in Reite when I found that the myth people were most keen to tell me was one I recognised from my pre-fieldwork reading. And they really were keen for me to hear it. The first major event of my life in the community was a day, put aside by all the important men of the hamlets, to gather and tell me this myth.

An aspect of my disappointment was that I had taken it for granted that this was no creation myth. While I accepted it as a fascinating indigenous commentary on colonialism and was unsurprised that my arrival elicited such a commentary, I did not see it as a story directly relevant to everyday life, but rather as a reactive interpretation of a history which had overtaken them. What I was being told – that this was their most important *patuki* (knowledge or story), and that it belonged to everyone (it was *pablik* [T.P.])[15] – I took to mean an undifferentiated claim that they had been disadvantaged thus far by colonialism. I do not mean to denigrate the marvellous work Lawrence did with this myth; the relevance of his writing is today still apparent. It had become just a little too apparent to me, sitting in my new house and being presented with something that evidently did not need further explanation.

However, when these people came to me with this myth, they said clearly 'this is our most central knowledge, our basic story (and understanding) of the world' (*patuki sakwing, patuki saporung*). My reaction to being told that this was *pablik* was merely that there was an undifferentiated claim on this interpretation, using the intellectual apparatus available, of peripheralisation. I was concerned that my fieldwork would be among people who thought that merely by claiming ownership of western goods they would receive them, and who were intent on making their claim through me.

However, what if what they were telling me *was* central to their understanding of the world, not as a reactive interpretation to a world over which they had little control, but actually as how they saw themselves as creative beings in the first place? Could there be such a thing as an origin myth which does not speak directly of origins, but speaks instead to Nekgini sensibilities and understandings of how things come to be visible, potent or agentive in the world? What if when they describe this myth as *pablik*, they were making a statement about it as common because, for people to be there at all, they must have this knowledge? These are the lines along which my analysis has proceeded since.

I provide a short version of the myth which makes no mention of the subsequent adventures of the younger brother who in some versions is said to be responsible for the creation of European material culture. There was much discussion about the 'correct Reite' narrative of this myth in connection with my work. Some felt it important to connect it to stories from elsewhere in Madang which they had heard while travelling there. These are the versions which say that in the end, the younger brother went away with all the knowledge necessary to make western goods. The village consensus however was that I should only record the myth as it had been told in Reite itself. As Gow explains, variation is central to myth (2001: 78–9). It facilitates the ability of myth tellers to make the narrative relevant to changing situations. Thus I point out how this myth has been made to serve different agendas. My intention here, though, is to elucidate a nexus of human action which has maintained its centrality precisely because it is how the world has come to be the recognisably human. It is known as 'Pomo' in Reite, after the place in which the elder brother made his palem.

* * *

After the sea had come and killed everyone except one man and his woman, who hung onto the tail of his loincloth while he forced the rushing waters aside, there were two brothers, an elder and younger, who lived together at the place called Pomo. They were there. We do not have hidden (secret) names for these brothers, they are only known to us as Wanikaak – the younger and elder. They lived there with a woman, their mother. The younger brother decorated her genital region with his design 'Yandi imang'.

She was shamed and hid her skin. Her husband felt pain now, and wondered why she had started to cover her body. He put all the cooking pots and plates on a shelf high in the ceiling of the house. He lay beneath them, and his wife went to the garden. When she came back, she said that he should move so she would not step over him, but he shivered violently and replied that he was too ill to move, so she could step over him. Once the food was ready to go into the pot and he still had not moved, she lifted her leg over him, and he saw something, so he told the wife to go up to the ceiling and fetch all the pots and plates. She demurred, and said she would be polluting him by stepping over him, but he said not to worry, it was between them. The man pretended to sleep, but he was really looking, so when the woman climbed up, and opened her legs, he saw her thighs and genitals, and saw the design that covered her pubic area and extended onto her thighs. He saw it clearly now. He said, 'Oh, this woman has been doing that sort of thing, that is why she is hiding from me. I am the one who should be with her.' The woman brought all the pots and plates down and cooked. They ate, and slept.

The man took thought, and decided to make a palem. He called for all the people in the area to come and carve their designs on the bamboo poles (Po tandagerurung) that he planted around the meeting house. He gave everyone a knotted rope (gnalo) so they would know on which day to come. He prepared food for them all. He didn't call for Reite first, but everyone else. On one day, he called one place, then next day another. Finally he called Reite, and all the leaders met in the same way we are met now. Last of all there was only one bamboo pole left and still he had not seen the mark. His small brother came last, and put his mark. The man asked each in turn which their mark was, and then he came to the mark he had seen on his wife. They all said, 'it is your small brother who made this mark'. He said, 'Ah, now I'm clear. I've called out for everywhere to come, and now I see it is my small sibling'. The mark is called Yandi imang.

That afternoon he went to see his small brother, and told him that they would cut a shield (sumber) tomorrow. This was the challenge of people before. They got up, and strung their bows and fought, trying to mark each other's skin. They fought for a long time, for days and weeks. They fought in all sorts of ways. The woman tried to stop them, but they carried on for days, months, years. The woman was sick of it. She dug a hole in the ground like a (marsupial) rat does (kasawi musi). She gathered stray marsupial hairs, tiny bits of chicken feather, a few threads from an old skirt, fibres from an old loincloth, and scraps from the ends of old thatch. Digging under the earth, she made a path which came out at the island of Arop. Then she dug again, and the path led to Karkar and Bagabag islands. The two brothers carried on their fight. The elder dug a hole in the ground, and told his younger to step inside so he could 'try' him with a house post. He wanted to kill his younger brother by beating down on him with a sharp house post. The younger brother chewed betel nut, and spat the red juices into a coconut shell. He went into the hole, but the woman had dug her tunnel close enough for him to transfer his body into it. When the post came down, the red betel juice made the elder think he had killed his younger. But in the morning, he heard someone inside the woman's house tapping his lime spatula against its container (koro). He asked 'mother, who is that? and she replied that it was his younger. The elder attacked him again, and now the woman was really tired of it. She took the younger along the path under the earth she had dug, they sang, and they came out at Arop. Because she had put the animal hairs and bird feathers here, this island was full of game animals. She put the thatch and threads on Karkar and Bagabag. These islands are full of people and houses. His big brother was trying hard to find him. He called out from outside the woman's house in the morning for his brother to come and fight again. He went into the house and saw that the two had gone. He was cross. He wondered where they had gone. It was afternoon now. He was worried, and he sat down and cried. He said 'Oh, small, I was wrong and fought with you, and now you have run away'. He didn't eat. The woman cooked, but he wouldn't eat. She was cross with him, and said, 'why have you changed your talk now? Before you didn't say "brother" to this man'. But he said to her – 'don't speak crossly to me, I might hurt you'.

In the morning, he carried his bow and arrows and his spear, and he went down to the beach to try and find his brother. He came to the beach, and felt hungry, but he didn't have food. He had been worrying too much to eat. The younger brother saw him from his hiding place on Arop. Big brother looked and looked, but didn't find him. He sat down at the base of a Kalapali tree. He chopped at the roots of the Kalapali and worried. He sharpened his stone axe. The small brother was watching him from the island. He made his design on a large stem of grass, and on the skin of a seed. He got tail feathers of a chicken (it was his sign), and stood them around the grass stem in the top of the seed. Then he floated it to his big brother. He sang to them. Big brother sat and looked and waited, and the nut and grass came floating up, and the sea tossed them onto the beach in front of him. The elder marked the direction the seed had come from, and then hollowed out a canoe. He sailed to Arop. The woman saw him coming and said, 'here is your brother coming'. But his younger brother had changed his face. He sent him on an endless wild goose chase, until finally the woman told him to stop playing tricks, and he revealed himself in the place where the elder had first landed. The elder said he had felt sorry for his younger and had followed his design. The elder ate the younger's pig, then he told his younger to come to his place. The younger brother knew he would trick him in return, so he stuck a chicken feather in the back of his hair. When he arrived at the beach, the elder tried to trick him and send him around looking for him, but the younger was wise to it. He ate pig, and then left. They had children at Arop, and then he disappeared.

* * *

I suggest that what we see in the beginning of this myth amounts to a static hamlet grouping – in effect, an undifferentiated sibling set.[16] Notice the ambiguity in the role of the woman, something Reite people comment upon;

> People say 'mother', later they say the wife of the elder, and later still they say that the younger married their mother. This is hidden talk. The younger had this knowledge, and they fought over it. The younger decorated the woman, and they fought over this. These two men established all the ways of doing things we follow now. They made the first palem. The younger marked the woman, and took her. People know that these two men are our origin. The children of these people began the palem at Ripia, at Reite and at Sarangama. We are the true origin point. These two arose here, and then went from here to other places, to the islands, to Madang and everywhere. That is why this story is found all over the place. Some have said (in this village!) that this is also the origin of whitemen and their knowledge. I do not know about that. The story we have here is only of the fight, the flight and the palem. (Porer Nombo in 2001)

The woman's identity is not fixed by her gender – there being no children there to show her to be in a productive relationship with either of the men present. Thus she is 'wife' and 'mother' and neither. Young women in Reite are referred to playfully as 'mother' by men, both parties enjoying the allusion to potential future sexuality and productivity; and women in a hamlet are undifferentiated when referred to collectively, *paring sulieng*, covering sisters, daughters and wives. In the opening of the myth none of the conditions recognisable as marriage, and all those internal to palem, are apparent. There are no children, no in-laws and therefore no maternal uncle in the story anywhere. The one woman is at times wife, and at others mother, to the men in the myth, but never is she mother to their children, until the very end when one of them lives elsewhere.

The first significant act in the myth is that of the younger sibling tattooing *Yandi imang* between the legs of this sibling-like woman. Others have interpreted this as adultery: 'adultery was a sure way to break up a family' (Pomponio 1992: 34). Reite people (although they have no knowledge of Lévi-Strauss) would say that marriage is, in fact, a sure way to break up a family.[17] As I will make clear, adultery has nothing to do with the imagery being played out here. It is of little consequence, then, whether intercourse is made explicit or not, although I point out the obvious question of why, if this were merely an act of adultery, this is not said directly. These are not people with puritan mores about discussing sexual matters openly. What is said to occur is that a man tattoos his design, the inspiration for which is thought to come from power resident in his own land, onto the body of someone like a sibling, or other palem member. He genders her, and in so doing, also genders himself as the recipient of her sexual gaze.

Now we come to the anger of the elder brother. Sensing a new relationship between himself and this woman who is part of his place, he tricks her into showing him her vagina. That the elder sibling should look for the source of the rupture between himself and this woman in her sexuality is significant. Having himself seen his sister as gendered, sexualised, and knowing it is not him that has been the cause of this, the elder is forced, not to punish her or secrete her to a place where this 'adultery' cannot be repeated, but to find out who is responsible. He instigates the cooking of pigs, and organises hospitality in order to see the designs of people around him.

In organising this feasting, the elder brother has recognised he has something to give away, has recognised he must lose his female aspect to the man who has gendered her productively, something he never managed to do. The play of many people trying their designs could be read as a comment on the fact that gendering, like all identity, is a reciprocal recognition between specific persons. There is no essential identity or gender, but only that created in specific relationships. Others come and make their designs, but these are insignificant; it is not in the view of these others that the woman has been gendered, and the dissimilarity between her sexualised appearance and these others' view of her is apparent.

Part of the myth whose meaning to a Western audience seems self-evident, that men fight over a woman because of jealousy or wounded pride, has wholly different resonances for Reite hearers. These centre around the fact that men always fight when one of their sisters falls in love and wishes to marry, thereby removing herself from them. In every case of a sister finding another man attractive, prior to marriage (i.e., a marriage 'of choice' is to take place) her brothers know with certainty that this man has caused her to regard him as desirable. It is said as a kind of refrain, *meri i no save laikim man nating* [T.P.] (lit. women do not like men [for] nothing), meaning not, as I initially assumed, that a woman has no interest in a man without money, but rather that she will have no regard for the man unless forced through the use of love-magic.

The anger that brother's evince in the inevitable fight with their prospective in-laws is a version of the same anger as that of the elder brother in the myth. The fact that the fight goes on indefinitely, and is eventually stopped by the actions of the woman, perhaps speaks of the correct resolution to such anger. That is separation. In the myth the significant act is the gendering in the view of a man who becomes other by the act of seeing a sibling woman as marriageable. In a similar way, the significant moment in the anger of brothers over the loss of their sister to a husband is not the moment that they catch the two together, nor the moment of her departure, but the moment that anticipates these inevitable consequences. This lies in her recognition not as sister, but as possible wife. Thus her lover's act with the love-magic is an act of definition, as much as was the act of tattooing by the younger brother in the myth.

My argument, then, runs thus: In the myth of Pomo, we have the origins of sexuality and therefore productivity as it is understood in Reite cosmology and practice. The *Yandi imang* design is an act of creation, and is the origin of separation between persons (gender, placement). The anger and fighting in the myth is not jealousy over a wife, but the anger of being separated from a sister, and this anger still exists today. This being the case, it is no wonder that this is a story which can also explain the separation from white people, from cargo, or from their deity. Whatever the separation, it is plausible because such separations are forms of the essential separation between kinspeople that generate the conditions for a recognisably human future. This time, however, is not in some historical sense 'in the past', like the loss of cargo was 'in the past', but is present and relevant to a loss that all people feel as siblings.

A brother creates future strangeness by separating those who will marry his sister in fighting with them. Ultimately, his children will forget there is a connection between themselves and this other man's children. This is where the preference for marrying a cross-cousin completes a separation made in the past; one might say this is why it is preferred. They are relatives, made different from you in an initial violent act, and then brought back to you in marriage. A sister is not made a stranger, the consequences of the violence done to her (her extraction) and her husband (the fight) are carried forward into the future to make her children strangers. If the axiom of kinship is that everyone is related, then this is a solution to the problem of how one finds anyone different enough to marry.

This throws the identity of Europeans, as understood by Lawrence, McSwain, and others, into a different light. As it has been understood, the Manup and Kilibob myth was presented as a rationalisation of the inherent difference between those that had cargo and those that did not. I am suggesting that the differentiation between the brothers in this myth is something that is built into things all the time. I often wondered why many people called me by the Tok Pisin kin term *kandere* (cross-cousin). From this analysis, it appears an answer could be given. As a person, I must be related. The assumption is that as I am from elsewhere, my relation is through a woman. They claim me (whites) not only as kin, but also as marriageable kin, made so by Reite people's own productive agency in the past. Pomo is not a one-off story about the past, but tells people (all people, hence the designation *pablik*) how creativity, the future, in fact existence that is recognisably human, comes about.

Reite marriage is always to some extent *ne naki* (to oneself), as all persons are recognised as kin to some degree. The separations involved in marriage are necessary whether one marries 'too close' or 'at a distance'. Thus it appears that Reite people are concerned neither with incest (all sexual relations are to relatives), nor with sexual distinctions as biological properties of individuals – that is, given from the outset and moulded by society. It is these latter ideas which make it possible for sex to occur between persons who are too close. Our metaphors for this are spatial, as are Reite descriptions. In their case, however, the description is accurate. Marriage to siblings involves conflict and separation resulting in the establishment of a new palem by one of the affinal sides. Thus physical removal is the start of a process of differentiation which produces affines and cross-cousins as distinct from their origin. Sex between persons who are 'too close' cannot persist in Reite because recognition of gender implies the kind of differentiation that generates new palem and new persons.

Genealogy and Biology; or Does Incest Exist for Nekgini Speakers?

The problem we face when looking at kinship terminologies is one of the (assumed) separation between term and reality. The problem Nekgini speakers face when they look at marriage is (effecting) separation between persons. Using genealogical models for analysing social organisation imports an assumption of the biological basis of relatedness and difference. As theorists, we imagine that kin terms amount to variable ways of ordering a base reality of procreation and affiliation (through society). The issue of marriage among Nekgini speakers highlights these assumptions. Do Nekgini speakers 'really' know the difference between siblings of the same parents, and those of distant parallel cousins, whether they call them by the same term or not? And are they less likely to commit 'incest' with 'true' siblings, for the reason that the recognition of biology is universal, as is the incest prohibition? Why should Nekgini speakers use terms which classify people together if they 'really' understand them to be different? What relation does 'true' genealogy have to the social definition of genealogy in a kinship terminology? How indeed are people differentiated? This dualism was first addressed by Lewis Henry Morgan over a century ago, and it seems to be an analytic problem that has not gone away.

If we think that all systems of terminological classification are both artificial and arbitrary (i.e., bear no relation to 'real' genealogy because we cannot find a universal principle by which the underlying and the conscious structures are related), we come to the position where kinship is viewed as a set of symbols (Schneider 1968) – a system of meaning, internally consistent – but arbitrary in relation to what is described. The basis of cultural and interpretive anthropology in linguistic models of exactly this kind is worth remembering here. The position that kinship is a set of symbols and has no relation to any physical or biological reality that subsumes cultural difference has been taken to an extreme in Schneider's study *A Critique of the Study of Kinship* (1984). In that book he argued that there is no such thing as kinship, or rather, there is no universal meaning in genealogy for the terms that we (Euro-Americans, anthropologists) use. Thus there is no way we can look at and understand kinship systems elsewhere. This is a *reductio ad absurdum* line – concluding, from the initial premise that human kinship is arbitrary, that there is no such thing as kinship.

Perhaps the source of the problem lies in an assumption that Nekgini people patently do not make, namely that classification is about entities. Our model of classification assumes that a priori entities need to be grouped together (classified). Differentiation is given by biology. Thus the project of classification arises through recognition of the reality, or nature (biology), of the pre-given entity. This works as much for gender as for recognition of siblingship. However, Melanesian assumptions are very different from this in that they assume processes and relationships, not pre-given entities. Nekgini people's, and other Melanesians' project is not to group like things together, but as we have seen, to differentiate, to make entities appear out of processes (Weiner 1994: 342). Thus when Nekgini people use kinship names in their speech, these usages are not classificatory or tax-onomic, but are part of the process by which persons are made to appear, in the perception of others, as standing in a certain relationship (say of wife, rather than sister). The relationship does not follow from pre-recognition of the person as of a certain biologically or genealogically defined type.

The history of relations, and of the places where kinship comes into being have their influence. So growing up together in a hamlet makes one 'siblings', or an affinal relation in a previous generation means types of 'sibling' are resident in different places (cross-cousins). They are related through a gendered separation in the past. When we hear kinship terms being used in these places, we need to view these usages as pragmatic acts, as acts that secure an effect, not ones that serve to express realities which are already specified by either biology or society.

We are presented then, in the study of kin terms, with the problems of how words relate to concepts, and of how concepts relate to the world; but we must remember these are *our* problems, the products of an epistemology that insists that knowledge is prior to action, that one knows the world by representing it concep-tually in the mind, and that language is the vehicle by which such representational knowledge is expressed and shared. However, if Nekgini-speaking people think about 'kinship', they do not have to contend with the distinction between real-life individuals (who for us are ready-formed as biocultural entities) and persons as constructed within the categories of relationship terminology. For the use of kin terms is part of the real-life, elicitory process that makes persons appear out of the relational field within which they are constituted.

The problems with kin terminologies, then, are problems with our epistemol-ogy. In our modern, relativistic approach, we attribute a generalised humanity to the subjects of our study, and imagine that they – like us – are formed through the superimposition, upon this substantial baseline, of particular and variable cultural forms. I suggest that if we are willing to look at the constitution of persons within cosmological lifeworlds, which include language as a mode of elicitation and agency (rather than classification, which of course is creative of a relation to the world itself) and where cosmology consists not of symbols or myths with little rel-evance, but speak of the imaginative and embodied make-up of persons themselves, we might accept something quite radical – namely, that humans are

different beings depending upon the relational worlds they enter into and participate in creating. Rather than saying that they have different cultures, which
carries the danger of essentialising our ideas of mind and substance (although it
need not necessarily do so [see Mimica 1991: 35]), we should say that they have
different constitutive lifeworlds.

We cannot model the constitution of persons, for Nekgini speakers, in the
terms bequeathed by modern thought: of individual and society, biological organism and cultural mind. Theirs is not a culture with Iroquois-type terminology
superimposed upon a substrate of 'real', genetic kinship. They do indeed share
substance, but this is not at all what we would imagine the substance of kinship to
be. That is why people in Reite see no fundamental difficulty in marrying people
who are, in principle, unmarriageable. Their myth, and the possibilities it gives in
mythic consciousness for relationships which accommodate what for other people
might be an unthinkable act, is not a set of symbols, any more than their terminologies are arbitrary in relation to the people to whom they are applied. These
aspects of the Nekgini social world assume a person's definition as an aspect of a
process in which change occurs.

Reite people talk about 'blood' (*asurung*). One of their objections to close cross-
cousin marriage is that 'blood has not gone far enough'. In agreeing that a
marriage is acceptable, men say '*blut i go longwe*' [T.P], 'blood has gone far'. What
is meant by blood here is a fascinating problem; but it is no longer a problem that
Nekgini speakers appear to be recognising a part, but not the whole, of our
descriptive system for understanding kin relations: that substance is contained in
blood. As Brenda Clay writes for Mandak people from New Ireland:

> The symbolic idiom most commonly used to convey the meaning of paternal substance
> is 'blood'. Western ideas of kinship must not be confused with this consanguineal refer-
> ence, for when the Mandak speak of blood relationships they are conveying something
> quite different from the American meaning of the term' (Clay 1977: 39).

The understanding of shared substance, called 'blood', may prove to be a problem in this analysis. However, it is a descriptive problem, one of finding the right
language to describe Nekgini cosmology. I move on to describing land as the basis
for substantial connection between people in the next chapter and thus elaborate
on the meanings of *asurung*.

Notes

1. I clarify at the outset my use of the terms 'sex' and 'gender' in this chapter. When I use 'opposite
   sex' I mean merely the relation of a male to a female. Thus in the definitions of cross-cousins – as
   in 'opposite sex cross-cousin' – I mean only that one is male and one is female. This does not have
   implications for sexuality as such. My use of the term 'gendered' implies an activated or productive
   sexuality in relation to an opposite sex person. Thus siblings who do not marry may be 'opposite sex'

– a boy and a girl – without the relationship being 'gendered', i.e. they are not sexually productive together; but cross-cousins who are 'gendered' in relation to one another, have a sexually productive relationship.

2. *Asi* is a reciprocal term used by grandparents and grandchildren.

3. Although in arranged marriages practised in the past a girl moved to her future husband's hamlet after her initiation.

4. All young people I know in Reite complain about the amount of hard work involved in fulfilling affinal obligations once married, and most postpone marriage for as long as possible. In the material on love-magic that I present below, it is as well to remember that it is rarely on the youth's own initiative that this form of sorcery is performed, but rather on his behalf by elder men of his palem, and at their initiative.

5. FFZSS is 'father's father's sister's son's son', e/yB/Z is 'elder/younger brother/sister'. The specific requirement of a child of your father's *tapi* serves to highlight how intricate the management of previous affinal relations are in relation to new marriages.

6. Rawirawi are given when payment is for a *body*. This happens in Matopo (and see Chapter 5). The Huli payment is for the acceptance of the union by the girl's kinsmen. Each plant carried relates to her future as a wife. The banana shows productivity, the flowering shrub long life, and the gorogor, peace. These are planted as a mnemonic of the goodwill between the affines, and thus for the girl's future life. With the preponderance of 'choice' marriage, this aspect has been lost. Porer Nombo, commenting on this, said 'Nau mipela stil tasol, mipela ino save wokim Huli nau' (we steal these days, and don't perform Huli). This does not mean that bridepayments are not made, but that wives are not brought to their husbands as part of a concord between the future affines. Therefore the niceties are not observed.

7. I use the Tok Pisin term from here on, as it was favoured in the conversations I heard most often. People in the hamlets of Reite enjoy speaking in Tok Pisin, especially when speaking euphemistically.

8. For example, I have witnessed fights over sexual unions between siblings which turned wholly on the issue of their marriageability and not on the union as a thing in itself. The problem, both in what was acted upon, and in the indigenous commentary given, concerned the promise of marriage entailed by sexual relations (in this case between siblings). In further support of this view, I cite Goodale's again. She writes that sexual activity is a statement of, and amounts to, the permanent establishment of a marital relationship. Kaulong have 'no concept of premarital sexual activity' (Goodale 1981: 276), although this might be overstating things rather for Reite people.

9. And see Leavitt (1990) who sifts the evidence regarding the incest prohibition, with the startling conclusion that there is no scientific evidence that incest is biologically detrimental to organisms or the gene pool. In other words, the myth of a biological rationale for the rule is so encompassing that it is never questioned, even by the scientists who cite one another in self-referential confirmation.

10. Other than those who adopt the 'familiarity breeds sexual contempt' argument.

11. I am writing this as a commentary on the point of view of an old man. It would be interesting to look also from the point of view of his wife – the woman who was his sister and became his wife. Unfortunately this is not possible for me other than in very general terms. It was men that used to talk to me about whom they married. Just because women did not discuss this with me does not mean they do not think about it, but I believe that in this particular case the consequences of this marriage were less noticeable for the wife. She did not have her relationships circumscribed in the same way; she remained the sister of the men who had eaten her bride compensation, and a sibling also to the men who helped her husband with this payment. I would also say that, unlike for a man, the recognition of agency as a woman is not dependent on one's visibility in exchange, and wealth/knowledge.

12. For example, 'The natives' claim to the cargo and mounting hostility to Europeans were stated clearly by the belief that the latter had obtained exclusive possession of a valuable commodity invented by a deity to whom they only had partial rights or no origin rights at all. If Kilibob or Manup created both whitemen and natives, then the whitemen should have given the natives their

quota of the cargo. If Kilibob or Manup had only discovered the whitemen in their distant home, then the cargo belonged primarily to the natives' (Lawrence 1964: 237).

13. See Gow (2001: 9) for a discussion of the drawbacks of this reaction to the place of myth in people's construction of their history.

14. This idea of a 'flawed' or incomplete theory comes from Alfred Gell (1998) via Edwardo Viveiros de Castro (personal communication).

15. Belonging to all.

16. The point that there is no productivity, and no significant gendering, is unaffected by whether this is a sibling set or a family of more than one generation. As the figures for marriages show, father/daughter and mother/son marriages are more common than marriages between siblings.

17. According to the Reite Komiti, there has been only one case of adultery that has come to his notice in his jurisdiction during the twenty years of his tenure. Adultery could not be said to be a preoccupation of Reite people.

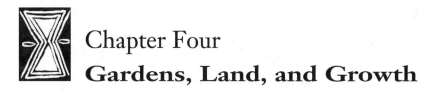

Chapter Four
Gardens, Land, and Growth

'One bush is the same as one blood.'
Peter Lawrence, quoting from Garia informants (1967: 125)

The analysis of terminology and marriage has shown that differentiation is something that people work to achieve. Persons appear as different things through time. What then of the central element in a genealogical model of kinship, the transmission of substance as an immutable element of identity? How do Reite people understand the processes whereby structures of relations appear, have effect, and are dissolved in life-cycles, (or over longer time scales), if *not* by relating them to pre-existing distinctions between substance as biogenetic inheritance? These are issues which usually invoke descent and thus lineality in kinship-based societies.

The idea that definition is an outcome of exchange relations in Papua New Guinea was developed by Roy Wagner. He tells us that among the Daribi, 'consanguinity relates, exchange defines' (1967). I began a discussion of definition through exchange (including the exchange of perspectives) in the previous chapter. What is not yet apparent is what a notion of 'consanguinity' (*asurung konaki* 'one blood') refers to among Nekgini speakers.

Time-scale is one way of introducing the themes of this chapter. If one was to film a garden over a year, and then play this film at high speed, what would appear? That the garden was in motion, was alive with movement and change. Reite gardens develop over a growing season from scorched patches of earth, bare tree trunks standing like dry sticks among the pitted limestone boulders, to lush, green expanses.

Taro plants wave large glossy leaves in the breeze, and yam vines cover the bare trees, making shady 'houses' (*ya*) for the tubers which inhabit the shelter at their feet.

Movement is integral, not contingent, to the perception of gardens by Nekgini speakers. Spirits come and go, bringing their children to populate the earth. Once grown, these children move away again, giving sustenance to people who also rely on movements between gardens, places, and kinsfolk for their growth. Land is not

Photograph 4 *Taro Garden after Four Months Growth*

static, but moves through animating and distributing its offspring. Taro itself is thought of not only as animate, but as migratory. Nekgini speakers find ways to talk about the power of land, about its animation. They link this power to the connections between people who reside and work together. Thus land itself provides a kind of continuity in relatedness. In doing so, it is the basis against which differentiating relations with others are visible.

Origin Points

People from Yawaspiring palem claim that they own the knowledge or story (*patuki*) for the origin of taro (*pel*).[1] The original strain of taro – *kapa* – was given to their ancestors by the deity 'taro' itself.[2] The tubers, and methods of growing them, were subsequently distributed to kin in other hamlets, and so on into the wider world. Taro (*Colocasia esculenta var. antiquorum*) is now the staple crop in this area, and is a prestige food required as a central element in the construction of a palem. It is infinitely preferable in local people's taste to insubstantial *embe* (sweet potato, *Ipomoea batatas*), and more significant than *wiynung* (yam, *Dioscorea alata*) which has a less prolific harvest.[3] Taro gardens are the pride and joy of Reite people. They provide an aesthetic standard by which other people and places are known and judged. Nekgini speakers enthuse over the particular look and feel of good heavy tubers, and the taste and texture of the close-knit starch. The harvest is temporally ordered on the basis of proximity to the origin place of taro.

It is told that before the discovery of taro, men and women had to boil stones with wild ginger, and drink the soup as a palliative for their hunger. They would wedge the boiled stones into the belts of their skirts and loincloths to fill the space left by their empty bellies.[4] Taro gardening has extensive mythic elaboration. The domestication of wild plant species (i.e., the beginnings of horticulture), in its indigenous significance,[5] can be gauged from the convergence of forms and images in the practice of gardening and in the knowledge of reproduction which these myths make plain.

Taro is associated with generation and growth predicated upon the recognition of gender. Women take taro 'babies' when they move in marriage. Taro requires a 'mother' to be brought into the garden to grow the child-tubers in her belly. Siriman (Kiap) Kumbukau described to me, as a matter of common sense, how taro follows (is distributed by) women (in marriage) and thus how women act like the peace-making plant *luhu*;[6] '*Meri i go, na taro save behainim em. Meri em olsem gorogor [luhu]*' (T.P.). He was referring to how men give their sisters' children their gardening practices in initiation, and thus the original strains of taro, along with the productive form of gardens revealed by the taro deity, have been dispersed. Siriman's common-sense statement about how taro moves belies his own complex mythic (cf. Gillison 1993; Weiner 1995) understanding of the relationships engendered by the growth of this staple crop.

Many ethnographers of Melanesia, from Malinowski on, report the special significance of gardening.[7] Trobriand garden- and weather-magic, for example, are owned and jealously guarded, charges being made if another appropriates them. Annette Weiner describes Trobriand origin myths as valuable and coveted forms of knowledge (and see Harrison 1992: 230). It is this level of importance that taro, and being identified as its origin, has for Reite people.

Gendered Productivity: The Tambaran

If in the previous chapter, I made gender 'disappear' as a definition *prior* to people's involvement in constitutive relations, it was to reinstate it elsewhere. During initiation, boys and girls are secluded with spirits that grow them into adults. Both are understood to be marriageable – that is potentially sexually combined with another – after this intense involvement. When arranged marriages were common, a girl's initiation was the responsibility of her future husband. That is, he provided the wealth and food that facilitated her relations with the spirits. Sexual maturity is something which is grown in bodies. Gender exists as perhaps *the* principle of productive difference in the Nekgini creative process, as I outlined in the last chapter.

Making gender appear as a detached principle is an analytic move on my part. I argue that qualities, attributes, and identity are *grown in* people through the actions of others. Entities are not pre-differentiated, thus social life does not 'make apparent' a more 'primordial' reality contained within bodies. Instead, creative endeavour succeeds through generating the difference that may be combined to productive effect.

Nekgini speakers call the processes of growth which rely upon gender *kaapu*. Kaapu are the spirits that grow adolescents during initiation into adulthood. They grow the child in a mother's womb. In other words, Nekgini speakers also separate the principle of gender from persons. Kaapu are their way of doing so. Gender is an attribute of persons who exist at specific positions, defined by their close involvement with kaapu, in a field of relations.[8] The idea that difference has to be grown in people is made clear in seeing the principle of gender as part of the rela-tional constitution of the growing body itself. The centrality of gender as the principle facilitating association with growth means kaapu appear as an important element throughout the Nekgini lived world.

In his early work on the Andaman Islands, Radcliffe-Brown (1922) posed the question of what it is that occurs when one sees the 'same' thing in different con-texts. Are they indeed the same things, or is it the contexts that make things that are, in reality different, look the same to the observer? One might say that this is a question at the heart of symbolic analysis. In what follows, I cite the spirits (kaapu) of the Nekgini world as a linking element across what would usually be thought of as different domains of activity, namely: agriculture, the growth of children, ritual initiation, and artistic production. I do so because Reite people themselves call what happens in all these domains 'kaapu'. Thus I follow their connections and analogies 'across' contexts, seeing 'the same' things in different areas of life.

The Tok Pisin word *tambaran* is often translated as 'ancestor spirit cult' (Mihalic 1971), or by reference to some variation on the theme of ancestor wor-ship and male ritual control. Gardi, in a book named *Tambaran*, writes

> It is difficult to put down all that this word Tambaran implies. It is the mystery barred to women; it embraces everything connected with the cult; with it are bound up tradition, community, ancestors, the dead. These Tambaran figures typify spirits and ancestors and are embodied in them too; they symbolise the strength of a tribe, they are sources of strength which render possible the life of men. (Gardi 1960: 14)

Although this would be a set of understandings Reite people might agree with, Don Tuzin comes closer to their understanding when he writes, 'Birth, death, fer-tility, sexuality and growth – these are the biological mysteries of which the cult claims privileged knowledge and control' (1980: 25).

'Tambaran' is used in Reite to translate the similarly polyvalent Nekgini word *kaap*, which is spirit, ghost, voice/tune, secret cult object, menstruation, and child-birth. Kaapu is the collective word used to describe the body of initiated men who watch over and produce the sprits during cult activity. Thus one can say 'the kaapu' or 'the tambaran' to refer to both the spirits, *and* the entity of men com-bined with spirits engaged in particular (kaapu) activity. As Niles describes, while introducing a recent book on spirit music among Waxei people of the East Sepik

Hills, 'Sounds produced by men... or through the singing of men and women are *for* and *of* the spirits concerned, but in many ways *are* those spirits. In some ways then, humans become spirits' (Niles 1997, original emphasis). Nekgini kaapu are most obvious in their manifestation as musical voices, produced secretly by men in seclusion with the spirits.

At a time during my fieldwork, wondering not for the first time what people 'really' believed about the kaapu I asked Porer, 'what really is the tambaran'? The clarity of his answer excited me, given that we were engaged in daily discussion of the meaning of Nekgini kastom. 'You have seen it and so you know what it is. What more can I say that is relevant? To examine it too closely will make it disappear.' Kaapu are indeed apparent in the effect of those activities which involve liaison with the spirits. They are also apparent in the outcomes of people's activities that produce things in the image of persons. Porer made it clear that thinking of it as something people affect misses the point, and would undermine the power of these actions. It is not the thing itself that is the focus of interest, but rather the creative power of a way of doing things. One could think of this as a way of saying that kaapu is a concept used by Nekgini people in many contexts to explain growth and change in bodies, and to claim agency in directing or organising the conditions for such change. He pointed out that by preserving the mystery of the spirits, these conditions are maintained.

In this chapter, I do with 'gardening' what Reite people 'do' with tambaran. By this I mean that I make gardens and gardening – the procedures within them, the forms they take, the labour involved, what they produce, and how they are thought to produce it – into an explanatory moment in the production of what we would call kinship. What makes this possible is the fact that these are domains which are linked by kaapu in Nekgini speakers' understanding. Or, indeed, it would be more accurate to say that these are domains which are habitually separated in our understanding and our analysis. Nekgini speakers do not make this separation of domains, nor of ritual work from agriculture, nor agriculture from kinship. Control of the powers of growth (kaapu) is recognised as agency, and has social effects, whether this occurs in gardens, or in producing persons. The outcomes are commensurate because the creative process is the same. Although, then, this is ultimately a chapter about gardens and taro, I come circuitously to the garden itself through presenting the power to grow things briefly in a couple of other contexts.

Women's Tambaran

Kaapu in Nekgini represents something of a departure from the information given in other literature of the region on tambaran.[9] In Reite it is said that women *also* have a tambaran (*parieng yara'kaapu*). This is very different from the tambaran reported by Tuzin for the Ilahita Arapesh which has no female counterpart, and from which women and children are rigidly excluded: 'victims in body and mind of terrorism systematically applied by men acting in the name of the *tambaran*'

(1980: xiv). Among Nekgini speakers, women are rigidly excluded from male kaapu activities. Musical water spirits (*kaapu tupong yara*) are hidden from women and non-initiates in a kind of consensual secrecy which Gourlay (1975), following Bateson's insights from much earlier (1958 [1936]), describes as '[b]oth male and female connivance in mutual deception and the subsequent rituals [made possible by that deception which] operate as interacting forces to ensure the survival and wellbeing of society as its inhabitants see it' (120). Yet men's kaapu is balanced by the power women have to grow children. This suggests significant differences from the Arapesh, where the 'tambaran cult is, .. dominance...' (Tuzin 1980: 73). In Reite, as Porer explained, there is *parieng yara'kaapu* and *ai yakaapu* (women's tambaran and men's tambaran). 'Tambaran is something which remains hidden, men and women hide it from each other. Women have tambaran for conceiving and growing children, for dying skirts red, for planting taro and for carrying string bags (*au/bilum* [T.P.]). Men's is [concerned with] adolescence, taro, *kiramung* (slit-gongs) and hourglass drums, and music. Prayers or rituals (*sawi*) using spells (*paru*) is an activity covered by the name kaapu.'

A woman's initiation into *parieng yara'kaapu* comes about at adolescence. At the onset of her first menses, a girl stays in her house, without lighting, or eating from a fire. Her brothers must find freshwater crayfish and bring them to her. These are burned on her fire, and the girl scorches her hands and feet in their flames.[10] This allows her to then cook and eat from a fire during her seclusion. She remains in the house, and her elder female relatives, often in consultation with her mother's brother, decide on a period of time that she will eat only dry foods baked in the embers of that fire. She may not leave the house other than to relieve herself, and must keep her head covered and her gaze to the ground when she does so. When this period (between two weeks and one month) has elapsed, *yapel sang kupiret* (cutting wild taro leaves) takes place. Her mother's brother arrives before daybreak to cook a hot (ginger) soup for the girl, and he again heats her hands and feet on the fire before her emergence. Her face is rubbed clean with yellow flowers and turmeric to make it light and shine, and a large betel nut (*sima tawapo*) is broken over her forehead. The girl is told to step from the house at dawn onto a leaf of wild taro, and break sugar cane as she does so. Looking up at the sun, and taking a small white stone in her mouth, the girl spits the stone into the 'eye' of the rising sun. She is taken into a secluded spot in the bush by her female relatives who take the mat on which she has sat during her seclusion and discard it. A coconut, on which she has been seated throughout the morning, is broken open and eaten. Then she is 'eaten' by the spirits (*kaapu't neaeni*).

During her seclusion, female kin on her maternal side (i.e., mother's brother's wives and sisters), and her father's sisters, engage in *rauang* (women's play). During *rauang*, women have the right (and duty) to trick men, steal their food, soak them with water, go naked through the village, and make lewd gestures and suggestions to men of the girl's hamlet and their close male kin. Women's play is by definition vulgar, and at times frightening in its intensity and anarchy, but men may make no angry or violent response during *rauang* on pain of subsequent claims for compensation against them.

While in seclusion, a girl is counselled on the correct behaviour of an adult woman: how to welcome strangers and kinsmen to her house, how to treat her husband and how to work, when to complain and what to do if there is trouble in a marriage, how to cook, to raise children, and so forth. On her emergence, the girl is unable to eat most foods. She has to find and cook them for her mother's brother, who in eating them, carries away the potential sickness and 'heavy-ness' associated with many foods. This payment (*yungyung*) finishes her initiation, culminating in a presentation of pig meat. The stated purpose of many of the rites during seclusion, and of the payments of tabooed foods to the mother's brother after her emergence, are for her to grow successfully; that means into a woman who is red skinned and fat, can carry burdens, bear children, and perform the tasks required of a wife and mother.

The theme of hiddenness and growth, the very essence of kaapu itself, is clear from this brief description. A girl spontaneously begins her initiation, yet she must be hidden away in the body of the house for her change from a girl to a woman to be completed. During this time, only older women and her MB have any contact with her. Menstruation is a mystery to unmarried men and pre-pubescent girls. She emerges as significantly different. It is her father's affinal kin that monitor and direct her growth and change, and that decorate her on her emergence.

Now this whole process of hiddenness, and of lodging an entity one wishes to change and grow in the care of another (affinal palem), is also clearly shown in the production and growth of an entity Reite people consider a type of person, namely the slit gong drum.[11] These drums (*garamut* in Tok Pisin, *kiramung* in Nekgini) are used to communicate over distances in a kind of code made from different beats and rhythms. They are also used to accompany *kaapu simang* (child tambaran) performances from within the *passae* (men's house). Significantly they have a voice, and this makes them, as are *pariwah* (hourglass drums), the focus of special attention during their production.[12] It is the aspect of voice (*punging*), so central to the musical kaapu of the male cult, that distinguishes them from other objects which receive no ritual attention during manufacture.[13]

Garamuts

Manufacture of *kiramung* has all the elements of Nekgini conceptions of origin, growth, power, and revelation that I want to highlight.[14] They are made in seclusion by men, hidden deep in the bush where the tree is cut for their manufacture. Women are not present at any stage of their production. *Kaap sawing* (wild tambaran) are brought to the place where a suitable tree has been cut, and are watched over by initiated men as these wild spirits 'eat' (see above, *kaapu't neaeni*) the insides of the logs, which men cut from a single trunk. Once the whole tree of logs has been hollowed, the *kaap sawing* are sent back into the bush, and *kaap simang* ('child tambaran', one of the *kaapu tupong yara*, spirits whose presence is known by their imposing and eerie voices) replace them. Men are said to be 'watching over' the work of the spirits as they eat and shape the logs. From the very first possible opportunity, the new drums are beaten to the accompaniment of the spirit voices, and thus are heard in the surrounding hamlets. The men watching over the kaapu are subject to *rauang* (women's play), as are those for whom the garamut are being made. After several months comes a final night in seclusion with the whole male cult when the new drums are decorated, their 'faces' cut and painted, and at dawn they are dragged along the paths to the hamlet of the man who receives the base of the tree as his drum. This man is the 'base' (*saporung*) of the work, the reason for it, and he provides the promise of payment for the spirits that have worked on his drum. It is at this point that women see the new drums for the first time. In the centre of the hamlet, they make as if to attack the drums, circling them, as the men protect them with their bodies. When they have been seen, promises of wealth in the form of 'ropes' (*rawirawi* – as in the rope to which a pig is tied) are placed on the face of each drum.[15]

A garamut is made for a man by the kaapu of his affines. This may be done at the time the husband and wife pay her brothers for her body (*parieng huli*), or at some later date. Affinal kinsmen come onto the land of their sister's husband (*apari*) and cut a suitable tree. The sister's husband will be the 'base' (*kiramung saporung*) of the series of garamuts, it is he that 'supports them', but he will have little or nothing to do with their construction. His affines bring their kaapu (*sawing and simang*) onto his land to eat the middle of his own tree, and shape it into something with a voice and a face. 'Making' garamut is directly equivalent in ritual procedure to the 'making' of adolescents into adults. The tree 'sees' the tambaran and is eaten by it, while the father's affines 'watch over' and direct the work of the spirits. When grown, the new person is decorated by its 'father's' affines, and emerges from their period of seclusion with the tambaran into view of an audience who judge their condition. Payment is made by the 'father' of the child/garamut to his affines for the work they have done in bringing their powers of formation and decoration to bear on the person in question.

Notice that the substance of what is made is supplied by a man himself; the tree used is his own tree and comes from his land (comparable in this respect to New Ireland *malangan*, where the carver provides the image on behalf of the owner of the carving [Küchler 1987]). What his affines transform by their labour, they reveal to him and the women of his hamlet group. At this moment of revelation, they receive promise of further payment for their work. This payment is called the same as the payment for watching over, and decorating, an initiate (*yungyung arsang*). Payment, then, is made for an elicitation of form from potential. The identity of the owner of the garamut is bound to this object which others form for him, from his own substance. (A man and his garamut, and a man and the beat by which he can be called, are closely identified. Both garamut and 'name' are supplied by other palem. In many cases the skeletons of dead men are placed inside their slit-gong drums, which act as coffins). Garamut are grown from bones (a tree), are secluded like adolescents, and are 'eaten' by kaapu. What is produced is something equivalent to a person; it has the appearance and voice of a person. Yet it belongs to the supplier of the original substance, and not to those who made it. The form of the thing is not its origin, and it is apparently origin which allows identification.

Hidden Growth

While things always grow, the power to control this is something people claim. The power to elicit this nurture from others is central to the development of a palem. It is how their children are grown. The difference between having the bush grow up in an area and having tubers grow under the ground is a product of people's agency in making affinal relations. If affines/maternal kin elicit form from children and trees (substance), paternal kin in turn elicit this labour and nurture from their affines. To make the growth of anything productive, and to produce the correct forms within this wider process, takes work. Growth happens; to ask why or investigate the mechanisms of this are not the concerns of Reite people. In fact the whole power of growth is such that in this rainforest environment burgeoning with life, it just occurs without anyone doing anything. This is the background of relationality from which people work to highlight forms they can claim as their own (Wagner 1977b). People do not know how things grow and they do not investigate this.

To go further: the hiddenness of growing tubers in the earth is mirrored in the hidden nature of the child that is in the belly of its mother, or the seclusion of children during initiation. It is not a Reite preoccupation to know *how* these things grow – that things grow is part of the taken-for-granted background to human concerns. Thus I asked many times what the process of conception is, and was always met with blankness. The very fact of growth appears as something that is hidden, and once this observation has been made, it is less surprising that there is no interest in observing growth as it occurs. *Paru palangpalang miyae wiyung ikori sak'weiyung gnu malankaet porikerweiyung* ('exposing *paru* (spells) will make them bad and finish [their power] like water [they] drain away'). The notion of containment, which permeates so much ethnography from Papua New Guinea,[16] is relevant here. For Reite people, there is a hiddenness about that which is contained, and it is in fact the out-of-sight nature of the thing that gives it its potential for growth (see also Biersack [1982]).

A corollary to this is that seeing something arrests change. For Nekgini speakers it is clear that revelation completes work, momentarily turning transformation (process) into an object (entity). There is a time for this. The folly of breaking open a container to view the contents is self-evident to Reite people. *Saseng patang'ani wangari weyungket kating keting* ('someone revealed to sight without preparation [at the wrong time] is ruined and dry [will grow no more]'). Who would murder a woman in order to see if the child she is carrying is growing properly? Who would dig up a garden to see whether the tubers in it are developing? For something to be hidden, then, is to imagine it in the presence of a power which effects a change upon it. Nekgini speakers call this power kaapu. It is no coincidence that the powerful in the world (sorcerers, weather-workers) are in control of the unseen. As Reite people often bemoan, 'there are ashes in our eyes, we cannot see the spirits and the dead'. The powerful realm of growth is all around – but it cannot be seen.

Households and Gardens

Turning now to the units which make gardens, I think it worthwhile to look at some contemporary ethnography from elsewhere in the region on the changes in household work patterns brought about by the introduction of wage labour and capitalist enterprise. Robert Foster charts the emergence of the household as a significant economic unit under the influence of colonial and post-colonial capitalist production on the island of Tanga, New Ireland. He argues that *kastom* and *bisnis* [T.P.] have become opposed there as different foci for the organisation and products of labour. Whereas kastom demands that labour and wealth be pooled by the matrilineage and that authority over it rests with matrilineal heads (*bikmen* [T.P.]), bisnis demands household autonomy and that the products of labour be consumed within smaller social units. The antipathy Tangan big-men see between the two systems of social production arises from the lack of authority they hold in the sphere of bisnis, and its consequent detraction from the encompassing image of the matrilineage as the source of life (Foster 1995: chapters 2 and 3).

In Reite there is a similar opposition between kastom and bisnis. The former is seen to be detrimental to the development of the latter. It is tempting to think that Foster's suggestions for Tanga may be appropriate here also, especially his sophisticated discussion of the interplay of autonomy, consumption and individuality engendered by capitalist production. Interestingly, however, the household as a site for production (rather than consumption) is not a departure from 'traditional' social organisation in Reite. Much as the Tangan matrilineage becomes paramount in funerary feasting and exchanges, the Nekgini palem is made evident through feasting and presentation – the presentation of the products of the labour of the hosts to the visitors/recipients. Yet it is individual household production that is pooled by palem members. They will each have separate gardens and labour drawn from individual households, and it is from these apparently individuated sources that the image of the palem as a single entity under one named person on a particular piece of land appears. Gardens are made to appear as the outcome of a particular man's work, and the division of labour between husbands and wives, whether or not he has had help from other palem members or wider kin. When grown for exchange, this appearance of individual production is essential for the appearance of the palem as an entity arising from a particular person's agency in a particular named place. Hence in making gardens for this kind of presentation, affines are not asked to help. However, when gardens are made with the labour and help of many, they are primarily consumed by single household units. This relates to the combination of husband, wife, and siblings in the presentation of a palem as a single entity which produces things at 'one door', and the reciprocal assistance offered by members of the same palem in each other's gardening activities.

A husband and wife have the responsibility to feed their household. In making his garden a man will often allow the reciprocal aid of cognates and affines, who will be given token produce from the garden, but who will not claim it as their due. Yet in making gardens for affinal exchanges, a man will tend to look to his own household, or at least palem group, for labour. That production centres around households does not reveal an underlying logic of capitalist production and consumption, but rather a Nekgini notion of the responsibility of men to make their land productive through ritual procedures, and thereby show their control over the potential for growth in the land they claim as their own. By making a household into a single entity – a 'body', from the door of which come other 'bodies' (children, food) – persons become conjoined, and identified, with places. The focus on individual men and women (household units) as the site of production, and of use rights over garden produce, is important.

Foster's analysis throws comparative light on Reite ethnography and highlights some novelties in relation to the general process of commodification. Here we have the apparent opposite to a simple contrast between clan and community work as equivalent to kastom consumption, and household work as pertaining to bisnis or the cash economy. This may throw light on the opposition to bisnis, from kastom, adhered to by many on the Rai Coast. It is the fact of reciprocal communal work that helps the everyday consumption by households, but when translated into bisnis does not result in reciprocal and balanced consumption (Leach n.d.[b]). This causes jealousy and complaint.

Gardening, not 'Production'

Each household clears and plants at least one large taro garden each year. Most households make more than one, often sharing land in second and third gardens with members of the same palem, or with close affines. Gardens made individually are usually those intended to be the basis of payments between affines. Much of the work in a garden takes the form of what anthropologists call 'ritual' (see Lawrence 1965: 209).While we make a habitual distinction between ritual and technical endeavours, as well as process and product, Reite gardeners patently do not. Process itself is creative, and it is the creative aspect of the relations involved that generate outcomes which are commensurate with other sources of value. Lawrence's assertion (1984: 17) that 'in agriculture – as in other major activities – Garia do not distinguish between physical labour and the religious ritual associated with it…' supports this.

Why should this be? While we may feel that some of their procedures are instrumental and others decorative or religious, for Reite gardeners, the enterprise is not geared to production in a straightforward sense. Instead their technique, and their register for effect, is the form of social relations themselves. Garden knowledge not only comes out of a history of relatedness and movement, it is the ongoing production of these relationship that a gardener seeks to energise. Thus procedures within the garden mirror the form of relations outside it. I come on to show how this is the case. The technology of garden production, apparently magical in that it has metaphorical or analogic effect, is aimed at securing 'growth' itself rather than technical competence in securing products. As I have said that these realms are not separate in Nekgini understanding of garden work, this description does not quite capture the issue. One might have to say that it is the techniques of elicitation pertinent in the social world which gives form to the everyday tasks of subsistence agriculture. Processes which have their roots in the garden as it were, are what we might call kinship. They are concerned with 'producing' relationships out of relationships. This work is never finished, hence, 'gardening' rather than 'production'.

The Garden Year

The principal operations of the garden cycle are cutting, firing, and planting. Judging the best times for each of these operations is always a delicate matter. Garden work begins each year in June and July. At this time new areas of forest are located and earmarked by men for new gardens. Cutting and clearing the undergrowth is mainly completed by women, and for a large garden may take up to a week. When the ground is clear, men come and either lop the branches off large trees, or fell them altogether. Both these activities are generally co-operative, with the garden owner providing an end of day meal (*sukarung*) for those who come and help with labour. No one is asked to help, however; they come of their own volition.

June and July are the hottest and driest months on the Rai Coast, with a prevailing north-westerly wind (the Rai wind). For the months between May and October, heavy rain is rare, and having cut the forest early enough for the undergrowth and branches to dry in the sun of the coming months, people wait, usually helping others with the heavy tasks of clearing and cutting. This is the time of year when people spend most time away from the hamlets, often living for weeks in rude lean-to shelters near their garden sites. Most hunting also takes place during these months when the leaves are dry and marsupials may be heard clearly at night as they move among the branches or on the dry leaf litter of the forest floor.

The next task is to burn off the debris in the garden, and to divide it into roughly equal sections of between 10–20m along each side. These sections are called *hokung*. This is achieved by laying the larger unburnt boughs of trees in tramline formations (see Figure 4.1), marking the edges of the garden, and the divisions between *hokung* (also called *tom* in Tok Pisin). Planting is the next major task, and this involves a specific and complex procedure outlined below. Again it must not be accomplished too early as the hot sun will shrivel the baby taro in the earth, nor too late, as immature taro can rot in wet ground. The growing season is short and precise, and a household that is late with their planting – because of the need to clear regrowth (after having cleared the garden too early), or because they misjudged the weather and the garden never became dry enough to burn properly – may well suffer hunger in the next year. Control over the weather is thus a significant aspect of Nekgini garden knowledge.

During the first weeks of October 1994 a neighbouring set of hamlets (Asang) beat slit-gong drums calling on Reite to hurry up and let the rains come or there would be trouble, as their [efficiently planted] gardens were shrivelling in an unexpectedly long dry spell. At that time I was not yet cognisant of the little discussed power of some men in Reite to make sun, rain, or thunder at will. It seemed absurd to me (when the complex set of beats was translated) that anyone could believe other humans were really responsible. I was amused that these people, having been too efficient, were now crossly waiting for the good weather to break and blaming their neighbours when it did not. However, my amusement was misplaced; they were really angry. Unseasonable weather is often attributed to the work of certain palem, and men who have knowledge of such things are very proud (although not usually direct in their claims) when there is thunder in the vicinity.

September is the month for planting. Women go into old gardens and collect old taro tubers which have been left over from the previous year. These tubers have, by this point, grown suckers, or 'baby/child taro' (*pel simang*), from the bulbous middle of the tuber.

Photograph 5 *'Mother' and 'Child' Taro Tubers*

There may be many 'children' from one 'mother' (*neng*) tuber, attached all the way around. There are many named types of taro, and the indigenous classifications are complex, taking account of shape, leaf or stem colour, origin, and so forth. I have been proudly shown gardens with at least fifteen named types, but in general for planting purposes, taro are divided into male and female – *pel'a aing* and *pel'a paring*. In collecting taro shoots, women keep the old 'mother' tubers separate, so this difference may be readily identified.[17] At the same time, the man who owns the garden retrieves two types of taro child, one male and one female, from the very centre (*wating*, see below) of his old garden to be placed in the very centre of his new garden. The male taro is *kapa iuing* and is an elongated variety, the female, round and red, is called *kendang*. These varieties were first given to Reite Yawaspiring palem by the *patuki* for taro. He revealed the correct form of gardens. Taro *kapa* is a variety thought to have surpassing savour and nutritional value, and fascinatingly, Reite people claim it mutates into other (female) varieties (*pel paring*) if moved from Reite lands and planted elsewhere.

The Eye of the Garden

As soon as the debris is burnt, a hole is made in the centre of the garden in which all the 'baby' taro is placed for storage until it has begun to shoot. In the meantime, and even before the ground is divided into *hokung*, the gardener (*wa saporung*) comes to plant shooting heads from long yams (*wiynung*) that have been looked after in the ground since the previous harvest. Chewing *manieng* (aromatic 'ginger'), he calls the name of the *patuki* for yam and sprays a fine mist from his mouth over the shoot as he carefully places it in a position to climb one of the bare tree trunks. This 'first yam' to be planted will be the first to mature, but if the shoot dries, a gardener fears someone in his family will die.

It was Musire and his father Hungeme who taught me the practicalities of garden making. They gave me a *hokung* of my own to plant and look after. I was not, however, given the names of the *patuki* for taro or yam, and though it was my *hokung*, responsibility for its growth and success remained firmly with Musire as the man who planted the *wating*. *Wating* translates as 'eye/shoot (*ting*) of the garden (*wa*)', or 'principle shoot of the garden'.

The man in charge of a garden's growth (*wa saporung*) rises before dawn on the day of planting, and without allowing anything to pass his lips, or relieving himself, he goes to the garden, already laid out in *hokung*. The day before he has collected all the plants needed to plant the *wating* (Nombo 2000). In the middle of the central *hokung* he prepares a small planting bed (*huri yakundet*), sometimes spoken of as 'preparing the pool' from which the taro deity emerged (*tapoing pfari yakundet*). In the cases I saw the *huri* was built up on the downhill side of the slope, like a terrace, to make a flat bed. A stem of *luhu* (*gorogor* [T.P.]) is split, and laid around the edges of this bed to make a border within which planting occurs. *Luhu*, mentioned at the beginning of this chapter, is a 'cold' plant. Enclosing the *wating*

Photograph 6 *The* Wating *of a New Taro Garden*

with its split stem prevents sickness among those who work there, and also prevents the taro showing (*alawung*) the gardener that someone in his palem will die by itself shrivelling and dying. The plants that are grown in the *wating* are all there to make the taro grow well, to make it sweet, and to improve the soil. Cordyline (*masau*), for example, makes the earth soft and allows the taro to spread its roots though the earth. It is planted by those who know to do so with the name of a place where the sea crashes against the shore, encouraging it to break the earth. Others merely plant it as 'decoration'. Other decorative and aromatic plants, a banana, a sugarcane, lowlands *pitpit* (*Saccarum edule*), and a stick for the taro-woman (see below) to hang her string bag on are all put in place. The leafy vegetable *tawau* (*aibika* [T.P.]) is planted over them. *Tawau* too has a name which he calls, the name of the last star to rise in the sky before dawn. This star gives water to the garden as dew (rather unattractively described as 'stars urine'), even in dry weather, thus ensuring the growth of the taro. It is said to be the watchman for the garden, and thus men who have knowledge of this name, and use it to watch over and water their gardens, do not eat *tawau*. The *pel kapa iuing* is planted in the very centre while the gardener calls the name and hums the voice of the male taro deity. It is told to look after all the women surrounding it. Once the taro is planted here, the gardener takes a stem of the plant *piraaking* which ends periods of taboo, and spitting the juices into the eye of the rising sun, he tells the taro *nekoneko kasip kundiyung'ket. Nangu silung palang kelukut* ('you are tabooed from everything, we meanwhile will be eating from other sources').

The *wating* in the central *hokung* is called the 'child' of the central *hokung* itself, which is the 'mother' of this child, and of the whole garden. Calling the name of the 'taro mother' (Mai'anderi – see below) the man plants in this prepared bed, as he tells her to come and reside in his garden, and look after her husband and children there.

The word *ting*, combined with garden (*wa*) is interesting here. The link made between contexts through this image of growth is significant. Others have found similar words denoting a 'point of growth' or 'shoot' across contexts. M. Strathern (1980) reports that the word *mbo* has a similar valance for Mount Hageners, one which Ingold (1996) has redescribed as 'any point of growth in the general field of human relations' (18). Additionally, in discussing the Barok word *bungmarapun*, Roy Wagner asserts that it exists 'at the level of image, not verbalised gloss' (Wagner 1986a: xv), and thus the 'meanings' that it has (spot of blood in a fertilised egg, the red eye of a starling) are contained in the image itself, and are elicited by its use, connecting contexts and making the things within them analogous to one another.

Ting denotes 'eye' or 'shoot'. It seems to denote the point of growth and development, even of life. Nekgini speakers describe the human eye as if it protruded into the world and made a physical point of contact with it, like a growing shoot does. The polite expression, equivalent to our 'excuse me', in Nekgini is '*kaka ting*', (lit. 'your eye'). It is used before disturbing someone's line of vision, as if this disturbance was a physical contact with the person. At the end of *Symbols that Stand for Themselves*, Wagner (1986b) describes the nose of a wolf in a manner

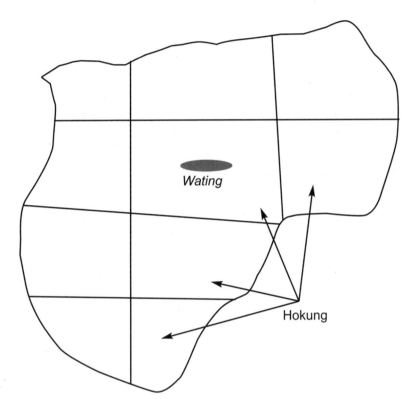

Figure 4.1 *Divisions within a Garden*

reminiscent of this, protruding into and engaging within the sensory array, and not merely recording data about it. A growing shoot, of course, propels itself into the world to seek light and sustenance, an active engagement with what the environment affords. Other uses of *ting* also denote significant, or powerful, points of growth. *Tupongting* ('water eye') are the springs feeding spirit pools where musical *kaapu* (*kaapu tupong yara*) dwell. The cutting edge of a knife is *nankiting* 'knife eye/shoot'. The fontanel of a new-born child is *nomangting (head-shoot)*. *Wating*, then, is the point of entry or growth of the garden's child – the taro.

Mai'anderi Patuki – 'The Taro Mother'[18]

As told by Urangari Kumbukau, Gayap Makon, Poiyong Salong, and Salong Poiyong:

> *An old woman was cooking food by Simonung stream, down at Nomang Sering. At this time, there was no food, and people lived on wild ginger, which they made gardens of, and they boiled this ginger with stones to make soup. A man from Marpungae had come to Simonung to file his*

stone axe on the stone that is still there with a groove in it. The smoke from the woman's fire floated down the stream to where he was, and he was enticed by the smell to follow it. Collecting his bow and arrows, he made his way to where the woman was hunched over her fire. She said, 'yes child, come and eat if you are hungry'. He ate his fill, and then left her, going straight home to sleep with a full belly. He did not tell his wife and children anything, although they wondered how he could sleep so well, while they were wakeful with hunger. When he continued to go each day to Simonung, and come back to sleep, his wife became suspicious. One day she followed him secretly. She hid behind a tree, and watched as her husband met the old woman, and she gave him taro to eat. The wife was enraged and jealous, and she rushed from her hiding-place and caught up her husband's stone-axe from where he had lain it down. She swung the axe at the old woman, saying she was still hungry and they had kept this good food for themselves. But the old woman told her to wait, and parting the hair carefully on her head, invited the wife to split her head cleanly. When the wife had split her head open, the old woman took up all the food that was around her – taro and sugarcane and pitpit and banana – and filled her skin through the split in her head. There is a spring there that is the blood of the old woman flowing. When there was nothing left but beans, and her belly was swollen mightily, she took up her bilum, filled it with beans, and placed it on her head. Then she left, and went to the East, to Maibang, and to Waping, where she stayed in the house of a bigman who lived with his grandchild. They made a bed for her, and she bore taro as if it were her child. Then she turned into a young woman.

Here we have short taro kapa, *taro* iuing. *Waping have long taro* kapa sangsung mararing. *They are both taro* kapa. *The long one saved Maibang people, and the short one saved us all here.*

The myth is full of potential for interpretation. I resist the temptation as there is much else to say about the garden itself. The sexual imagery, consistent with procedures I go on to describe, is a central aspect of knowledge of gardening. Mai'anderi's name is called by men planting the taro in their gardens. It is said by men in Reite that Mai'anderi must be attracted to the garden if taro is to grow, and as will be seen, when the harvest begins it is essential to tie her down there so that she does not leave, taking the taro with her. She is told to bring her children with her when she comes, if possible from other people's gardens, and to look after them in the place prepared for her by the gardener.

In the *hokung* surrounding the *wating*, a man plants *kendang*, a *pel parieng* variety that is said to have been one which Mai'anderi took away with her. These female varieties grow up around the *wating* and encourage the rest of the garden, in which *pel ai* (male taro) is planted primarily, to grow quickly. They are called the 'mothers of the garden' (*wa neng*). They 'pull' taro from other places, and look after it while immature. The growth of the *wating* itself is responsible for the growth of the rest of the garden. The food in the *wating* is not eaten. Men plant and look after this central *hokung*, and women will never enter it. The 'smell' of their bodies would drive Mai'anderi away.

Having finished the *wating*, the gardener begins planting taro without the same ceremony in the other *hokung* of the garden. His female relatives join him at this point, along with other kin who wish to help with this laborious task. Using a digging stick, one man breaks the ground at between one- and two-metre intervals, and following him, others come and place two *pel simang* in each hole, their shooting tops pointing up the slope, around 15–25cm deep. While planting taro, one is admonished not to look outside the garden, especially onto another man's land, nor to think of other people and places, lest the taro leave the garden being planted and settle elsewhere (see Clay 1986: 88–9 for similar practices among Mandak gardeners). I learned to plant one *pel parieng* at the centre of each *hokung*, the growth of the 'woman' encouraging the male taro surrounding her to grow. When taro is planted in all the *hokung*, banana suckers, sugar-cane and lowland pitpit are planted in spaces between the taro plantings. The large indigenous wing-beans of the Mai'anderi myth called *puti* are also planted at this time. However, recently introduced maize, which provides a valuable supplement to the sparse diet during January and February, is not planted until the taro shoots are 10–20cm above the ground. It grows fast and is known to inhibit taro growth.

Finally the gardener goes to the edge of the garden, and adjacent to the path used to enter it, plants a number of *pel paring kendang* and a cordyline. This is for the frog (*kerukeri*) which is said to destroy taro crops, and prevents it from entering the main body of the garden. He returns home to prepare a meal (*sukarung*) for those who have helped with this work. After a day's planting, women are admonished to sit properly and behave quietly. They must sit cross-legged so that the *pel parieng* will have a round base and retain its bulk, and they must not be involved in breaking firewood or the shells of nuts, nor in making a fire, as such things are detrimental to the tender shoot (*ting*) of the plant. It was said that if women who have planted taro behave decorously in this way, men's efforts to grow the taro quickly will be successful.

These efforts do not end once the taro is in the ground. It is forbidden to return too often to the garden, and there are ways of preventing trespassers. Often, men plant yam and taro with certain names and substances that cause boils in any that step over the plantings. The growth of a tuber underground is likened to the growth of a boil, swelling the earth, and eventually bursting it. Men return to their gardens after some weeks, and throw white ashes from a fire made in the bush, over their gardens. While doing so they hum the voice and call the name of the male taro deity. They may do this up to three times, and it is said to speed the growth of the tubers. Finally, earth is built up around the base of each plant (*pel nala'reita*), providing space for it to grow its tuber. Women are told to avoid the garden for many days after such activities.

Hokung vary in size and number in gardens, depending upon the terrain, the number in the family of the man planting the garden, the amount of ritual work expected in the coming year, and so forth. Usually, a *hokung* is set aside for each member of the household. A second taro garden may be planted, in combination with affines or other relatives, in which a couple of *hokung* will go under the name of the family as a whole. If preparing to stage any ceremonial payment, or complete ritual work, it is usual for a man to make a garden solely for this purpose. He will at least dedicate certain *hokung* in one of his gardens exclusively to it.

In gardens I measured, I found the following variation. *Hokung* were between 100m² and 500m², but mostly neither quite as large or as small. A square or rectangle of 15–20m on each side seems fairly standard. For what it is worth, numbers of plantings in a large and a medium *hokung*, as recorded in taro gardens in 1994 and 1995, are shown in Table 4.1. A typical taro garden, then, may be for anything between one and ten persons, with *hokung* calculated on this basis. Winedum, an elderly but hale man, still plants his own garden each year, making two small *hokung* about 10m × 10m each, while a large family such as that of Palota Konga (five children) may have eight *hokung*, all 20m × 20m square.

Table 4.1 *Numbers of Root and Other Crops Planted in a Garden*

Species	Hokung 20m × 20m, Number of Plantings	Hokung 20m × 10m, Number of Plantings
Taro	256	203
Yam	7	4
Banana	15	8
Pitpit	9	6
Maize	51	32
Wing-bean	9	4
Sugar-cane	7	5
Cucumber	5	3

Notes: Figures are averages for large taro gardens, of which each household may have one or two, the second shared with affines or palem siblings.

Reite people also make gardens of sweet potato, of Chinese taro, of yams imported from the coast – *mamie*, and occasionally of green vegetables, tomatoes, and melons. None of these gardens are divided into *hokung*, and not all households will have all, or indeed necessarily any, of them in any one year. Sweet potato and Chinese taro are the main staples after taro, both eaten during the hard months of January and February before beans, maize, and cucumbers are ready in the new taro gardens.

Feeding Garden Spirits and Closing Paths

By the end of December, corn and cucumbers start to ripen in the taro gardens. Along with beans, they are welcomed as an addition to sweet potato and Chinese taro. Old people say that before Chinese taro was prevalent, or in fact recognised as a food (there are tales of its use in sorcery when it was first introduced), these first crops were even more significant. Before harvesting the first crops (*mai masalo*: wing-beans, spinach [*sapi*] and indigenous cucumber), the garden owner goes alone into the *wating* and takes from there beans, *sapi* and *tawau* which he puts inside a bamboo tube and seals. Then, taking a cucumber, he breaks it over a stick and skewers the halves on posts at the edges of the garden. Calling the names of all the areas of land in the garden, he invites them to come and eat. Then he takes his bamboo home, and cooks it over the fire. When it is hot, the man opens the bamboo, and heats his own leg, arm, and shoulder joints and those of his family with the steam from the vegetables (*masalo ket'a tarik artiking artundet* 'burns legs and arms on new foods'). The bamboo is taken by the gardener to the bush, and tied to the base of a wild banana (*wear'a pundarur*) or a vine. People say that often this brings thunder and rain. This completed, his family, but rarely the gardener himself, may eat new crops from gardens other than their own, and harvest beans and corn from their own garden. The gardener will keep a close eye on the taro in his garden, adjusting his diet according to its growth. Explaining this 'burning of skin', Porer Nombo told me that it strengthens the skin of those who might otherwise become ill from the power used in gardens to ensure growth. Adult men rely on the work of *tawau* and *sapi* to give water to their gardens and watch over them, and say that to eat these things is to 'turn back' and eat that which you have asked for help. To do so invites aching joints and arthritic pain.

When most of the leaves have fallen from the taro plants (between March and May), and the tubers have swollen the earth around the base of the stem, the gardener collects *pununung* (meat and fish) for the first harvest of the year. When he is prepared, and at the time appropriate for his palem to eat new taro, he returns to the garden at dawn and 'blocks the path' (*sernung tang'et*) of the taro. In a procedure similar to planting the *wating*, he collects bark, leaves, sticks and red dye. These again make the taro firm, glutinous, thick-skinned, savoury, and sweet. Rising before dawn, he goes to the garden, and splits the leaves into two, leaving one at the edge of the garden before proceeding into the *wating*. The gardener must be *kundeing* (following taboos) in order to fasten the garden spirits there. Spirits apparently roam around at night, but return to the tubers (*tuwiret*) before dawn. This is the time to catch them. He tidies the *wating*, removing dead leaves, straightening the plants, and tying their straggling growth into bunches. Standing sticks of *titikung* (the tree in which the taro deity hung a string bag of taro) in the earth to brace the growing plants is supposed to follow the example of the taro deity, and encourage taro from elsewhere to come into the garden. The leaves of this tree are part of the mixture collected the previous day. The mixture is shredded, mixed with red dye, and then buried at the base of the *pel kapa iuing*, and the *kendang* at the centre of the *wating*, admonishing both not to chase children away, but to comfort and support them. Spraying aromatic ginger from his mouth, the gardener mixes the remaining shreds with earth from the *wating*, and throws it to the four directions, telling it to go and fetch taro children from elsewhere and bring them home.

Moving to the edge of the garden again, he takes pitpit and sugar-cane from the *hokung* nearest the road, and plants them on either side of the path that enters the garden. If the garden is fenced, he will plant them immediately on the inside of the fence where those entering and leaving the garden habitually step over it. Cutting

Photograph 7 *The* Wating *is Tidied Before Harvest*

staves of *titikung* to about 1m in length, he pushes these into the ground on either side for Mai'anderi to hang her bag on, and makes a small frame for the cordyline stems and other leaves which he has brought. Then, taking the shredded leaves and bark, he buries a baby taro *kapa* and a *kendang* on either side of the path. He smears them all with red paint, and finally ties an aromatic herb for her *naie* (skirt). While doing this the garden specialist sings the name of Mai'anderi, and calls for her to return to the place that she left and bring taro with her. Here he does not throw earth, but admonishes the spirits of the taro to stay in the garden, and look after their children there. The gardener then cleans his hands on the leaves of a banana, taro, or yam that he thinks is particularly fine.

The work to 'close' the path (tie down the spirit) is said to ensure that the taro will be strong and sweet, but most of all that it will last a long time in the garden. When Mai'anderi has been brought and held in this way, one can remove taro from the ground in a *hokung*, but next time the gardener goes to look in the same *hokung*, taro will still be there. The *wating* is said to be the child of the central *hokung*, which is the mother. The child is the taro, and the mother is Mai'anderi. Space and welcome are made for the mother and the child in the centre, and then she distributes her taro over the whole garden. This is how Reite men spoke of the reason behind their work, although more often they would say this was 'the way' to make a garden, and *patuki* had ordained it so. Taro removed from the garden is replaced by Mai'anderi, who is encouraged throughout not only to look after the taro that is there, but go and steal it from other gardens as well.

All the way back to the hamlet, leaves of immature taro, wild ginger, and leaves associated with individual palem are left along the road. They line the steps of the house, and follow the taro into the house where the tubers are kept overnight. (Taro following the path to the hamlet can thus find its way.) Children are admonished not to play nearby so the taro will not be disturbed. In the morning, women peel and break the taro tubers with pig bones, and they are cooked with *pununung* to be eaten by the whole family. When it is ready, everyone takes a piece of *kendang* (female taro) and, pretending to eat the piece, they remove it from their mouths and hurl it at a pig, to make the pig cry out. Porer explained this as follows:

> This is because we do not have food and go hungry for some time before taro is ready. Pigs are the same. We give a bit of the new harvest to the pigs. It is the mother taro, *kendang* which we use to hit the pig, the one we plant only in the centre and at the edges of the garden. When you hit the pig, they get up, cry out, and eat the taro. Then the taro spirit (kaapu) will be afraid of the pig, and rush back to the garden where it can look after all the other taro. You have pulled it with you to the hamlet to eat, but it mustn't stay with you, it would be bad if while it was roaming about it got caught or lost, and was lost to your garden. We say the pig cries and makes the village strong; the hungry time is over, like when the clouds part after rain, we say *saret* – the place is strong again; *yapaei saret* – the village is made strong.

A pot of taro is cooked with a forest bird for the *au*, knives, axes, and so forth used in the garden, and pieces of cooked food placed on them.[19] The man who planted the garden breathes a name (*paru*) over the cooked taro, and passes it under his left arm behind his back, where it is taken directly into the mouth of each family member. It is said that it is better then not to return to the garden for many days, but to leave it undisturbed, and to eat the food stored in the house. From this day, taro will be the sole food in the house for some time. Many people, including children, are tabooed from drinking water as well, living from the cooking water of the taro. This is because of *pasuwikeruae*. *Pasuwikeruae* is sickness caused by eating other foods in conjunction with, or soon after, eating the first taro of the year. It is said to result in extreme hunger, as taro is likely to ask, 'why do you eat me if I am not enough?'

The Order of the Harvest

Garden procedure is closely related to weather working. The order in which people harvest taro is still significant in making differences between palem histories apparent, and amounts to a kind of ritual hierarchy. And this relates to weather. Offering *mai masalo* to a vine is one aspect of this. In the past, there were those who cared for a red clay pot, *kukup'ou*, which when asked, made the sun shine fiercely. These were the people called *salili*, that is, the last to eat taro each year. When the *salili* had begun to harvest their taro, they would put red paint on the pot and with the sun hot, people would cut their new gardens. When the gardens were ready for planting, they would remove the paint, and the rains would come. Porer rationalised this in the following way, 'it is obvious that these were the people who discovered/revealed taro. They were the ones who supplied the foods, and so everyone had to eat before them. If anyone waited and ate later than them, they would ask "was it your ancestors who revealed this and gave it to us?" Salili are the fathers of this, they are strong and will not become hungry and harvest before their time. They are the fathers of taro and the fathers of the sun.' This ordering of the harvest in Reite is still practised today. Breaking the order of palems was a serious offence, yet there seemed no stigma attached to eating sooner than other palems. At one time I was told those who ate first were responsible for rain, and those last for sun. Eating taro, and offering the new harvest to one's palem spirits and ancestors is thought to bring their power to life. In Maibang, people once fed me taro before I had eaten it in Reite that year. They impressed upon me the importance of *telling* Reite people I had been given taro – that they had started to harvest it already. When I did so, people in Reite scoffed at such haste, saying that they were the 'origin' or 'base' of taro, so it was indeed correct that others should eat first.

Gardens, Land, and Substance

In the above ethnography, particularly the information about the *wating*, one sees a dual-sexed productivity – a man and a woman, one placed in the land, the other drawn to that place – becoming a single productive entity – a garden, or in the context of childbirth, a household. In both cases, that single productive unit (body) produces offspring – the offspring of the woman – which is provided by the man, and grown by a hidden force attributed to the place itself. Now this internally sexed unit, the married couple, or the gardener and the taro mother, appears as one whole: a household in a hamlet with a 'door' at which their work (children, garden food) is revealed. Revelation of a slit-gong is not when it is played in the bush prior to its emergence. Revelation of garden produce is not when a man pulls tubers from the ground and his wife places them in her bilum. The revelation of the birth of a child comes not inside the house or when it is born, but later when it is given a second birth from the back of the house itself (see Chapter 5). In all these cases an internally gendered unit gives the appearance of being one entity, of being undivided – a garden with a single entrance, a household with a single door, a tambaran performance by a single place – when revelation is effected. The true moment of revelation occurs when the outcome of this union is shown to others: when taro is placed in large bowls with meat and distributed to other households in the hamlet, or when it is piled on a platform in an exchange.

Moreover, this is not only the revelatory moment, but in fact a reproductive moment, in that it is at this time that units gain social identity and are externally gendered by the response their appearance elicits from others. In making things appear from 'one door', thus appearing to come from a single whole entity, a Reite couple mask the separation between male and female. The produce of a garden is made to look like the outcome of a single body. I have pointed out the analogy to the emergence of the child. This makes the palem, like the garden, a productive place in which the origin of the container which gives form to the growing child is masked. Thus the child emerges from the house/garden as if this house (place) were the body which formed it. Substance and form are seen as the power of a single place. Yet we have seen that in both cases formation has to be elicited from another.

We will see in Chapter 5 that a child does not develop without the influence of its mother's brother. A child, a garden, or palem, has growth inside it. In a garden, a 'child' is placed there, by a man, in the belly of a woman. Although he only plants once, he returns to the garden a couple of times, singing the tune and name of the male taro deity. All I could ever elicit from Reite people about conception was that a man must have intercourse with his wife three times. *Asuriyinda nekring patandi* 'a man's blood makes a child appear/develop'. A man places a child inside, but there is no explicit knowledge of the actual process within. What is hidden is kaapu. For gendered adults, contact with the power of life and flow in the other gender is hidden, as things that are seen do not grow.

The issue of substance, and of continuity, appears to be dependent upon the place of growth rather than on the transmission of some property inherent in men and/or women themselves. Seeing his sister married into another palem, residing on different land, a man may see part of himself as there. The movement of wealth towards him demonstrates his connection; but placement makes the critical difference to substance and form. His sister's placement elsewhere makes her productive efforts part of the appearance of that place, and thus these productive labours do not make an internal contribution to his own place. Her external contribution is as an affine who provides social containment and recognition in the form of wealth. His elicitation of wealth from her dwelling is recognition of her placement, of his identity as a separated brother (affine), and as a mother's brother to her children. His positioning in the land as (part of) another named place, and in the exchange network of affinal relations, is appropriate to receive exchange items which confirm or develop an identity as a mother's brother, a wife-taker, or an exchange partner.

One might say that the influence of place results from what Ingold (1994c) has called 'dwelling'. Growth does not take place in isolation, but rather in what I have termed a field of nurture, constituted by the work of others. The role of the father is not primarily to pass some component or substance to the child, but to establish the conditions for growth. Growth is thus not merely expressive of something inherent in the child, but is generated by the land and labour of those whom the father calls kin and his spirits. For Nekgini speakers, it is their generation of places and persons through labour on, and knowledge of, the land, which results in growth. This power to grow things is channelled and used to produce offspring (children, taro, slit-gongs).

The generation of persons and of places are mutually entailed as aspects of the same processes, those of growth and recognition. As Casey puts it 'bodies and places are connatural terms. They interanimate each other' (1996: 24). Reite people's perceptions and actions make us question the conventional dichotomy between the study of kinship (as social organisation) and agriculture (as subsistence economics). Landscape has a temporal dimension, and people's tasks and activities within it constitute both the people and the landscape itself (Ingold 1994a).

Identity depends on generation in different places. Difference is what emerges from the productive separation of persons and their discovery of and control over entities that constitute the powers of fecundity and growth in the land itself. In Reite, they talk about relations with different kaapu, different *patuki*, different land and spirit places. This interplay is based on the idea that it is the tambaran that grows things. Tambaran – kaapu (spirits) and *patuki* (stories) – are physically placed in the landscape. Substance comes from land in that it is the power in that land which grows persons. 'Other people' provide recognition, land provides substance – namely: knowledge, stories, songs, voices, tunes, bodies, animals, and so on. These provide the conditions, the 'field of nurture' by which things grow. These powers that grow things (stories, songs, voices, tunes) are heard, but not 'seen'. Recognition of the products of growth are seen (revealed for inspection), while the powers that grow them are 'kaapu'.

Regeneration

At the end of Chapter 3, I suggested that as an image of connection, 'blood' was problematic because it is too suggestive for anthropologists used to a genealogical model of biogenetic kinship. I left a problem, what does *asurung* amount to for Reite people? An answer emerges from this ethnography of gardening.

In Chapter 2, I described how descent is only one of the elements around which people form groups. Residential, ritual, ceremonial, maternal, and paternal connections all influence the identities and obligations of persons. Thus Lawrence described Garia people as having a social organisation based on an 'ego-centred security circle'. Strathern (1992b) has shown how such a social organisation might arise from an understanding of the person as the focus of many relationships, because within their make-up, they embody the relationships which constituted them.

In Reite certain relationships are privileged (that of the mother's brother/sister's child, for example), but kinship is ramifying. Yet there is a kind of 'lineality' to be divined, founded on the continuous creativity of the land of each palem group. In producing persons, Nekgini speakers imbue the locale with an identity. Persons are generated by places. It is here that I would locate the importance of paternity.

Land, and knowledge of an area's stories and spirits are passed to men by their fathers. As I discuss at the beginning of the next chapter, the father seems tangential in some ways to the emergence of his child. It is the mother's brother who has prominence in their education and development. Yet Reite men are proud of their fathers. It is the father's name which men invoke for their own protection and succour in time of need. One's father provided one's name; and names are linked to land and to ancestors. He also, of course, provides payment in the form of wealth for his children's bones from maternal kin. Now in order to make this presentation, he has to have control over the kaapu of the land on which his son resides. He also has to have control over the *patuki* of taro and yam, and possibly others, in order to produce gardens of food, to procure meat, and so forth, from that landholding. His attraction of a woman to that land provided a mother and maternal kin for his children. In other words, he provided the specific field of nurture in which his children could grow.

Ideally, among Nekgini speakers, one takes the name of one's grandfather, and gives to one's son one's father's name. The connection with the father then is this: he has produced himself and his son(s) from the land which the son(s) claims to own. His control over the spirits and growth of that land is a version of the son's, and his knowledge made possible his children's existence. Notions of ancestry, descent, and the transmission of substance should be replaced here with something akin to replacement or regeneration.

People in Reite are willing to follow connections through the mother or the father. People are easily convinced of 'sibling-like' relationships with their mother's family, although these people are in theory their cross-cousins. Without pronounced clans or stable moieties, it is not as if one's future affines will necessarily be the affines of other hamlet residents, or of one's brothers.

However, when it comes to land, men face a different situation. They have an understanding that to control land and remain on it is a 'male' principle. People are aware themselves of a tension between this as a principle for connection between persons, and the reality of the kinship connections they operate. People other than those to whom they are related through men and current residence can claim connection. This finds expression in a phrase I heard often (in Tok Pisin) while investigating the make-up of exchange groups or the rationale behind calling certain people certain kin terms: *ol mama save faulim mipela* ('our mothers confuse us'). Mothers convince their sons that they are equally connected to their maternal kin as to their paternal, and they are right, other than for another aspect of Reite relationality – common identity with respect to growing things. Because women move in marriage, the 'substance' their children share with their siblings in other hamlets is distant from that which a man shares with his palem siblings.

Within Nekgini speakers' sociality there is convergence between the kind of 'relational personhood' with which Strathern solves the problems that Garia appear to present (1992b), and a relationality based in – and including constitutive relationships with – the powers and ancestors in and of the land itself. That the claim of 'substance' (i.e. what we would recognise as biological connection) is made through this land tells us about the ideas of 'substance' itself for Reite people.

There is a contribution made to identity, relevant to our understanding of palem as social groupings, which is made by the father, but this is a contribution tied up in his placement on the land. Could it be that an answer to the question of what is meant by *'asurung konaki'* 'one blood', is that people thus defined are too close to marry in spatio-temporal terms? The phrase refers to the separation necessary in a kin network before marriage is advisable or acceptable. Such separation is achieved through separate residence, and therefore the accumulation of substance made different by different relationships over time.

The continuity of creativity is inherent in places themselves, and in the lands that men pass to their sons. Substance, as the form this creativity takes in persons, thus does, in a sense, follow a male inheritance. My point is that this is not inheritance based on the passing of some internal component which the growth of the child expresses, as in a genealogical view of kinship.

Male Continuity, Female Movement

Mai'anderi may have originated at Simonung water on Reite lands, yet she is known of, and her name is used for taro planting, all along the Rai Coast (Lawrence 1964: 204, 1965: 17). As the myth tells, she left with food in her belly, and gave birth to it elsewhere. She must be induced to return if Reite gardens are to grow. Yet all we know about Reite sociality and thought would suggest that to have an affinal connection, to draw a woman to one's lands, one must exhibit power. Control is thought of as the prerogative of men, as it is men who stay put, who draw others to them, and who maintain continuity in creativity through the repetition of names and practices handed down from male ancestors.

In other places I visited – Maibang and Waping in the Ngaing language area to the east – they use Mai'anderi's name and the procedure she gave them for planting taro. In fact, the myth as I heard it from Kundi Pawayin in Waping was more complex and detailed than the version my Reite informants told me. There is a reason for this.

Reite have a second myth for the discovery of taro, apparently parallel, and not explicitly connected to the story of Mai'anderi. It is *this* myth which Reite people refer to when they say they have the origin of taro, and are its base. It is the name of this taro 'man' which gardeners in Reite use to plant and grow their taro, in the care (containment) of Mai'anderi. This taro *patuki* is not known beyond Reite. I give it in full because it tells us much about the issues I have brought up in this chapter.

Samat Matakaring Patuki[20] – 'The Origin of Taro'

Told by Siriman Kumbukau:

The first man came, and after him, came Pomo, and after this came taro.

DW wanted to sharpen his stone axe to make a garden of wild ginger. He went down to the stream that runs between here and Asang [Simonung]. Now there was a man there who had the voice of the tambaran. This man didn't need ritual paraphernalia. When he breathed, everyone heard the tambaran. In Asang and Sorang too. Everyone could hear him, and they would say 'who has the tambaran', but it was just this man. A man from Reite went down to sharpen his axe, and at the water there was another man, this man with the voice of the tambaran. He said, 'Ah kandere' [sister's son, cross-cousin], and came and held his hand. He told the man that he lived underneath the stream there, 'you stand here and watch, I'm going into the water'. He went inside and took a bean, and spat it on the water which dried up. Then he brought the man inside his house under the water, and the water returned, but they were hiding in the house of the storyman.

Now he started to cook taro. He cooked it with salt wood (paap), and he cooked beans. He took ginger and cooked it with the beans. Now when he opened the saucepan, DW was sick, he vomited all the rubbish that he had inside him, the wild ginger and stones and wild taro. The vomit went down into the water. The man asked "finished", and he said "yes". So he gave him the cooked beans. They were the first real food that he ate. They acted like medicine, killing the sickness that came from all the rubbish he had eaten before, the ginger heated his liver, and his head cleared. Now the man blew on a piece of taro, and gave it to him to eat from under his arm-pit. (We follow this way now.) He ate a piece, and then was given a basket of taro. The man told him to go and give it to his wife and children in the same way as he had been given it.

He came to Reite, where his wife and children were eating wild ginger and stones. He washed all the pots out, and he cooked with the salt wood, scraped ginger, fried beans and cooked the taro. He called for his children, who smelt the food and vomited. He asked if they had good thinking now, and they said yes, so he put food on their plates. He blew on the taro and gave it to them from under his arm. They ate, and then slept quietly. But all around them, people were crying out with hunger.

Plate 8 *Samat Matakaring. Katak and Taropang Demonstrate the Taro Patuki*

In the morning, the man went back to the stream carrying his bilum. He knocked on the ground (the mark of his knocking is still there). He took a bean, and spat it, and the water dried up. He took out a loincloth, and gave it to the storyman, who put it on, and was happy. He made a bed, and piled taro on the bed. The Reite man filled his bilum with taro from the bed.

He went back to the village, and told them they would go and make a garden the next day, he hid his thoughts, and told them they would be making a garden for wild ginger. He went to his house, and filled it with taro.

The next day they all cut the gardens, and at midday, the taro was cooked. They all came back from the gardens, walking slowly, as they were so hungry. Then they smelt the food that was being cooked in this man's house. All of them vomited until they were completely empty. He prepared everything in the way he had been shown, and when they had finished being sick, he put their food on plates for them. He told them the names of these things: Beans – puti, ginger – warivi, salt wood – paap. Everyone ate then, he didn't forget anyone. They all ate ginger and beans. Then he went and got a skewer. He speared the taro, blew on it, and gave it to all the big men, then to all the children, and then to all the women. They didn't eat too much – they were soon full up. He called the name Pel samat *– you and I are eating taro now. They were all happy.*

He told them that the next day they would plant the gardens. Some people wanted to know where he had got the taro, but he told them, 'sorry, this is tambaran, I can't tell you where I got it. Tambaran showed me. Later you will know.'

Now the next day they all went and made a garden. He had enough food left to feed them all. He told them to come and see him when they had finished the garden. When everything was dry, they burnt the garden. The first of the torches was blown out, and kept, and a second one lit to help burn the garden. Then they came and told him they had finished.

He told them to go and put the half torch on a vine, and then rain would come and put the fire out. They did so. Then he told them to breathe his name over the wating (the eye of the taro, where they plant aibika and banana, where women cannot go) and plant it. Then he gave them baby taro and told him to do the same thing over the taro, and plant it. They planted the whole garden. The women weren't allowed to go to the place where the men had planted the wating and the baby taro. They planted taro in other parts of the garden.

After a few days, they had finished the gardens. He told them that when the shoots came up, they had to tell him. After a week, the shoots appeared, and the DW went to the patuki, and told him, 'kandere, the shoots have appeared'. He brought earth and ashes from his fire, and told them to call his name, and to throw them over the taro shoots. They did so, and the taro grew strongly and quickly. They did this three times, and the taro was big enough. (We still do this to make the taro come up.)

He told them to make a passae, to bring up pigs and collect meat from the bush. They did all this, and the storyman said, 'OK, now you have seen me, but you will be the only one. Women cannot look at me. I am a spirit of yours, I am taboo. You can call my name and plant taro as I have shown you.'

The man made the passae with a place inside for this (story) man, and with a part for all the men to come and sing and 'watch over the tambaran'. He told him, 'kandere, the house is finished, and the house for putting the taro is finished too.' Then they went to look at the taro, and the beans which were dry and the cucumbers which were red. The man told them to break the tops of the cucumber and put them around the place on sticks. There was another set of words for the cucumbers, and for the beans. Then they told all the women and children to come and eat the beans and cucumbers. They did so, and were happy. This was while the taro was still growing. When the beans and cucumber were finished, they knew that it was time for the taro now.

They decorated the taro gardens and nominated the day for eating taro. The place where they had planted the wating and taro first, they were to leave until later in the year. All around they could harvest the taro.

Now he gave everyone their day for eating taro.

He called for them all to come, and made a big ceremony. They all came, and he held pigs for them all to come and get them. In the afternoon, the man went to the water where he had first seen the storyman, and collected the tambaran. He brought the man, and hid him inside the house. No one but this first man saw him go inside the house. He closed the door on him. They all ate, and they were happy with the new taro. They sang and beat the drums and the tambaran sang quietly, and all the men followed his lead, and the celebration for the taro lasted all night until the morning.

All the people from other places came, and were decorated with all the food from before, wild ginger and fruit of trees and so forth. When they saw Reite they were ashamed, but Reite said that they shouldn't be ashamed, all these rubbish things are finished now, and he gave them all baby taro. They all came up, and smelt the food and vomited. He did with them exactly what had been done with him. All the taro was heaped on a bed, but they didn't deal it out immediately. The sun was high in the sky, and they came and killed the pigs and cut them up. Now the man told them to deal the taro from the bed. It was after this that they were given the baby taro for them to plant themselves.

Now the man killed a pig for the people of Reite, and the tambaran. He was buying the work of all who belonged there for making the gardens. Now they danced and sang. The storyman inside told them to come and get him and take him to the storyplace. It was the man who had first brought taro. He then said to him, 'you have seen me now, and that's enough. Later you will not see me again, but I have given you breath, spirit breath to call my name and plant the taro. I have given you tambaran and my voice'. He then sat down and turned to stone. The man came back weeping to Reite, and now the stone is still there, and we pray over the taro as he taught, and have the tambaran.

Pel Patuki is tambaran. Using the power of his voice, and through the revelation of knowledge, taro is grown. It is clear in fact that the musical tambaran (male) were a creation of the taro deity, and that it is this tambaran which grows tubers in a garden. Prior to the myth, there was no growth in the image of the person, thus no tambaran. The creation of *ai yakaapu* as a male cult in fact appears as the outcome of the universal acceptance of taro gardening. The enclosure of tubers in the garden mirrors the enclosure of the man in the house, and the male control over this form of growth appears as the counterpart to the female power to grow things (children) by her own tambaran – that concealed within her body. Both are required for the production of offspring (tubers). The process of growth is the same in different contexts – and this process is attributed to the power of something which is hidden. This power is located, and its placement engenders the connections that people have to land, and the emergence of places which gather together land and people into loci of creativity. Social entities are named after the land on which they exist (palem), and this is a direct result of their generation by the powers of those lands, drawn together in the bodies that animate them, and regenerated through work in each generation. The taro deity causes Reite people to give taro away, pass it on to others with whom they thus enter exchange relations. The form in which taro was presented was as a palem, that is as a platform with taro piled on it, decorated, and with a pig to accompany it. We will see (in Chapter 6) that this construction is clearly valued as a body by Reite people. Thus we have the beginnings not only of the male cult and the potential that this gives men to grow tubers, boys, and garamut, but also the beginnings of exchange relations with other places in the image of bodies. What is explicit in this myth, then, is the connection between bodies, grown while they are concealed, from substance in the land; and the role of these bodies as the basis of exchange relations with other places. The musical (male) tambaran turns out to be that which is contained by the generative (female) one. Bodies are potentially either. In practice, they are made one or the other by, amongst other things, movement or fixity.

* * *

Thinking that I had grown during my time with them, my hosts and friends said laughingly that when I had arrived I had been a 'young boy', 'all bones', but that by the time I left, I was 'fat'. The growth from youth to adulthood they ascribed to the consumption of real food: to taro. Taro gardens themselves are archetypal images of the processes of growth, and being sites for the production of the substance of persons, this interdigitation between the growth of tubers and of persons is more than symbolic slight of hand. Establishing the conditions of growth for children and for tubers are seen by Reite people as similar enterprises. Their treatment should also be the same. One may often hear an old person counselling restraint upon an exasperated parent with the phrase *pel'ma uret yama raewaeung* ('do not harm your taro leaves'), encouraging tolerance for wayward children, as squashing their vigour by mistreating them will retard their growth. I have been interested here in these cross-overs between the domains of production and reproduction, and thus in this chapter I examined what we might know about Reite understandings of growth and substance from pursuing their own emphasis on the centrality of gardens.

Reite people claim to have the origin of taro, to be its owners, and this is demonstrated in the ownership of its name, the tambaran of its origin, the specific and jealously guarded form of the *wating*, and so forth. Yet this is not enough to grow their taro. There is also a mother of taro (Mai'anderi), and as in the myth 'Pomo Patuki' I examined in Chapter 3, though she originated in Reite, she was separated from them in an act of violence which caused her to leave. As they do with the younger brother in that myth, Reite people attempt to reunite what was separated, making the difference a productive one. In Samat Matakaring Patuki, Reite people have the origin of their own placement. Taro is a version of the bones of their land. This is the source of their pride in taro. However, the myth is only a part of the knowledge needed to grow taro. Its complement is provided by Mai'anderi. In Samat Matakaring, recognition is provided by the exchange relations generated in distributing taro. The myth of Mai'anderi's departure posits a separation, and thus a different point of growth, for the one who comes and contains Reite tambaran, who elicits the form of their children. Her movement, and a garden's placed-ness, genders the combination. As Kiap (Siriman) told me in the comment with which I began this chapter, gardens and taro are sites for the generation of human relationality.

Notes

1. It is a claim acknowledged by their neighbours including those of other language groups. Morauta (1974) reports specialisation of 'clans' with regard to types of 'magic', in the area around Madang town. Garden magic, specifically that relating to taro, was owned by specific people.
2. *Pel patuki*. The actual names of the characters in this myth are the names used when planting and harvesting taro. They are *paru*, secret names/spells, passed from people in Reite to their children and sister's children to ensure that taro gardens grow correctly.
3. Although it would be wrong to give the impression Reite people are not proud of their yams as well. New yams from the beach (*mamie*) (cf. Harding 1985), recently introduced, are grown by young men who delight in the novelty of their gardens with mounds and stakes. On the whole, gardening – and particularly producing early, novel, or fine foods – is of great interest to Reite people.
4. Kahn (1996: 177) reports a similar story in Wamira in the east of Papua New Guinea.
5. '…the activity that concerns people the most is agriculture, which is also a virtually perennial task.' (Lawrence 1984: 16)
6. *Zingiberaceae hornstreditia scotiana* (T. P. *gorogor/gorgor*).
7. 'A fuller insight into the way in which the proceeds of their gardening are utilised will show why the natives devote so much work, attention, and aesthetic care to their gardens. Only after we have seen in detail how the crops are taken out of the soil and stored; how they are displayed several times in the process – cleaned, counted, and adorned; how they are cajoled by special magic to remain stored and not to stimulate the appetite of greedy human beings, how they are redistributed, renamed, and classified by sociological categories, only then shall we be able to appreciate the value of the crops to the Trobriand farmer' (Malinowski 1965 [1935]: 81).
8. This does not contradict the previous chapter in which I argued that gender is established in the recognition of difference, and that love-magic is a common instrument in dramatising this recognition. Love-magic relies upon the assistance of kaapu, thus the differentiation-through-love-magic described in Chapter 3 has as its background the substitution of relationships to both men and women in the palem, with relationships to kaapu, in order that love-magic can be performed. Men remove themselves from relationships with women and children, and enter into intense communication with kaapu to generate power for use in love-magic. They become *kundeing* (see Chapter 6). Relations with kaapu define, and aid, the practitioner of love-magic in his emergence as male in relation to his intended counterpart.
9. Thus I use the Nekgini word from here on.
10. I understand that the association between *kindam* (T.P. – crayfish, prawns) and menstruation which was often made, results from the way these crustaceans turn bright red when cooked, and from their rapid movement. Running water – especially the streams running from *tupongting* (spirit pools) where one is most likely to find *kindam* – is also associated with women (coldness and flow seem the relevant attributes here).
11. Slit-gongs are idiophones; long logs with their centres gauged out, leaving a slit along the top. They usually stand on end, and are jolted with wooden sticks to produce sound (see Leach 2002).
12. cf. Tuzin (1980: 57). Harrison writes of the concept of inside, or centre (*mawul*) in Avatip, which presents striking similarities to the notion of voice (*punging*) in Reite. Interestingly, the quality of animating bodies is what these indigenous concepts draw together. 'Once a trading-canoe or a slit-

drum has been carved, and given a personal name in a special ceremony, it becomes animate. Its *mawul* (in the sense of its xylem) becomes *mawul* in the sense of a mind. As a carver once told me, as he was hollowing out a slit-drum and removing the soft xylem: "we men have a *mawul*, and so we are able to walk around and talk. It is the same with a slit-drum. It too has a *mawul*...'" (1993: 99–100).

13. *Utung* (wooden bowls) for example, which are made from the same wood, coloured and decorated with carved designs in similar fashion, are not made in conjunction with spirits.

14. I was able to witness the construction of a series of *kiramung*. The opportunity was provided by a grant from The British Museum to make a collection of contemporary objects from Nekgini-speaking hamlets. To include garamut in the collection, it was necessary to commission and sponsor their construction. The collections may be seen as 95.16 in the National Museum, Port Moresby, and Leach.95 in the stores of The Department of Ethnography of the British Museum, London. Documentation of the construction and use of Nekgini artefacts exists as a British Museum 'Ethnodocument'.

15. Making garamut is involved and complex. I have only given an outline here of the procedure as a detailed analysis of this ritual is not my purpose here. For more detail see Leach (2002).

16. For example, see Gell (1975), Mackenzie (1992).

17. In the simplest observation, 'female-taro' (*pel'a paring*) has a shorter tuber and is rounded at the base. *Pel'a aing* is more elongated, and has a pointed base. The female taro has a reddish tinge under the skin, while the male is white.

18. cf. Lawrence (1964: 17; 1965: 205). And see Leach (1997, Appendix 1) for the Waping version of this *patuki*.

19. This is also the procedure followed for venerating ancestral bones and *kaapu* at this time, and is associated with the power of weather-working.

20. Map 2 shows the place called Samat Matakaring, after which this *patuki* is generally known.

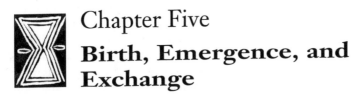

Chapter Five
Birth, Emergence, and Exchange

Firs bon yu mas wokim ol disela samting. Sapos yu gutpela man bilong lukautim pik, na yu laik kamap olsem topi *yu ken lainim bilong olgeta pikinini. Nogat, em nogat nau. Yu wokim, bai yu gat planti save bilong wokim kastom, na bai yu kamap* topi *man.* (Porer Nombo, September 1999)[1]

Wok bilong kandere em bilong mekim pikinini i kamap wanem kain man. (Pinabin Sisau, October 2000)[2]

In Chapter 4, I examined the notions of growth, containment, and substance. Things in the image of persons are grown in a field of relations. While this is a general observation, each thing grown emerges from specific relations. Distinctions are elicited, and placement is crucial. Land is not the backdrop to or the container for life, it is the source of substance. As such, it is where consanguinity is created.

I turn now to the payments that are made between hamlet groups that are separated by marriage (affines). Presenting ethnography on life-cycle payments, I discuss them with the following in mind. Reite people marry their cross-cousins, yet we have seen that people are only nominally related or distinguished by genealogy. Nekgini speakers do not appear to have moieties. Members of a sibling set are likely to take wives from different places, resulting in complex networks of affinal, sibling, and cross-cousin relations in any one palem generation.

The importance of the mother's brother is strongly emphasised in Reite people's account of their own growth, and in their exchanges. Long ago, Radcliffe-Brown (1952a) proposed that the significance of the mother's brother is due to his ambiguous position; while a closely related male, he is nevertheless outside the child's lineage. Given what we know about consanguinity in this place, this gives pause for thought. Nekgini speakers, as we have seen, do not have lineages, they have palem. The mother's brother is indeed outside the palem of the child, so in what way is he connected to that child?

The literature on marriage and alliance assumes that groups created by marriage exchanges endure to give society its structural form (Lévi-Strauss 1969) even if this transforms over time (Leach 1956). Even in the case of elementary structures, the definition of groups as wife-givers and wife-takers rests on a notion of linealities as well. Thus discussions of the relations between affines turn on issues of descent, or recruitment (Wagner 1967: xxvii). In this literature, payments which flow from a sister's child (ZC) to her/his mother's brother (MB) are thought to compensate for substance. They are made by those who have the right to affiliate the child to their lineage to compensate for the substance contributed – in the formation of the body of the child – by those who cannot affiliate them (for example, see Wagner 1967, Weiner 1988). In other words, in much of Melanesia, payments to the MB have been interpreted as balancing the input of the two parties (lineages). This connection is imaged in the substance contained in the body of the child. The child is a composite of maternal and paternal substance. In payments to the MB, the substance provided by the maternal side is bought off, leaving the child unproblematically affiliated within the paternal clan.

For Nekgini speakers, not only is the notion of lineality based on genealogy problematic, but this image of the body as composed of substances provided at birth by two sides is absent. I believe that these two facts are crucially interdependent. Reite people claim that the father's palem alone provides a substantive input to the make up the child. How then are we to understand affinal payments for their children that look like payments for substance?

The Transactions Between Affinal Kin Focused on Children

People in Reite are clear that the payments made between a MB and ZC are not a price put upon that child. They view them as recompense for work done in making the child into whatever kind of person they are to become. For every payment made, people will say *wakai nuing uruweiyung* (leave/omit inside of this kind become) That is, *nuing*, the inside or awareness of a person will be not be attuned to kastom, ('of this kind') if the payment is not made. If a child or adolescent fails to observe the dietary restrictions placed upon them by their MB, or the power given them fails to have effect in making gardens, they will be told *gnurung nuking ureiting'gnu* (your insides have become of this kind of person now). I quote from (the now deceased) elder, Hungeme; 'This means, for a child who makes all their payments, he will grow into a good man who has understanding of making kastom and developing a name for himself. Later, he will make a name for his child also. Adolescents who do not do these things, *neko sasaeng palang* (a child who is nothing) will never manage even small kastom work. (These phrases apply to first-born children).'

Table 5.1 *Life-cycle Payments Made Prior to Marriage among Nekgini Speakers*

Name of Payment	Procedure and Wealth to be Given	Boy	Girl
Eemung uret	'Face them'. Woman's bothers come, give decorated spear and coconut to newly pregnant girl. Return of betel nut and coconuts.	—	—
Nek sulitikung	'Washing the child'. Mother's brother receives the child from back wall of house. Palieng to MBs.	✓	✓
Yungyung	'Heavy foods'. F and M of child cook post-partum taboo foods and give to MB.	✓	✓
Unamau pusiraeo	'Not to be carried'. Cuscus (pununung) draped over shoulders, MB removes and eats.	✓	✓
Maal rongairni	'Fasten loincloth' – eel tied around child's waist, MB removes and eats.	✓	✓
Ming kupiret, tari talang'yenda	'First haircutting, rubbing dye into skin'. Pig, rawirawi and palieng – to MB.	✓	✓
Po asumiket	'Spiting [cooking juices of a] pig'. Cooked pig with wealth given to MB's. Child spits out juices spooned by MB into his/her mouth.	✓	✓
Kalawung	'Present'. Child cooks a pig for his/her M and F and their same-sex siblings. Small items (household goods) exchanged.	✓	✓
Yaan utae	'Inside the house'. First menses, girl secluded. MB receives tabooed foods to finish her seclusion – as in yungyung. Pig and meat – to MB.		✓
Matopo katiret yuna'wae	'Tie-up [your] body and give them'. Pig tied up and given with rawirawi and palieng to MB.		✓
Kaap wangiret, matopo katiret yuna'wae	'First view of tambaran, tie-up [your] body and give them'. Pig, rawirawi, and palieng given to MB.	✓	
Yong utae	'Hide in the shade'. First view of tambaran of the sea. Pig and palieng to MB who performed initiation.	✓	

Notes: There are three ways to give pork to a MB: cooked (with or without wealth), live with some wealth but no 'rope' (*rawirawi*), or live with a palem of food, and *rawirawi*.

Rawirawi (braided rope which secures a pig, draped with betelnut branches and shooting coconuts, given with palieng). Must be accompanied by a palem.

Palieng (wealth) is utung (wooden bowls), eemungin'a (dog's teeth face-band), upii (clay-pots), kombi (bailer shell), tesang (cash), maal (bark cloth), laplap (cloth), klos (clothes).

It will not necessarily be the same MB that receives on each occasion. Whoever washes the child will be given *yungyung*. The *umamau pusiraeo* and *maal rongairni* payments may well go to different MBs, or even to grandparents. The MB who receives pork for *po asumiket* will be substituted for another MB to receive *matopo*. In this way, relatives in many places are recognised.

Yong utae is a recently introduced form of initiation to which all young men are now subjected. It is additional to (does not replace) *kaap wangiret* and *matopo* for the first-born male child.

In the table, I have listed the payments made by a first-born child, male or female, to their maternal kin. It is vital that first-born children, potentially the future heads of sibling sets and palem leaders, achieve these payments. Others may make them, or not, as they and their parents see fit.

Sibling Order

First-born children are the children in myth who listen to their ancestors' advice, who make good, and live up to expectations. As palem heads, they are expected to 'go first' in all things, and in doing so elevate their younger siblings. Having 'come first', they are the first tangible outcome of the relationships which may make a new palem. *Paap waring* (for the eldest sibling in a group) means 'real' or 'first' (cf. Pomponio 1992: Chapter 4).

However, it is said that if a younger brother has 'stepped over' and 'gone ahead', his elder will inevitably lose interest in making affinal payments in the form of a palem, hence there is a restriction upon this occurrence. Making one's name here (becoming *ai topi*) is not merely a matter of giving gifts of meat, wealth, and produce to affines, but of making these gifts into the decorated platforms called palem. An elder brother whose position has been usurped by a younger sibling, it is said, will never achieve the construction of a palem, and will always take the easy route of giving exchange items away, 'on the ground'. His ability to encompass others in forming a palem has been usurped. If a younger male sibling marries before his elder brother, he must cook a pig to compensate the elder.

Photograph 9 *A Payment Given Away 'On the Ground', Serieng, 1994*

Sibling order is an issue in slit-gong construction (mentioned in the previous chapter). All work that is done on the fallen trunk proceeds from the base to the tip, the base section going through each stage of completion before the next one along. Thus it is always the drum and the man who is 'the base' of the work (the man in whose name the tree has been felled) that is thought to support the others. Those who take a slit-gong from any position other than the base rely on this base man's strength, just as younger siblings look for the support of their elders in making their affinal payments.[3] It is possible for a number of brothers to receive a garamut from the same tree, in which case the birth order of the siblings must be reflected in the order of their position along the trunk. The base man must be the eldest sibling, and it must be his affines that produce the garamut for him. A concern with sibling order and prominence are integral to smooth internal relations, as well as effective external relations, in a hamlet.

In many myths told in Reite, a younger sibling, against the advice of the eldest sibling, will cause himself, and even the whole of humanity, to suffer because of his idiocy. There are also many Reite myths in which a younger sibling instigates changes which bring beneficial things to following human generations (cf. Tuzin 1991). In the myth 'Pomo' (Chapter 3), one can see that although it is the younger brother who disrupts a primordial existence, it is through this that productivity and life as it is now known come into being. Nekgini speakers also accept that there may be innovation in the most basic matters of sibling hierarchy. In one Reite palem with which I am well acquainted, a younger of two now old and respected siblings is openly acknowledged by his elder to have surpassed him in making food (kastom) to be given to others, (be those others humans, patuki, or kaapu). He is said to 'have gone first' and has the greater say in palem, community, and other[4] matters. He has taken over the position of the first-born. Nevertheless, ideally each aspect of the life-cycle of a first-born ought to be complete before his younger siblings attempt it.

Birth

Children are never born in houses in Reite hamlets. It is said that to spill the blood of childbirth in a house to which men come would make the house cold and the men lethargic, unable to hunt or climb trees after birds. Having women's kaapu 'step over' (*ya lolondeweiyung*) the house would also have the effect of making pigs step over the fences around men's gardens and eat the immature taro. Usually, children are born behind the houses, on the ground covered with a mat of *piui* (*limbum* [T.P.]) bark. But immediately after the birth is completed, the mother takes her baby inside the house and is secluded there with the father until the umbilical cord (*waspiring*), cut from the placenta (*kotung*) with a bamboo knife, to a length measured between the mother's elbow and her wrist, is dry. The placenta itself is dismissed as 'rubbish' (*samu*) and is hidden in the ground in a hole dug by the birth attendants and placed there by the mother herself (*kotung tap ureiting*).[5]

When the length of cord has dried and breaks off, it is taken carefully and put in the father's small bag of personal items (*au tandang*); as 'first blood', it 'watches over' the baby. The father collects together a wooden plate (*utung*) and valuables including bark loincloth (*maal*), dogs' teeth and pigs' teeth (*palieng*). He sends word to the parents and brothers of his wife to come and receive this payment for washing the child for the first time.[6]

During their seclusion in the house, the mother and father are restricted from eating foods which are considered heavy (*neko nekitering*, heavy things). Soft white 'female' taro (*pel parieng*), original strains of plantain (*kalipoa*), and long yams (*wiynung*), in particular, make the child, and its mother and father, unable to perform everyday tasks. They may also bring sickness, particularly for the baby. Such foods cause one to have 'no bones' (*wimbiking malong*) that is, strength for work.

The mother's father, mother, and her brothers, attend to washing the child (*nek sulitika*). The baby is placed on top of the loincloth and is surrounded by the valuables in the wooden bowl. A hole is broken in the wall at the back of the house, or in the floor at the back if it is a raised house, and the baby passed through this into the hands of its maternal kin. (In some houses there is a separate small entrance through which the women of the household can come and go while they are menstruating, and if this is in the rear of the house, it will be used.) When people talk of this event, however, they invariably speak of making a split in the wall of the house for the baby to be passed through.[7]

Receiving the child, the maternal kin take it into the forest near the house, and wash it for the first time with water, and then with the juice of fast growing 'wild bananas' (*Heliconia sp.*), not in fact 'bananas' at all. A strong and quick growing vine known to have an abundance of sap is found, and split open, so that although still part of the growing trunk, it is flat like a piece of cloth. The mother's brothers place the baby on this and pass it over to the mother and father who, receiving it, pass through a split made in the same vine at another point in its length. A wisp of the baby's hair is taken, and placed in the cavity through which they have passed, and the vine is then wrapped around with smaller vines and leaves to close the break. The growth of this vine afterwards ensures the well-being and growth of the child. Returning from the deep bush onto a path, the paternal kin of the child now engage in a pretence of making small gardens, building houses, climbing trees, making traps for marsupials, and so forth. The baby will therefore be able to perform these tasks in later life.

Early in my time in Reite, I was eating with my neighbour's affines. My neighbour, Yamui, had lost his wife during childbirth in 1990. Sitting in his in-laws' house, he saw the wooden plate he had used to pass his first-born child to his maternal kin, and commented to me first on his loss, and then on his pride that he had managed all the payments for his children, so that their mother had not been ashamed. The plate was used regularly for serving ceremonial food.

Growing Up

The next rite, *yungyung*, involves foods tabooed at the time of the birth. The mother's brother takes away the 'weight' of these foods for the child by taking a bit of the tabooed item, passing it around the neophyte's head and then either spitting it into the setting sun, or containing it in a bamboo tube and breaking this container against the trunk of a *shish* (*Stercuia*) or *kapiak* (*Alocarpus altilis*), trees which carry heavy bulbous fruits. These rites always take place on the land of the father. It is 'his' trees which carry the weight. Giving these foods to the mother's brother is a form of politeness, and payment for taking the heaviness from the child, or for 'providing the power to grow'. All those foods considered dangerous for the new parents and their child will be cooked and given to the maternal kin of the child before the parents eat them again. Eating pork, however, is a major event in a first-born's life cycle, and usually comes later.

The meat, eggs, crustaceans and nuts for *yungyung* are presented tied around a kind of mast, or backbone, standing in the centre of a large dish. For the rite, the child will have a rattle bracelet made by their mother and father out of dogs teeth and decorative beads. This bracelet is called *zingsung*, and is removed by the MB, only to be replaced by a similar one he has made himself. The symmetry foreshadows later exchanges between the two which also involve the replacement of wealth from the child's natal kin by wealth from his or her parents affinal kin. *Zingsung* is the child's first body ornament.

As the table of payments shows, the child's first clothing, her/his appearance on the shoulders of her/his parents, first hair cut, first wearing of skin dye and so on are all completed with payments to maternal kin. These payments elicit recognition of the child's development, and make this apparent through causing the maternal kin to receive items associated with this development. Until *maal rangairni*, the baby is kept naked, not fastening a bark loincloth (or nowadays a nappy) until the father has placed an eel around the child's waist. The mother's brother is presented with the child. He takes the eel from the baby and replaces it with an eel that he provides. Similarly, a baby may only be held against the chest for the first months of its life. When the father has hunted a large marsupial, he drapes this around the baby's shoulders. The mother's brother comes and *pununung pusiring endikindo* 'carries the marsupial of the baby'. In this case, he makes a small return of *palieng* (hard white shell or tooth-wealth). It is said that the right to present the child in certain ways has to be elicited from the mother's brother; the right and the elicitation, one could say, are achieved in the payment and its method. The alimentary imagery here is also significant.

It is the restriction on eating pork which usually lasts the longest of those restrictions begun at birth. Particularly in the case of a first-born child, the mother's brother (*wau*) ensures that this restriction is observed, and eats the 'child's pig' before the child itself may eat the pig of anyone else. In the case of girls, what often happens is that the rites of emergence as a person, or 'cutting of the hair' (*taruyara*), and those of buying the bones (*wimbiyung kimeret/matopo*) are combined, and it is at this stage in the girl's life that her *wau* spoons the cooking juices of pig into her mouth, so that after this time she can eat pork. In the case of boys, the payment for their bones, and for the first use of decorative body paint is often postponed until they are adolescent and 'see the tambaran' of their mother's brothers.[8] Mostly, first-born young men of fifteen years or more have neither 'seen the tambaran' (been initiated by their mother's brother), 'held paint' (been decorated and thus been 'seen' themselves as initiated men), nor eaten pork, as they are waiting for the time their *wau* 'shows them the tambaran' before making a grand presentation for their body, and for their right to be decorated and to eat pork.

That there is no rigid order in these payments, that they differ slightly depending on the proclivities of the parents, the proximity of the maternal kin, the desire of the child itself to work to contribute to these payments, birth order, and so forth, shows not a chaotic approach, but rather a pragmatic one. One large payment that satisfies the recipients is as good as several drawn-out smaller ones which deal piecemeal, as it were, with aspects of one's recognition as a person. It tends to be the case that where there is animosity between affines, where women have been stolen by love magic without any consultation, or especially where one side has denigrated the other, payments will all be carefully noted, any absence drawing satisfaction at one's power to render the other unable to meet his commitments.

A second kind of emergence, or even birthing, occurs when the child's hair is cut for the first time, and when he or she first wears red skin dye. These rites are known as *ming kupiret, tari talang'ende*. A first-born does not have his or her hair cut, nor do he or she wear decoration until the MB arrives on a specified day, and takes the child away into seclusion to wash him or her with turmeric root (*kapuipui*) and paint his or her skin with red skin dye. (As in the example given at length below, this whole rite may be combined with initiation. A male initiate will be secluded in the men's house of his own hamlet, and thus both his fathers and his mother's brothers will be on hand.) Returning to his/her parents, the child will be decorated with *palieng*, that is dog's teeth valuables, cut bailer shells, and pigs tusks. Then standing in public, this wealth will be replaced, like item for like item, by the MB. They may put a little extra in the child's string bag, saying this is 'for eating their pig'.

Ming kupiret, tari talang'ende demands the presentation of a pig, if possible a payment which involves the construction of a palem, and thus includes a 'rope' (*rawirawi*) which secures the pig and is draped in wealth.[9] It is said that cleaning the child, and cutting the child's hair for the first time brings the MB into contact with *samu* (polluting or dangerous substances). In return, the man who takes charge of this work receives the pig, and the wealth around the rope. The process of making them clean, and decorating them with red dye and white valuables allows the child to parade herself or himself and appear in ceremonies, dances, and so forth, in the future. The facilitation of this emergence, along with the contact with *samu* warrants payment in the form of a *body* (palem), and thus an asymmetrical element at this point (the 'rope' [*rawirawi*] and pig). However, it is emphasised strongly that in all other ways, the maternal kin are replacing the child's own wealth, not taking any extra. What is also worth noting about this form of payment in this context is that, appearing as a 'body' (a palem) the payment is explicitly acknowledging the presentation of a body in return; and that can only be the form the child may appear in resulting from this rite. The Nalasis elder, Pangu Utering, said the payment is made because now the child '*inup raun na soim skin bilong en long narapela hap*' (T.P.; may move around and show their skin in another place). I draw attention to the imagery of white, hard wealth items – dogs' teeth, pigs' tusks, and shells that the child now has the right to display on her skin – showing her bones, as it were. As will be recalled, in the first payment where the baby is passed from the house to the maternal kin, valuables of this kind are placed around the child, but not on his/her skin.

Cutting hair is significant as a return to social life after a period of mourning. In mourning people remain enclosed in their houses and do no work. Cutting the hair in both these contexts is a birthing of a kind, where, as with the drying umbilical cord, an image of disconnection is created: either disconnection from the past state of mourning, or disconnection from the untended, invisible state of a child undifferentiated (enclosed by) their hamlet kinsmen. In both cases a severance from the past is accomplished by people from the hamlet of one's fathers affines.

Seeing the Tambaran and Buying One's Body

This example of initiation includes a payment to a mother's brother (*wau*).[10] It comes from an account by a Reite man, who told of *kaapu tupong yara wangareiting* ('seeing the tambaran of the water').[11]

When you want/are ready to see the tambaran, you and your father grow a pig. You make a garden with his help, your maternal kin do not know yet, but you do not share this garden with anyone else. It is just for you to give away. When your father sees it has grown well, he will tell your mother's brothers: in my case [from] Marpungae. They told all their family from Asang and Sorang, from Serieng and Reite, and the men came with their tambaran and hid on all the little paths around Reite Yasing. Their tambaran all cried suddenly (not the tambaran for dancing, but of hornbills and other birds). When the women heard this they jumped, and ran for their houses.

I wore a loincloth, and held fragrant leaves that they had put in the fire to make them smell more, then my fathers and brothers told me to close my eyes, and they stood around me, fencing me in completely. Marpungae all came to my front, and made a noise to make me open my eyes, and when I did I saw all the tambaran there together. I spat manieng (aromatic 'ginger') over them, and opened my eyes and saw them. Then the tambaran came and 'ate' the men who were surrounding me, and ate me too, pummelling me in the ribs and back, and clambering over our skin. They don't do this without thought, whatever the men watching over their tambaran hold in their head while the tambaran eats you, will make you grow in that way – there are stories for growing taro, for being a fighter, or for being attractive to women. There are also bad tambaran stories, ones which make you lazy, or want to have sex with old women. When I had seen the tambaran, it ate food that women had prepared, and then my maternal kin all left for their own

Photograph 10 *Palieng. Body Decoration and Exchange Valuables*

hamlets after having hidden me inside the passae. (It is at this moment that the mother's brother transfers power to the child, teaching him spells. His subsequent seclusion is said to be a chance for this power to stick to him.)

While I was in the house, I was tabooed from drinking water and from eating from the hands of women. My fathers and brothers provided me with dry food cooked on the fire.[12] While I was in the house, for five weeks in all, the tambaran of the water, brought by my mother's brothers was there and making music during each night, watching over me. At this time, my mother's brothers and my father came and told me many things about being a married man, about how to behave towards others, and many things about power – to grow taro and yams, for fighting, for making women fall in love, and for watching over the tambaran, both for dancing and the tambaran which eats the inside of garamuts. My father gave me school in all things too, about how to make kastom; to make food, and a palem.

During this time, my father's tambaran cut a tree for a post, and with the women hidden away, piled dry coconuts around this post to the top. Having completed the mast, the tambaran came into the house, and they beat the garamut signal for coconut to let my mother's brothers know we were getting ready. Then my father and his brothers and my brothers made a bed at the base of this mast, and he gave the women a day to go to the garden we had made and bring taro, yam, banana, and put them by the bed. Then they told me that at dawn I would pile the taro on the bed. Before dawn, my father took me to the spirit place of the Pomo story,[13] and I was told to climb a tree there for the topmost leaves. No one showed me which tree. Not having had water for three weeks, I was exhausted, and only made it half way. People said this showed I would never manage to make large food presentations, and would have no pigs at my door.

I pushed the leaves from this tree into the base of the bamboo which forms the backbone of the taro pile, and then tied all the sides of the palem (kawarieng) to hang yams and bananas. Then I spat fragrant leaves at the base of the backbone and placed one taro tuber there before they told me to go and hide again. The women went and hid in the bush for all of this. My brothers now piled the taro on the bed. Then they decorated the food (pel) with yams and betel nut and other things – the taro is the food, the rest decoration for it. Then they brought the pig and tied it beneath the bed.

Now they beat out garamut signals, first for coconuts on a mast, then for taro on a bed, then last for capturing a pig. When they had done this the women came back and my maternal kin were summoned. Yakai (the wau maring) was leading, and he took me off to the bush, and washed me with water from wild banana stems. The tambaran then brought us back to the passae where they put a loincloth (maal) on me and held paint for my skin. Then Yakai and his kin left the house and sat outside eating prepared garden food, so they would be strong to carry their pay home. My brothers came and put decoration on my skin – palieng – they gave me a bilum with money and shells in it, put dogs' teeth around my maal, and on my head, and a chicken tail in my hair. Women were banished again, and the tambaran of my fathers brought me outside, leaving me there, standing, and returned into the house where it sang as my brothers beat the garamuts. The women came back, and threw water with fragrant leaves onto my skin, making me clear so they could see me, and then I stood before the view of everyone. While they watched, my maternal kin came and changed the decoration on my skin, taking my brothers', and replacing it with their own. They replaced it exactly, they could not have anything for free, nor did they give me anything more than I had. Giving something is for when you give a rope (rawirawi) (as a payment). Things on your skin are to be changed (like exchanged for like).

When exchanging things is finished, it is time to buy your bones now (wimbiyung kimeret). You start with distant maternal kin, calling their names and giving them all a small amount of pay. Finally, I gave the rope (rawirawi) *and pig to Yakai himself. I held the rope up, and put four young growing coconuts around it, then hung money, dogs' teeth, betel nut and pigs' teeth over it. An unrolled bark loincloth, tail downwards, was also wrapped around the rope. I lifted these things and gave them into his hand, then everything else went to them – food, coconuts and the pig.*[14]

Returning to the house, I drank weak soup and spat it on the house post, and in the next three days, I made ready food for my father and brother's tambaran. I cooked a small pig and food, to pay them for looking after ('watching over') me. When I had fed them, they beat a garamut from the tambaran of Marpungae for me: they beat my father's name, then 'child', then 'no', and then beat my new name, which came from a tambaran spirit song belonging to Yakai from Marpungae.

My fathers and brothers were with me all the time I was secluded, and when I made food it was their tambaran that did all the work, but my maternal kin showed me the tambaran first, and gave me power to grow, they gave me paint (tari sawing) *and decoration* (palieng) *to appear in, a name [as a garamut beat] from the rhythm of one of their tambaran songs, and stories* (patuki) *of theirs for making kastom* (Kerimang Nombo-Ingem 3/95)

The paint that maternal kin put on the skin of the child (*tari sawing*) – be it during hair cutting, or after viewing the kaapu for the first time – is commented upon often and fully by Reite people. An outside observer might remark that the taboo on painting the skin, and the times of painting it, make a foetal image – of rebirth, glistening bloody newness. Reite people focus on the brightness and shine of the paint at this time. It is said that one can tell the (moral) state of the child from the brightness of his or her paint, whether it will be a 'good' person – a man able to find meat in the bush, grow taro, marry; or a girl able to carry loads, listen to her kin's wishes, bear children – and also the state of the relationship between the maternal and paternal kin. If the paint is dark it might be for a number of reasons. Immature sexual contact will pollute the child and impede its growth: this will show in the paint the mother's brother puts on its skin. If the mother's brother has consumed *samu* (dirt/blood, poison substance), or if there is a dispute or bad feeling between the paternal and maternal kin, the paint the mother's brother uses will appear dark. The initiate is explicitly an image of growth which refers to the particular relationships that have formed them.

What Kerimang describes above – the distribution of pay to a series of maternal kin, rather than just the principle initiator – has a complex rationale. The payments made by the child to their MB are principally part of the relationship between *affines*. One can reasonably say that although the focus is on the child, the onus is on the parents to complete these transactions. They are affinal rather than intergenerational obligations. As such, their completion has the effect of liberating the first-born child (and younger siblings) from the obligations of the parents. Thus children are free to make new relations of their own. Even marriages between successive generations of the same palem are managed *as if* they were new relations being forged in each instance. The logic is generative, as I have mentioned; by this I mean the payments between affines in effect begin the process whereby sibling order is transformed into a relation of authority between sibling palem. Each man and wife combined make palem. In doing so they become a named entity, and free their children from their own affinal obligations. Thus each palem group's offspring are a new sibling set, possibly a new named place.

The reason for giving payments to a succession of named maternal kin in instances such as Kerimang's above is 'to help one's mother'; that is, those named are those who did not figure prominently in the body payment the mother and father made for her own body (Chapter 3). If the mother has satisfied all those with a claim over her in her own *matopo* payment to her brothers, her child will name only one principle recipient, his or her initiator, who receives and makes a return (*kaiyung*) on the *rawirawi*. Other MBs will have a share of the pig, but will not receive *palieng* (wealth) in their own name for the first-born child.

Kerimang's narrative contains other points. The payment of *matopo* entitles the (male) youth to a unique beat on a slit-gong drum. This beat will be associated with him for his lifetime, and used, just as a name is, to call him and his wives and children. The beat is isolated from the rhythm of one of the spirit songs of his father's affinal kin, his *wau* (MB). Thus in a most public and enduring way, the wau acknowledges the emergence of the boy, and provides the vehicle of his recognition. As with hair cutting, with which the sequence Kerimang describes is often conjoined, wealth on the skin of the neophyte is provided by the father to be replaced with identical items, by the wau. Finally, it is the tambaran, the kaapu of the wau who 'eat' the initiate, and thus not only ensure his growth but also the kind of man this process will ultimately produce.

The Tambaran of the Sea

In the last thirty years, a new form of male initiation has been adopted by Nekgini speakers. It is a form of ritual from the coast, and is called 'the tambaran of the sea', or *yong* after the shade of the secluded area where boys are hidden. In it, a maternal kinsman, although not necessarily a close one who could claim a body payment, performs a minor operation on the boy, and then looks after him during his recovery.[15] Most young men, first-born and otherwise undertake it, and indeed for those not born first, this is a major change. One might say that one effect is to speed up exchange (Strathern 2001). As all boys now undergo a process of seclusion and thus attention from a 'wau', there are more instances in which pigs are exchanged. While in the past the first-born's initiation and *matopo* payment encompassed his younger male siblings, who ideally would be secluded with him and thus initiated at this time as well, in the current (dual) system, younger siblings have their own moment. Reite people see this ritual, at present at least, as something separate from the major obligations between affines. It is something young men want, and thus they do their best to facilitate it. Yet the initiation Kerimang describes above is at present the major focus of attention for first-born male children, and perhaps more importantly of the payments for emergence which maternal kin receive.

In fact there was discussion of an attempt to make the payments for the work done by a wau in looking after his charge in the *yong* cover the work done in showing a first-born the tambaran of the water. This was angrily resisted in Reite, where it was argued that the two must be kept separate. Particularly important was the fact that when seeing the tambaran, a child makes a *matopo* or body payment, and in many cases completes the body payment of his mother at this time. He receives a 'name' on a garamut at this time as well. In other words, it was felt that the initiation, newly introduced from elsewhere, could be additional but could not replace the myriad connections between affinal kinsmen made apparent and discharged through a *matopo* which accompanies initiation. People's identity and obligations are too closely tied together with the form of their spirits, and their position as affines (still receiving wealth for their sister), for these aspects to be sidelined in the emergence of a sister's first-born child into adulthood.

Finally, in an outline of the payments made by people to their mother's brothers, there is a requirement for grown men, initiated into the tambaran and who want to carry one of the decorated head posts (*torr*) in a performance of kaapu music (*sare*), to present their mother's brother with meat on the occasion when they first complete this feat. The posts carry designs said to come from, and to be inspired by, the paternal kin's land, and are owned as such. However, when a man first carries one of these heavy and cumbersome items, he approaches his wau who establishes the number of days that he avoid all contact with water and women. On the night of the performance, the man ties together a rope of meat and other prestige foods (*pununung*) – Malay almonds, bush fowl eggs, fish, crayfish, pig and marsupial meat, and birds – (the roped protein is called *zingsung*)[16] which he hangs over his shoulder, and, checking he can carry the *mangmang* (carrying frame) with it in place, he then puts it aside until the morning. At dawn, his mother's brother comes and removes the *pununung*, and leaves drinking coconut and betel nut 'to wash the pain in his legs'. It is said that without this payment, without the power his mother's brother gives him for it, no man would be able to carry a post for the full length of the night.

The payments listed in the table of life-cycle payments are necessary in the sense that to become a person whom others respect, they are the minimal conditions on which future exchanges can be built. Any attempt to give payments for, say betrothal or marriage, prior to the completion of these payments brings demands to complete other obligations first.

Here then, we see a series of procedures which ensure that the potential personhood in every child unfolds in the proper order. In other words, it is a temporal sequence that is being enacted in a child's relations with its mother's brother, rather than a series of fully self-contained rituals that have a set form in themselves. There is a sequential movement from umbilical cord, genital covering, to hair, skin, and bones. This sequence corresponds to a series of thresholds that have to be crossed as a person grows through his or her life cycle.[17] But what relation does this complex emergence have with understandings of the role of the mother's brother in the anthropological literature?

Photograph 11 Zingsung. *The Payment of* Pununung *to a Mother's Brother*

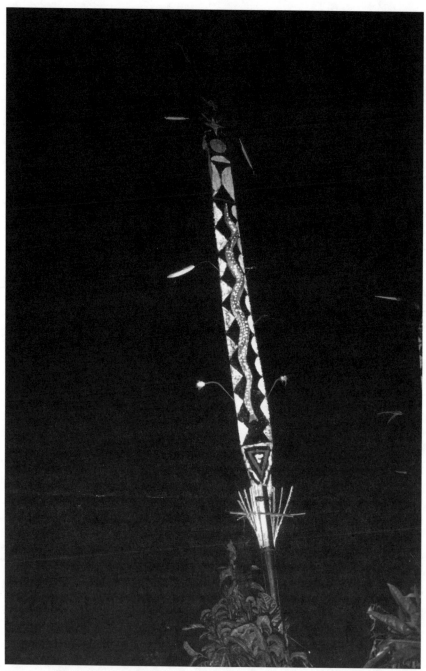

Photograph 12 Torr *Post Carried in* Sare

Mother's Brothers in the Anthropological Literature

Goody (1969) has drawn attention to the emphasis on lineality and filiation in the classic work of Radcliffe-Brown and others. The privileged role of the mother's brother is explained as a by-product of the principles of lineality and descent. The natural affection between a mother and her child was extended from the socialising nuclear family to her kinsmen, and the closest of these – the maternal uncle – therefore took an indulgent role with her children in contrast to the father and his kinsmen, who provided authority and represented the hierarchy of political (clan) structure.

> Since it is from his mother that he expects care and indulgence, he looks for the same sort of treatment from the people of his mother's group, i.e. all his maternal kin. On the other hand it is to his paternal kin that he owes obedience and respect. The patterns that arise in relation to the father and the mother are generalised and extended to the kindred on the one side and on the other. (Radcliffe-Brown 1952b: 25)

and

> The pattern of behaviour towards the mother, which is developed in the family by reason of the nature of the family group and its social life, is extended with suitable modifications to the mother's sister and the mother's brother, then to the group of maternal kindred as a whole, and finally to the maternal gods, the ancestors of the mother's group. (ibid.: 27)

Now in analysing my material from Reite, my emphasis has so far been on the relation of the mother's brother to the sister's child, but it is important to note that the father's sister/brother's child relationship is also important to Reite people, the one substituting for the other in certain circumstances. Because the father's sister is female and the mother's brother is male, their knowledge and powers are different. I have documented cases, however, where the spouse of a father's sister will take on the role of a mother's brother for a man or a woman on their initiation. In other words, the 'special' relations are with cross-sex siblings of the parents, whether they be maternal or paternal. This means with people from another palem.

What tells most against Radcliffe-Brown's position here is that the relationship to the mother is wholly different from that to the mother's brother. In fact, as seen in the table of life-cycle payments, one is made by a boy *before* his initiation, to his mother, for her nurture, and in which she is dealt with separately from the mother's brother. In this payment for nurture, the father receives a share – he is combined with the mother as recipient for the payment – thus *kalawung*, the gifting of cooked pig to the mother and father – establishes a kind of equivalence between them, rather than between the mother and the mother's brother.

When a woman marries into a palem, she becomes 'as sibling' to the members of that palem. Her co-wives are her *paap/wanik'ei* (siblings), as are her brothers-in-law. Relations within the palem replace an external cross-sex relation (between cross-cousins) with a form of same-sex relation which has, as its model, the relation of closeness and mutual aid that siblings bring to each other. Yet the actual relation between husband and wife is different again. They become a social unit, a palem, from which other bodies are produced. I have already examined how internal relations of productivity work – how in gardens, although two different elements come together in one process which produces offspring, these two elements come to look like one thing – one garden and its produce. Thus the internal differentiation is hidden in the moment of production, and those for whom the garden has been grown merely see a palem producing garden food (see Strathern 1988: 133–7). In a marriage, one can detect a similar process. A woman brought from outside is integrated into the palem. Children that are produced are said to come from and belong to the palem, they are the appearance of its productivity. In a garden, it is necessary to bring a productive other (Mai'anderi) to grow one's taro, but this other is hidden when the results are produced, just as the taro itself is hidden in the belly of this other to grow it. Internal productive differentiation becomes a single identity on the production of objects or persons which have to be seen by another in order to have an identity, and in order to give their source its own undifferentiated identity. Internal contrasts are encompassed and momentarily obviated by the internal/external contrast.

To move on, where Radcliffe-Brown emphasised filiation in his interpretation of the role of the mother's brother, Lévi-Strauss placed the emphasis on affinity. The 'mother's brother/sister's son' relation was seen not as an extension of attitudes arising within the nuclear family, but as one component of a universal structure generated by the incest taboo, and the consequent exchange of women in marriage (Gillison 1987). In his debate with Lévi-Strauss, Radcliffe-Brown conceded that in so-called Dravidian systems, of which examples could be found in Australia and Melanesia, affinity is built into the kinship system. In such systems, as Goody puts it (commenting on the debate), 'a cross-cousin marriage rule means there is no mother's brother relationship which is not at the same time an affinal, or potentially affinal, relationship…'(Goody 1969: 47). What is particularly interesting about this with regard to Reite material is that this recognition of the mother's brother is an acknowledgement that he is poised at the fulcrum where filiation turns into affinity, and vice-versa.

In Reite, mother's brother/sister's child relationships are 'affinal', because they make apparent the previous separation in a sibling set between a brother and a sister. We would have to agree with Radcliffe-Brown here: that separation in previous generations between specific kin has gone part way to creating difference in this one (cross-cousin terminology). As we have seen, it is possible to make anyone different, but with 'affines', Reite people already have kin who have been actively separated in the past, in anticipation of further social action (recombination). Rights gained by a mother's brother when his sister marries are jealously guarded; they are rights to receive wealth from her offspring. What this means is an expectation of recognition. Putting people in a position of recognition, as I argued in Chapter 3 elicits the possibility of future marriage, as well as opportunities to appear in receipt of wealth. Edmund Leach follows Lévi-Strauss, claiming that the role of the mother's brother is of an affinal nature. Goody (1969: 86) warns, however, that to take such a view is to risk ignoring other kin connections between affines which mean that relations to the mother's clan are not just affinal (exchange based).

However, where the indigenous perspective posits continuity even with affines (their children are your children), and where difference is what is strived for (there is, as it were, no inside and outside to kinship), 'affinal' relations need careful analytic attention. This is the case in Reite understanding as well. The constant need for exchange, and the Reite insistence on equivalence in exchange, points to the idea of an exchange of perspectives, leading to difference. Wagner phrases this differently, but his argument in 'Analogic Kinship' (Wagner 1977a) is relevant to my position here. He writes:

> The analysis of joking, avoidance, and respect relationships initiated by Radcliffe-Brown (1952) and Eggan (1937) deals with culture specific homologies between sociological kin roles and a set of 'given' genealogical relatives. Kin differentiation (the genealogical 'grid') becomes an invariant control against which the sociological alignments and stresses of various tribal peoples are contrasted (625).

In what Wagner calls 'homological schemes' of kinship analysis,[18] differentiation is given by genealogy, and thus relations in society use these distinctions as a template to define the roles of individuals. It is the validity of this natural differentiation, as an assumption made by analysts, that Wagner calls into question. In the case I examine here, we have seen that exchange in Reite comes about because of the active separation of kin into affines. Lineality, if it exists, is not given by genealogy, but by placement and recognition. Recognition by others is of a place and the kin relations which constitute it as a nexus of agency and production. Thus a person's identity is not given as a role (sister's child) specified genealogically, but as a recognition of his or her otherness. This otherness is a perspectival position, maintained by those separated from the place of one's residence in the past by the completion of marriage. A person's identity is established in the very relations of his or her emergence. Perspective is based upon position, and position is achieved in the processes of generation. The anthropological literature on the mother's brother has established where we do not need to look.

Affinal Payments and Lineality in Reite

I am going to draw attention to the aspect of social 'visibility' effected by all these ritual meetings with the mother's brother. The payments are for emergence, for first wearing clothes, for being carried as a human child (as opposed to a marsupial one). They are subsequently for the initiation of various aspects of the child's emergence as a person; that is; as someone who can wear wealth, eat meat (which comes from a source beyond the natal household), wear paint, carry decoration, and so forth. In short, the objective is the emergence of a social presence. What we see in the relationship to maternal kin is the unfolding of the appearance and powers of a Reite person. In the patterning of the elicitation of wealth and growth by the mother's brother from his sister's child, and in the reciprocal elicitation of nurture and knowledge by the sister's child from its maternal kin, the aspects of Reite personhood are laid out in their temporal development. This is for the very good reason that being seen as a temporal entity – one with a relational past, and one which anticipates future relationships – is exactly what is being effected.

By making a temporal sequence out of the unfolding of the person as a socially visible entity, those who see this are placed in a position of recognition. The substantial input comes from the paternal clan's land and their labours (as in placing the child in the belly, producing eels, marsupials, pigs, wealth). Brenda Clay's ethnography of Mandak on New Ireland highlights some interesting parallel notions of substance and identity.

> In Mandak procreation ideology, the male progenitor provides the blood, bone and internal organs of the foetus which is fed in it's mother's womb. The male procreative role involves a prestation – a gift of substance to his offspring.... The symbolic idiom used most commonly to convey the meaning of paternal substance is 'blood'. (Clay 1986: 39)

Her interpretation of this ethnography is interesting:

> While maternal nurture partakes of the female side of the sexual dichotomy, paternal substance provides the male complement. Thus an association of male, exchanging, and cross unit relationships opposes the maternal nurture elements of female, sharing and same unit relationships. Idioms of paternal substance focus on male prestations of substance at procreation, while maternal nurture idioms emphasise the continual provision of sustenance by females. The former are concerned with relationships that are *other* than oneself and outside ego's social unit; the latter marks off social ties which are of the *same kind* as oneself within ego's social unit (ibid., emphasis added).

In the Mandak matrilineal system, the role of the maternal and paternal kin are opposite to those in Reite, and there are, of course, other differences. Yet the notion of substance as a paternal input, and of social identity as the responsibility of the maternal kin, mirrors my own interpretation. Mandak people have relations to others – paternal kin – which in Reite are those to maternal kin. Relations to paternal kin in Reite 'mark off social ties which are of the same kind as oneself', and those to maternal kin provide social identity through exchange.

In Reite, people emphasise the visibility of connections, and thus of the relations in which persons appear. What occurs in the house – and we must remember that the birth itself did not take place there, so this is not about a first moment of physical emergence – is that a point of connection drops away. Cutting the placenta away from the baby, but leaving the umbilical cord, gives a temporary image to those inside the house of a residual connection to them of intra-uterine nurture. Keeping the mother and father out of sight until their nurturing connection with the baby finishes of its own accord, and leaving it to the mother's brother to 'birth' the baby – by receiving it from the body of the house for the first time – make mother and father together, as one, the producers of the child. All that is initially visible from outside the house is the baby's connection to the mother's brother. The first social event of the baby's life is its emergence from the house the father built to enclose it, into the hands of the mother's brother.

One could find a symmetry here between the container supplied by the maternal kin for the baby (the mother) and the container supplied by the father for the child, the mother, and himself, from which emerges a socially recognised being. That the baby emerges from the 'body' made by the father's hamlet (at their 'door'), rather than from the mother, is a masking of the containment provided by the maternal kin. This is compensated for in the rights the mother's brother jealously guards to be the one who provides a perspective on the child; to be the one who makes his sociality visible in receiving wealth and food payments from the child throughout her/his life. My analysis here proceeds along these lines.

Now we see here everything a patrilineal system would have: a payment to the mother's brother for the child which would amount in other places (Weiner 1988; A.J. Strathern 1972; Wagner 1967) to a payment for lineal affiliation to the paternal rather than the maternal clan. As Marilyn Strathern reports in an overview of marriage exchanges in Melanesia: 'the fact that a person is internally differentiated (as established by the exchanges deriving from his or her parents' union) may well have to be acted upon either to obliterate some elements or to ensure a balanced constitution' (Strathern 1984: 51, numbered references removed). The essential nexus of relations that is involved in any affinal exchange, namely among mother's brother, mother, father, and child, is still there (Lévi-Strauss 1969). But I suggest that the affinal tie in Reite positions and defines the attributes of the other. Payments in this case *are* the relationship between affines, they do not substitute for, or replace, another (substantial) relationship.

What is the significance of creating the house as an intra-uterine space containing mother and father? I suggest first, that it actively confirms what Reite people have a tendency to imagine – that the mother and father are as one unit, who produce things 'at their door'. Secondly, it confirms that in their similarity, they are unable to provide social recognition for the child. Thirdly, the role of the maternal kin in providing substance is denied.

Now in a system of a patrilineal type, social recognition comes from affiliation to the paternal clan, implied in such payments as those that the Foi, or Hageners (Strathern 1998: 14–15), make to maternal kin. In Reite, affiliation is the process of emergence. That is, payments are made, not for substance *per se*, but to establish the correct form of relations with other hamlets, and for the position of those making the payments as affines (not as siblings) to be maintained. They carry on through payments made to 'arrange' marriages for the future (Chapter 3).

The intra-uterine image of growth is replaced by an external image: the vine and the hair replace the umbilical connection, and the growth of these items is linked to the child's growth into a recognisable human being, able to perform everyday human tasks. This is a clear clue to the role of the mother's brother in 'growing' the child. Reite people 'know' that children grow anyway; but powerful growth is that which stands forth, as human, from the common background of plant or animal growth.

This helps to explain the different aspects of imagery in the procedure through which a child passes. As a new-born the child is placed in a bowl, and surrounded by teeth – a possible image of what was literally said to have taken place 'in the past', namely that the child was eaten by the mother's brother. However, the image of alimentary encompassment, everted when the child comes to eat pig himself or herself, is also one that could be of nurturance – of encompassment in a reproductive sense.

In eating pig, the child is shown to have the potential in his or her own right for such a productive encompassment and his or her personhood is literally shown on their skin at this point, as he or she is everted – red paint glistening beneath white valuables on the forehead and chest. An image of paternal bones is replaced by the bones given her or him by their maternal kin. A different eversion, from internal to external, is effected, this time producing her/him as an entity with insides, with bones of their own to be seen. The idiom of gaining power from the tambaran at adolescent initiation for both boys and girls is the same image of eating and encompassment, with the emergence from seclusion after being eaten by the tambaran of one's maternal kin fulfilling the same eversion of a body with flesh and bones on the outside to be seen. Buying bones turns out to be exchanging bones (the replacement of the father's wealth by that of the maternal kin), thus the person a mother's brother produces as an entity for regard (as in when adolescents emerge from his or her period of seclusion) carries a part of himself. Yet this part of himself is in another place, and thus while he can provide social recognition for the child (give them wealth to display), he cannot claim them as his substance. The bones he gives them are no longer his own, they belong, along with the mother, to the land on which the child grows.

Continuing the contrast with more obviously lineal systems, I refer again to the work of James Weiner. For the Foi of Lake Kutubu, Weiner writes that, 'a man must be compensated for the loss of his sister's procreative powers, for he considers her children as much his as their father's. But a man does not have the right to give pay to his sisters' husbands to affiliate his sisters' children; lineality is the prerogative of husbands even as it is the "natural" power of wives' (1988: 90). Now in Reite, men claim the children of unmarried sisters (who have not been paid for) as their own. Marriage is effected by payments that move the woman onto the land of her husband, from where she produces a payment for her body.[19] In Reite, payments to affines embed or re-embed a woman as a member of another productive place. The payment for the child establishes a connection, but as the child is located somewhere else, this connection is made into one of exchange rather than siblingship. The movement of persons is traced by the movement of wealth in the other direction. One does not exchange with 'oneself' (*ne naki*). Thus payments for the nurture of the mother's brother cannot be about substance.

Reite people claim to have no knowledge of the process of conception, nor of the contributions of the mother and father to the child's make up. If however you ask a Reite person, 'how does a child get inside a woman's belly?', they answer immediately, 'a man puts it there'. What this points to is that there is no maternal/paternal division of the body in terms of its conception, and in this, the Reite ethnography seems very different from that of, say, Foi or Hagen. To explore the ramifications of this I suggest that this 'lack' may be connected with another 'lack' in Reite ethnography – namely, clear lineality. That the presence or absence of substantial connections to maternal and paternal groups is made clear in the image of bodily make-up, and that such imagery is a function of lineality, we might accept as canons of Melanesian ethnography on kinship and clanship (e.g., A. Strathern 1972).; but the notion that the privileged position of the mother's brother follows from the recruitment principles of groups, dates from an earlier period of anthropological debate.

Women and Place

Women move between places. What does the 'lack' of lineality mean for their position? If they are not thought to be 'between' lineages, then are they conceptualised as 'between places'? Does this in turn result in a permanent peripherality to palem? Bolton has recently elaborated the particular and different (gendered) relation that women and men have to place on the island of Ambae in Vanuatu. She suggests that Ambae women may not stay on land, but by bearing children 'to' the land, they exist in an intimate relation to place also (Bolton 2002). This suggestion is worth pursuing in the context of Reite.

In more than one instance, Gillian Gillison (1987, 1993) takes up Lévi-Strauss's notion of the 'atom of kinship', focusing on the same nexus of relationships that I have identified in Reite – between child, mother, mother's brother and father, and explores its usefulness in understanding Gimi affinal exchanges. What Reite people call payments for bones (*matopo/wimbiyung kimeret*), Gimi call 'head payments':

> A woman remains affiliated to her *ababana*, her father and other paternal kinsmen, all her life, but her brideprice compensates for their loss of her as a wife... Each time she bears a child, their loss is renewed and compounded.... Head payments, as Gimi explain, are a repetition of the brideprice: 'we pay for a wife, then when she bears a child we pay her M and F *again* for the head. First her brother eats the brideprice and then each time she has a child he eats it again!' (Gillison 1993: 53/54, original emphasis)

The crucial relationship for Gimi, Gillison suggests, is between the son-in-law and his wife's father. This, as is clearly seen in Gillison's approach to the apparent exclusion of women in exchange, or the Gimi approach to identity, assumes a different core (to Reite) from which identity is reckoned – that being, for Gimi, men's exchange relations. She writes:

> Before marriage, a woman functions, like her brother, as an object of exchange, as one in whose name and on whose behalf her father presents head payments to her mother's brother. But once a woman marries, she drops out of circulation among men: her daughter and son replace her and her brother as the impetus of payments from her husband to her brother. A woman is 'killed' at marriage, punished for her mythic desires in the sense that she is no longer an object of exchange between her father and her mother's brother, no longer a child the two men continually transact to life, and that unlike her brother, she does not inherit her father's role as a donor of head payments. (Gillison 1993: xvi)

But if, as in Reite, a wife and her husband form a productive unit of a sort which resembles siblings, yet produces children, then she is not 'killed' or excluded at all. Like a boy (whose bones are bought), she goes from being a *reason* for exchanges (marriage payments) to a constitutive part of that which *produces* reasons (children).

To be productive is to work in combination with a place. A hamlet that is known for producing a palem is a combined entity which hides and keeps hidden what is being grown/transformed; thus a man and a woman become a part of a palem and produce children, making a name for the palem. A wife is incorporated into a place because of her separation from another. The contribution she makes to the child is one of nurture and labour, but not of any substance she has brought with her. These things are generated by, and thus attributed to, a palem, a place. Her bridewealth recompenses those who have grown her. Women are no more 'killed' in marriage than are their brothers, and it seems to make more sense to think of them as altered and productively spliced with another, rather than 'killed'.

A man 'eats' (receives payment on marriage) his sister, not his sister's daughter in Reite, for he has already 'eaten' for the sister's daughter in the payment for her mother's body on marriage. Old men forsake the journey to receive pay for their sister's daughters, saying they have already eaten this, and send their sons instead, who as kinds of siblings do still have some claim, based on past support. Fathers do 'eat' for their daughters, but then the relationship is between the father and his daughter's husband, and the 'eating' removes the father, not the daughter, from the circle of exchange. He can no longer claim anything of hers, and her offspring are the business of his sons. These are some of the differences the incorporation of wives into palems, which organise a field of relations in the processes of production and reproduction, make.

One interesting contrast here is in generational involvement, and another is the interpretation of women as existing only as objects in men's exchanges. I would say that in Reite, a woman's identity, based on palem membership (as is that of her brothers or husband), is for the most part inseparable from her; hence the trauma

of marriage, and the rapid reincorporation into the new palem as part of that productive place (producing her own bridewealth from there). The severance with the
parental generation highlights this severance from her natal place, not her 'death'.
Reite women work with their husbands to pay for themselves, and to pay their
husbands' other obligations, as if they were one unit. They receive payments for
this man's sisters, for his sister's children and so forth also as one unit, and they
(husband and wife) work together to produce and provide wealth, garden food and
so forth for this hamlet's payments to others. 'Visibility' is never in a woman's
name – as is also the case in Gimi exchanges – but here the name is of the palem:
it comes from the land from which presentations are made, and this is what is
remembered. Memories are not of the names of men (which are secret in their
true form anyway), but of the names of places from which a palem emerges.
Women, both before and after marriage, are fully members of the palem that they
work to highlight – that they grow food and pigs for, that they dance and sing for.
As full members, they are buried in the land in that place; thus they have the name
of the place and work for its appearance and visibility.

Visibility and Recognition

The payments made to the mother's brother can be understood by thinking in
terms of what I am calling 'visibility'. That is, about the emergence of a socially
effective, temporally sequenced, whole person who is visible, as such, to others. As
an affine, the mother's brother's palem provided a sister/wife and in doing so,
recognised the power of the father to define and extract a person from them. This
amounts to a recognition of visibility, of power to make themselves apparent as a
particular thing (a desirable person/place, a man). In turn it defined, for this palem
group, the status of another palem (the wife-givers). This process of mutual recognition, and thus definition, continues into the next generation. For the child, the
mother's brother provides a kind of containment, from which, again, there emerges
a social entity. Through his work, a child's development is directed, and also *recognised*. The mother's brothers register the child's emergence into adulthood.

In order to illustrate the effect of recognition, and the potential implications for
movement, gender, and exchange, I end with a description of the final moments of
a night of singing and dancing (*sare*). This kind of performance is called *tambaran
singsing* in Tok Pisin, as it utilises the musical water-dwelling spirits (*kaapya tupong
yara*) of the male cult. The voice of the *kaapu neng* (mother tambaran) are the cen-
trepiece of the performance. Tambaran performances work as love-magic. On
certain occasions, palem have the right to take their spirits and perform in another
hamlet. Both men and women travel to the host hamlet, although separately.
While men hide the paraphernalia of the spirits in their midst, and accompany
their voices with singing and on drums, the women of the performing hamlet circle the male dancers and lift their voices in accompaniment.[20] It is the finale of one

of these performances that I describe. They are said to move people, make them feel emotion, and thus make the performers visible, present in the thoughts and regard of the audience. This effect carries an obligation to compensate the audience, those who have been emotionally disturbed. Those made to recognise the dancers and their spirits, and feel desire or empathy for them, consider this an imposition. This may be taken as evidence of the importance of social visibility, and of the ambiguous effects it is perceived to have on others.

Moving People

The crowning moment of a *sare* performance in Reite (and its surrounding hamlets) is when the sun rises on the dancers. It is a time of deep emotion. The light of the rising sun brings colour back into a grey world, where for hours there had been just noise and movement. Suddenly the grey-black of the body of the tambaran,[21] and of the satellite women circling them, becomes pink, red, and then a myriad of yellows, oranges, reds and greens as the flower and leaf decorations of the dancers, the paint on the *torr* posts and the brilliant red croton leaves on the *mangmang* (housing of the *torr*) come to life. At dawn the *maal* (lit. genital covering) of the *kaapu neng* is secreted to the *passae* (spirit house) so it is not revealed by the morning light, and men join in a group, facing each other and lifting their voices in the songs of the spirits they have watched over and sung with during the night. The joy of the dawn, and the relief that the exertions of the preparations, decoration, and dancing are over, give rise to happy smiles and songs sung with gusto. Women who may have been fading into the watchers, sitting nursing infants around the constantly burning fires at the edge of the dancing, rejoin their lines and circle the men again, lifting their voices in the song.

It is at this moment that people cry. It is said that the sun turns their insides towards the dancers, they are swept with emotion and lose control. There is a quality to any dawn seen after being awake all night, and a relief to see a new day beginning. But where the tambaran has been, there is also an accumulation of exertion, of tiredness, and of having been involved in an extraordinary and exquisite discharge of energy. This leaves an open feeling in the torso, as if the winds of the world could blow through one. One is tearfully grateful, like a child, that the winds are kind ones, that the sun is warm and the world and its inhabitants are beautiful and brilliant. This was my spontaneous response to the dawn on every such day that I witnessed.

For people in the hamlets of Reite, this moment is an opportunity to practise *Kaapya tangawakting* (the spirits [*kaapu*] cause crying/wailing [*tangawak*] to occur). While mixed grief and joy is the response I experienced from a night with the tambaran, Reite people anticipate this moment and seek to enhance it through magic. If successful, people show their emotion by following a palem group home (*nuking tangawei apiting*, [those whose] inside's cry, come). *Kaapya tangawakting* is when the dancing group works to achieve this effect through special activities at the time the spirits are brought from their dwelling places in *tupongting* (spring-pools. lit. 'water shoot/eye'). Particularly at risk from this kind of magic are those who have denied the power of the visitors – nothing brings a response here like denigration of a place's power.

However, the knowledge for *kaapya tangawakting* is used sparingly. As Gayap Makon used to joke with me, making people feel for you is all very well, but it must be paid for. Gayap used to temper his enthusiasm for telling me stories of the tambaran's power with seriousness (not the usual tone for talk about the tambaran),[22] saying that this technique is not used much because Reite people were tired of losing large quantities of wealth. At this point, it is these payments for moving people which I want to bring to the reader's attention.

When the sun has risen fully and the singing is finished, the kaapu eats for the last time, and when ready, word is sent to women from the visiting hamlet. They set off ahead of the men who follow with the kaapu, crying as it moves through the bush, and accompanied by the men on their hourglass drums (*pariwah*). At each road junction, and along the paths, the kaapu leaves signs of its progress: flowers and croton (*ringe*) leaves from the decorations of the men. Anything they see on the way home – betel nut or bananas, for example – the tambaran can leave croton leaves at the base of, and it will be sent after the kaapu by the owner. Thus the route of its progress to its own lands is marked. Other things also follow the tambaran home.

Now it is said that any *birua* woman (from the host hamlet) who cries will follow, and that those who follow the kaapu will not leave again. Kaapu can make a woman obsessed with a man. If a woman follows the dancing group home, it is correct for the men of that palem to try and placate her – turn her insides again, as they put it – with gifts of wealth and clothing. Sometimes these gifts are enough to make her leave. If she still wishes to stay, however, people meet and discuss the possibility of her marriage to one of the men in the hamlet. I was given evidence of cases where this resulted in a woman marrying a man other than the one who had performed the rites to make people follow. A palem's members are in this sense 'one man'. The in-marrying woman comes to a place and a group rather than to an individual.

Men who follow must also be paid before they will leave.[23] Betel nut and drinking coconut (*taka turing*) are given first. Dogs' teeth, pigs' tusks, loincloths, wooden plates, and clay pots (collective: *palieng*) are gathered and presented to the newcomers with plates of garden food. '*Em nau, bai nogat wari, yu baim aiwara na lekpen bilong ol pinis, nau ol bai hamamas tasol.*' (T.P.: There now, they will not have emotion/worry, you have bought their tears and paid for their painful feet [from following you], now they will be happy.) While it is the tambaran itself that draws marriageable women, and causes emotion, it is the performance of additional power that causes unmarriageable people physically to follow (*kaap tupong koker'eta sariken ai tangawakit apiting* – 'spirits water washing, sing/dance men cry come').

Reite people are explicit that the payments that are made are for moving people. *Yu lukim singsing timbuna bilong mipela, na yu wari i stap. Mipela mas baim yu long ol pe bilong timbuna long disela as* (you see our ancestor's/ancestral singing/dancing and you are anguished. We must pay you with wealth for this reason.) The metaphor of 'movement', as a way of describing emotion or pleasure, is unambiguous in Reite. It describes not only what people feel, but what they are caused to do by this feeling – physically uproot themselves and come to throw themselves on another's hospitality. Though it seems that part of the payment is for the physical movement, tears are also paid for – internal movement, and its consequences – have to be acknowledged as if they were of detriment to those moved. Reite people perceive the removal of women from their natal hamlet and siblings as an act of violence as we have seen. There is a conjunction between aesthetic effect, and violence done to the emotions, also reported from elsewhere in Papua New Guinea. This has a lot to do with what aesthetic forms evoke. In Reite, crying during a kaapu performance by older people is often because the person has been reminded by the spirit voice of someone deceased, who in the past was associated with this spirit. These people will also follow to be near the spirit of the deceased, and extract wealth in compensation for their anguish.

In his ethnography of the Kaluli *gisaro* ceremony performed around Mt. Bosavi, Schieffelin (1976) describes a violent response by those who see themselves coerced into a painful memory of their dead relatives, by dancers who enact the spirits of those who have died. Anger seems an understandable response as Schieffelin contextualises it, and in my description of marriage I have tried a similar contextualisation of the response of siblings to the loss of part of sibling set. In *gisaro* too, people are paid for being 'moved'. Violence is a response for the pain of emotional disturbance. Gifts are made by those who have caused emotion to those thus affected. In addition to the violence they cause, the dancers give their emotional victims wealth in compensation. Simon Harrison notes the ambiguous nature of aesthetic production more widely in Melanesia. He writes that:

> The notion of capturing or exercising power over another person's spirit is a fundamental model for a whole range of transactions experienced as aggression or domination: killing, cursing, blessing, bewitching, or arousing strong and disturbing emotions such as desire.
>
> My point is that it is also the model for what we would call 'aesthetic' experience. (1993: 123)

Reite *sare* has the kind of aesthetic impact on an audience which Harrison draws attention to. 'Acts having this highly-charged aesthetic impact on others are experienced as aggressive assaults on their emotions' (ibid.).

The practices surrounding *kaapya tangawakating* show clearly that people are thinking payment must be made for things other than loss of substance. As Gell writes for Kaluli and their neighbours, '"Sociality" in Foi and Kaluli terms, is crucially bound up with the demonstration of sympathy' (1995: 251). The payments between affines, and then between a MB and his sister's children ensure the growth of a child. In working to achieve this growth, the MB ensures the future effectiveness of that person. This carries dangers, or if danger is too strong a word, then we should say it leaves members of his palem open to the potential of being moved and dominated. The child is given power by their MB. A sister's child is a person in whom the MB both has an interest, and yet is differentiated from. In organising their growth and witnessing of power in kaapu and other activities, the relations with maternal kin make a person whole. The interpretative extension I see is to say that the payment is also in anticipation of what the person so developed will be able to do with this knowledge. Payments then are for work, and for the potential future made possible by this work.

* * *

Theories in the literature about the importance of the mother's brother turn on the notions of recruitment and substance. I have argued that recruitment is not at issue for Reite people since children belong unambiguously to their place of residence. Further, I have argued that the issue of substance is misleading in this case, as there is no internal division imagined in a person's make-up between maternal and paternal substance. This clearly relates to the apparent lack of lineality in Nekgini sociality. If bodies are assumed to be the products of places, substance is provided through the nurture and labour of those resident in these places. Male landholding makes this look like a form of patrilineality. And it is, except that the continuity is in placement and work, not internal specification/identity. Such an assumption forms the basis for a genealogical model of kinship. In Reite, maternal/affinal kin have the role of containing and directing the growth of the child. This role is exactly the role of one who gives social identity by providing boundaries to the form in which a person appears. Form is specified externally, as it were, by the perspective others take on the person viewed, and what they can elicit from them.

In Nekgini practice, one does not exchange with one's own people, with one's siblings. Siblings are in a relation of sharing whereby connection is daily made apparent. Where there is no exchange, there is no position to view, no perspective which can be gained on parts of the self. Herdt highlights a version of this idea, albeit referring to a time long past:

> What would it be like to have lived your whole life without ever having seen your own face? Think on that for a moment. One can see the products of one's labour in gardens or hunting, or see one's trappings – clothes, exuviae (fingernails, hair, spittle), and waste products (faeces, urine). But one cannot fully see what Westerners call the 'self', the primary referent of which is our face. Sambia *see themselves only in the responses of others*: smiles, body posture, grimaces, gestures, interactions. (Herdt 1999: 54, original emphasis)

Whether one has a mirror or not, *recognition* of achievement is gauged by the reaction of others: '[s]ocial action itself consists in "presentation"' (Strathern 1988:

189). Thus the self can be known by what others are willing to give in return for a child, a body, or a wealth item. The mother's brother, already made distinct by his loss of a sibling to the father, provides this perspective on a child's growth. Each affinal payment has a logical position in a developmental sequence whereby a child moves from total containment to visibility as an active social person (producing from the land). The development of a social identity is based on the premise that someone will incur a future loss, future separation, because of these achievements. Thus the payment is also for a kind of nurture or labour which the father and mother cannot provide. 'Things must appear so as to elicit recognition from others.... Relations, ... are thereby reified in the manner in which they are differentiated from one another' (Strathern 1988: 298). The separation between the two kinds of nurture is that between growth, and containment/recognition. Both are necessary to the emergence of a person. The type of work is definitive of the respective positions (maternal or paternal kin).

Notes

1. 'You should do all these things for your first-born child. If you have skill in pig husbandry, and you want to become a respected leader, you can line up these payments for all your children. If not, then not. If you do, you will gain immense knowledge of making kastom and become a leader (*topi*).'
2. 'The work of the uncle determines what kind of person is grown.'
3. Support in material wealth, organisation, and knowledge of how to make a successful palem.
4. Siriman is acknowledged by his elder brother Urangari to have "gone first" even though he was born second. In part this stems from Siriman's close association with Yali Singina, whose influence on local thinking and practice of kastom persists. Cooking pigs for Yali and for other kastom work positioned Siriman as *topi*, or a leader who carries a gourd lime container and whose position is based on his generosity and popularity.
5. It is partly the handling of this rubbish (*samu*) that is the basis for small payments (*kalawa*) by the mother and father to the birth attendants (always senior women).
6. A more typical payment now has added a length of trade store cloth and between 2 and 10 kina cash.
7. cf. Gillison (1993), on Gimi of Eastern Highlands.
8. The way initiation is talked of in Reite.
9. I remind the reader that the palem in this instance refers to the raised platform on which taro is piled, decorated with yams, bananas and betel nut, beneath which a pig is tied, and a coconut mast erected. This use of palem, or in fact the use of palem to mean kin group, is wholly consistent, as kin groups are said to be those which make a palem together. Where a palem is constructed, the spirits (kaapu) of those lands from where the labour and produce to build it has been drawn is present, and the kaapu itself lays the foundations for the taro bed, and for the coconut mast. The making of a palem, as I will show in Chapter 6, is the moment *par excellence* of the efforts Reite people make to show themselves and their places of origin as social entities.
10. It is remarkable that the word for mother's brother is the same among the Iatmul of the Middle Sepik (Bateson 1958 [1936]).
11. I leave the Tok Pisin word 'tambaran' untranslated in this man's account so the reader may see how it was used in Reite in the 1990s.
12. In most cases the task of 'watching over' the initiate would be performed by a young cross-cousin, perhaps the son of the mother's brother who would be named in the later payment. In this case,

because of the requirement that the carer also give up drinking fluids, the boy to be chosen for this task was too young, and left the initiate to the care of his own brothers.

13. Pomo *mundutor*.

14. Although not mentioned in this particular account, the named MB may make a return for this *rawirawi* payment – of coconuts, money, and valuables, and even of a small pig if he is so inclined. Making such a return frees him from the responsibility of contributing to the man's bridewealth payment, or other payments he may be called upon to help with. In many instances, a man's MB will help with his obligations anyway, but the desire to make a balance in all matters of pig exchange remains a priority, in order that no one may say of the maternal kin – 'they just eat pig for nothing' (i.e., provide no tangible evidence of their relationship by making a return).

15. If I sound coy here, it is to preserve the secrecy of the event.

16. The same as the name given to the rattle-bracelet of dogs teeth which is a child's first decoration.

17. My thanks to James F. Weiner for discussions of this material.

18. The schemes are homologous because they are whole systems with the same internal differentiations, thus thought to be 'the same' in all but their interpretation.

19. Interestingly (although not unexpectedly) claims on children seem highly dependent on location and co-residence. Thus in marriage, a man's sister moves to her husband's lands, and from there works to pay for her own body. Her children thereafter, with more or less help from their parents, use this land to produce their own body payment. In the one instance I am aware of where a woman became pregnant without this movement, the child unambiguously belonged to her natal hamlet. He was given land by his MBs. Body payments were given to maternal kin from another hamlet, thus making his MBs as F to him in all practical respects.

20. A sample of *kaapu neng* performance by Reite villagers may be heard as track 10 on the CD accompanying Leach (1999).

21. The group of male dancers is called 'the tambaran' because they both hide and embody the spirits.

22. Although spirits are both dangerous and powerful, men tend to laugh when mentioning them.

23. There are examples in contemporary Reite of men who have been drawn from other palem and stayed. These men were eventually paid for 'like women'.

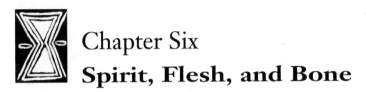

Chapter Six
Spirit, Flesh, and Bone

The Palem as a Body

I have outlined a process which generates and regenerates bodies as recognised social entities. Processes of differentiation, growth, and emergence culminate in exchange. The process of creating these bodies organises the productive efforts of persons and generates named social groups. As Wagner says of Daribi:

> the elicitation of social collectivities by indirect means is more than a mere rhetorical device among the Daribi; it is a style or mode of creativity that pervades a whole range of their activities. (1974: 108)

The culmination of my description, and perhaps of Nekgini social life, returns us to the notion of the palem.

The activities of the *kaapu*, (tambaran), are central to this description. Reite people repeatedly cautioned me against revealing the objects, form, or activities that constitute the physical presence of the kaapu. In deference to their wish I make my description as full as possible without at any time telling the reader of the mechanics of the performances. There are published sources where an interested reader may find out more about Rai Coast tambaran performances (Lawrence 1965; Niles 1992; Reigle 1995). My position on this issue is clear. It is not for me to present information, even in a form unlikely to be seen at the present time by Rai Coast people, on an aspect of Nekgini people's practice which they consider powerful *because* it is hidden. Tambaran performance is part of contemporary life, integral to the process of making persons as I outline. It includes innovative aspects, while conforming to *kastom*. In other words, it is very much 'alive'. In this book I present the tambaran in the way it is presented in public speech in the hamlets of Reite. I hope that readers will tolerate the use of euphemism in order that, as an ethnographer, I can keep faith with Reite concerns.

Photograph 13 *Sarangama Receive a Palem from Asang, 1999*

Palem as Platforms for Taro

When people make specific payments to affines (Chapter 5), they construct a palem (Chapters 1 and 2). In this sense, a palem is literally the platform on which taro is piled and wealth displayed. In contributing to the construction, people become 'a palem'. A palem is constructed anew for each and every affinal presentation, but is only accepted by the recipients if the payment given is for a body.[1] A palem (the group who construct the platform 'at their door') is named after the piece of land on which the platform is built, and the platform may only be constructed at the very door of the person who is making the payment.

The gathering of wealth, garden food, labour, and meat for the staging of an affinal payment in the form of a palem, is a serious undertaking. The construction of a palem crystallises for a moment peoples' affinities, connections, and separations along a simple divide between members and supporters of a kin group who make a payment for a body, and the receivers of this payment. Each time a palem is made, a different crystallisation of kin relations is likely. In many cases that I have recorded, those who qualify as both affines and cognates choose which side to join on the basis of past exchanges.

Significantly, all other residents of the hamlet that make a palem are classed as 'one door' with the maker of a palem; thus the structure is at their door also. Non-co-operation in palem construction by members of a hamlet would almost certainly lead to the break-up of the hamlet. It would imply a dangerous lack of unity and sympathy. Hamlet members are not only 'one door', but become 'one palem' through their part in the production of the presentation. Their future identity, and that of their children, remains that of the palem in which they reside until they move away and are involved in the construction of a palem on another named piece of land. Memories of past support ensure that when people do move, they consider themselves adding and transforming relations, not removing them.

Palem are constructed on specific occasions, and to be given to specific affines; therefore each member of any hamlet gives wealth to different people from the named palem site. It is not unusual for obligations within a hamlet group to cross-cut one another, thus people often choose whether to help kin in other hamlets making a palem, or to receive wealth from it, even though their own siblings and co-residents may choose the opposite. Those living together produce a palem on their hamlet site, but in the context of subsequent exchanges made beyond their residence this palem *konaki* (single palem) may well divide, and some members help others to make their palem on another site with gifts of food and labour; while other members go to the presentation on the side of the receivers.[2]

Male landholding and virilocal marriage result in hamlet sites, and therefore palem sites, that do not necessarily change rapidly. It is both acceptable and in many ways preferable to use the *passae* and hamlet site of one's father. Without rigidity in their recruitment, palem often have histories of many generations; but the history is one of a site that gives its name to those regenerating a palem there, not of a lineage.

One will often find a palem on the borders between lands owned by the members. Ideally, people who are 'one door' co-operate in everyday tasks and share garden food. They may garden different land, but bringing its produce back to the 'one door' (especially contributing to the production of a single body when a gift to affines is made) makes them appear as one entity (hamlet), as of one place. The image of being from 'one door' may be taken further. The offspring of residents of the same palem are siblings by definition. They emerged from the same body. Hamlet members share enclosed spaces such as the *passae*. It is this appearance of coming from one place which is most pronounced when a hamlet dramatises its position and existence through the ritual cycle which leads up to, and produces it, as a named palem.

An Assemblage of Body Parts

Learning about the activity of making a palem, called *turum maliemung* ('gathering everything'), was one of the most satisfying moments of my conversations with Reite people. One can see the old palem structures like high tables in different states of decay when one walks through most hamlets. They do not look impressive in this state, yet I was curious as to their use. The answer to my questions – that these are what one piles taro on in a marriage payment – was, as many answers seemed to me during fieldwork, both accurate and yet incomplete. It was not until near the end of my first long stay that I found myself sitting up on one of the high platforms, outside the house of Palota Konga, one evening in Sarangama hamlet. We were waiting for, and then eating, a supper of taro. Palota and I talked with Porer Nombo, Nangu, and his father Winedum, about what I was using for a bench. To see us all so animated was a pleasure I have not forgotten. These men seemed to feel, as did I, that the fact we could bring together so much of what they called kastom by talking about the palem was a justification for all the work we had completed together. Yet it was a surprise to us all. I am not offering it as evidence. Yet the happiness of these men with the kind of conjunction and explanation that social anthropology makes as the basis of its understanding was deeply satisfying.

The palem consists of a platform built around one metre from the ground. It has a top surface of about four square metres. Four upright posts carry cross-beams, onto which split palm-boards are lashed to make a table-like surface. A bamboo pole is placed vertically in the centre of the table. It stands a couple of metres above the platform's surface. This pole is called *wising wimbing* (backbone). Sticks are lashed to the tops of the leg-posts, extending them upwards, and to these uprights, a loose frame of smaller boughs is tied with vines (*kawarieng*). This frame fences the table-top on three sides, leaving only the front open. A roof made from sago palm thatch may be raised over the platform.

To the immediate right of the front of the platform is erected a mast – a straight wooden pole which can be 15–20m high. Coconuts are tied around this mast in a pile, rising as high as possible (with the coconuts available) from the ground. Within the body of the basic structure, a pile of taro is made, supported by the

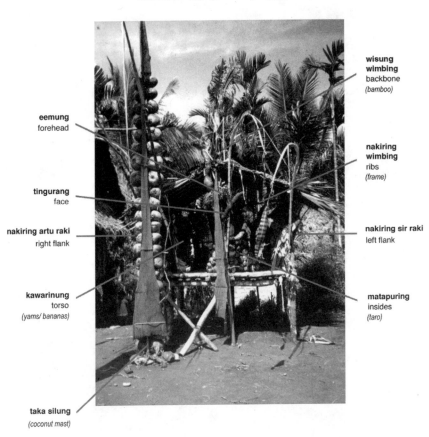

Figure 6.1 Turum maliemung: the palem as body parts
turum maliemung - gather everything together

eemung
forehead

tingurang
face

nakiring artu raki
right flank

kawarinung
torso
(yams/ bananas)

taka silung
(coconut mast)

wisung
wimbing
backbone
(bamboo)

nakiring
wimbing
ribs
(frame)

nakiring sir raki
left flank

matapuring
insides
(taro)

Figure 6.1 Turum Maliemung: *The Palem as an Assemblage of Body Parts*

central bamboo pole (*wising wimbing*). Taro is piled in a particular order beginning with taro *kapa iuing* (the first strain of taro). As with other aspects of the construction, building the pile is the work of the tambaran.[3] The man making the presentation must place certain leaves in the base of the bamboo pole called the 'backbone', and as he does this, he must entice Mai'anderi to enter the structure by calling her name. He then departs, and the tambaran piles other taro tubers around the central bamboo. Long yams, bananas, and sugar-cane are supported on the frame around the edge of the table, to which they are lashed. Betel nut branches festoon the outside of the frame, and bark cloth is hung from the mast and the roof beams. When those who are to receive the payment arrive, a pig is brought forth and, ideally, tied to the legs of the structure.

Photograph 14 *Winedum of Sarangama*

Porer, at first doubtful in his answer to my question as to whether one could see the taro pile as a body, began thinking it through by telling the myth of Mai'anderi (Chapter 4). As he told the story he became more interested in the fact I had asked about the construction in this way. In the myth, Mai'anderi fills her belly with taro. Moving to a new place, she gives birth to the tubers as if they were her children, and lays them on a bed of the kind I was perched upon. Porer said they are told to think of this *patuki* when they construct a palem, and also of the bed as a strong woman who carries the taro. Taro, as Mai'anderi's child, is the 'inside' the structure. Thinking of the way yams are used to surround the taro pile, Porer suggested that they were the other body parts, the bananas which are hung from a structure of sticks around the edge of the bed were flesh, and the betel nut branches were skin. He pointed out that as with a body, as with skin, paint is applied to the surfaces of the garden food, and it is decorated with (bark) cloth.

Armed with this idea, we questioned the others present, particularly Winedum, the oldest and most knowledgeable man in any of the Nekgini hamlets.[4] He named for us the parts of the structure:

wisung wimbing	– backbone (bamboo pole by which taro pile is supported).
matapuring	– insides (the taro pile).
kawarieng	– torso (yams [kawundet – to surround, or close off]).
nakiring wimbing	– side bones/ribs (frame).
nakiring artu raaki	– right flank.
nakiring sai raaki	– left flank.
sakareng	– back.
pakuping	– chest.
yamentaming eemundaki	– open front (face).
eemung	– forehead.
taka silang	– mast with coconuts tied around.
passae nareng	– decoration (meat hung on a frame) for the men's house.

As can be seen from these names, the structure is clearly imagined as an assemblage of body parts. With his son Nangu, Winedum recounted a myth attributed to the area around Madang town in which a woman gave birth to a yam. The tuber was cleaned and prepared, and once planted, grew. He said that in Reite, it was taro to which a woman had given birth. In Reite myth, it was a man who put the taro on a bed and dealt it out. They made the specific connection between this man dealing taro out, and the way they dealt (female) children out from their hamlets. (I reported this indigenous connection between the movement of women in marriage, and the spread of taro tubers to new places, in Chapter 4.) The pig could be seen as *mak* (Tok Pisin – 'standing for') a body, he said, and the taro is what is in the belly of a mother – it too has the potential to grow children. Winedum emphasised the containment of the taro pile – *matapuring* (the inside)[5] – by the structure which surrounds it. The mast of coconuts, which must stand right by the bed, could be the man (who deals the taro), Porer commented. Then one would have the bed with taro as the inside of a body, the pig tied beneath as replacement flesh and bone, and the mast as the donor of the child.

Obviously pleased we were catching on to something he already understood, Winedum then told us how the *tingurang* (eyes and nose) of each coconut tied to the mast must face the front because '*taka em olsem man*' (coconuts are like a man). The original coconut palm was a man, and when you raise the mast, it is as a man, to which coconuts are tied,[6] and the pig fastened. The mast is a man, and the bed is a woman.

Wising wimbing, the bamboo in the centre of the taro pile, is what keeps the whole palem strong, he said. The same bamboo is kept after a payment for a wife, and will be used again to support the payment for the child. 'This has strength or power. Like a man putting a child in a belly has power. It is this strength which makes the taro pile stay together until the receivers come and break it up to take away. It is like the strength given to a child. If there is a dispute or anger among the parties, this will make the taro [pile] collapse. The same as a child – which will die in the womb [in similar circumstances].'

> *Ol save tingim man, na meri bai sindaun klostu long en. Na ol narapela bai kam na kisim hap skin bilong en na karim i go kaikai. Mipela sa'tok* matapuring rataopinaetung – *kisim namel bilong en na kaikai. Ol bai kaikai skin bilong mipela nau, na ol brata bai no inup kaikai. Stat long taro i go olgeta long pik – makim stret skin bilong mipela na givim.* (Winedum, 6/95)

'They think of a man, and a woman placed close by. And others will come and take some of their body and carry it away to eat. We say *matapuring rataopinaetung* – take the insides/centre and eat. They will eat our body now, and our siblings cannot eat. Beginning with taro and going all the way to pig – [we] make a faithful representation of our body and give it [away].'

The mast to which the coconuts were tied is taken down after the event. It is broken up for firewood, and this wood is used to make a fire on which meat is cooked for the tambaran a man has called upon to erect the mast, and line it with coconuts. As Winedum explained:

> You do not use the platform to cook with – everything has been removed from it. But the man; his bones are still there, and the man making the presentation will use these bones to make a present to the men and spirits of his own land who worked hard to help him in his work.

He went on:

> when the tambaran piles taro for you [for your presentation to affines], and when the tambaran erects the coconut mast, you *may not* watch this procedure. You must hide.

Why? Because they are making you. They are faithfully making your body and you cannot watch. This is the plan of *patuki*. You make this work first for your mother's brother, and later when you have a wife you will stand as if you were [a] tree while they [affines] come and take. A girl child will do this same work for her mother's brother, and later her brothers will come and take and eat her.

In the description given by Winedum (which ends here), there is a clear identification between the person who gives the presentation, the produce they give, and a physical body. The need for seclusion while a body is formed is emphasised, as is the idea that each aspect of the construction is a person – the bed is constructed to be a woman (yams, bananas, betelnut) with taro as her insides, the mast to be a man made of bones (wood) and meat or 'heads' (coconuts). A pig is given as a replacement body of another kind – one made of edible flesh and blood. The names of the parts of the construct show clearly that it is an effigy which is put together.[7] Yet Winedum also draws attention to the fact that some things remain after the removable and consumable parts of the bodies have been stripped away. This is significant in my analysis.

The two items left when the palem has been stripped by the receivers are both called *wimbing* – bones. These items are the mast around which coconuts were piled and the backbone of the taro. The first is used to transform raw meat into food edible by spirits, the second to heap taro around in a future presentation. One might say they both strengthen or add rigidity to bodies.

The person in whose name the palem is made must feed their supporters and tambaran with meat. This is provided by the receivers of the payment. Thus affines will bring a small pig, or wild game meat on a frame (roughly shaped like a pig) if they have no pig to give in return, when they arrive at the donor hamlet. This meat is placed at the door of the *passae* (tambaran house) to which they have been drawn. Garden food accompanying the meat will be laid on leaf mats beneath the meat. This present (*kalawung*) is called *passae nareng* (the decoration for the *passae*). It is commonly belittled as a small thing (*nek'kek'ek*) and insignificant. Yet it is required that the receivers help the donor in this way by providing payment for those who helped the donor with labour and their spirits. It is called a return payment, but has no significance in terms of future debts between the parties.

It seems aesthetically satisfying to me (a moment of closure or completion) that this meat is cooked using the strength (bones) that a man claims to himself, and which are not exchangeable (the coconut mast is broken up for this purpose). The image is clearly one of partible flesh, gendered as female where appropriate to the affinal relationship, and immovable bones, gendered as male mainly in that they stay put. The gendering of these items makes sense when one thinks of the payments as a return for products of a piece of land which are moveable – as women are moveable in marriage, and their inverse – products or aspects of a place which are not moved from their source, as are men. The gendering of the items at this point is not particularly significant. The aesthetic of gender as a whole, however, is central.

The work of the tambaran as an agent of growth does not end in the garden. The decoration of the hamlet, the construction of the palem and the power to draw affines to the exchange is all within the work of the tambaran. The final throw of the event is when the tambaran itself is foregrounded in dancing. *Pununung* is essential to feed the spirits through all this work. My interpretation is that the tambaran itself amounts to an aspect of a place; that along with designs and land, it is like the bits of the structure which are not removed – the 'bones' of a place. Reite people go so far as to describe *mundutor* (spirit places) as 'the bones of the land'.

Relations with Spirits

For a man and his wife who wish to produce an affinal payment in the form of a palem, their first responsibility is to produce abundantly from garden land. Reite people rely on their knowledge of their lands, the names of taro deities (*pel-patuki*), and revealed procedures for ensuring the taro grows correctly, that it replenishes itself in the garden, tastes sweet, and so on (Chapter 4). People have few pigs here, and one pig is all that is required for an affinal payment (i.e., it is not the only item given). There ought to be dried marsupials and other hunted game given in these presentations, and also some left-over to feed a man's own tambaran when it is first called to the hamlet. Hunting successfully involves the knowledge of names, places and events in the land on which he hunts, and what Lawrence (1964: 17) describes as 'strict taboos on food and sexual relations'. Growing pigs likewise is accomplished speedily when a man has knowledge of esoteric names, procedures, and specific mythic places, from which substance for the pigs' growth is drawn.

When his garden is ready to be harvested, a man enlists the support of the kaapu which reside in pools, formed by springs in the limestone landscape. These spirits are summoned from their different pools on land owned by his close kin. They are brought to the hamlet *passae*, where they are kept out of sight of women. Kaapu actively contribute to the preparations for the palem from there. Their presence is known by their musical but eerie voices, and by the presence of the men of the cult who accompany them night and day on slit-gong (*kiramung*) and hourglass (*pariwah*) drums. While the kaapu are in residence, the owner of the production must keep them fed with meat. The tambaran moves around during the day, busy with preparations. It is sent to bring newly dug taro and yam back from the gardens, to cut the timber for the palem, and to erect the coconut mast. Surrounding hamlets hear of all this work. Everywhere the tambaran goes, the spirit voices call, warning women and children to hide themselves.

It is strictly forbidden for women to see the paraphernalia of the men's kaapu. They are sent to gardens to unearth taro, but then scatter at the approach of the tambaran, and hide in houses when the tambaran works on the palem. There are classes of female who do not count as women in this sense, however, and thus do not observe these restrictions. Girls prior to puberty have the same restrictions as boys before initiation. They may witness tambaran activity as long as they are not conscious of it as such. Women past menopause are free to see the tambaran. It is common in fact for old women to enter the *passae* to sweep in there. When I questioned a group of men about this, Urangari, a senior man, answered me in Tok Pisin – *ol man iya* – 'they are people'; undifferentiated by gender. It is the activities of the parallel tambarans which gender people who in turn grow others. Post menopausal women have moved into a stage of their life-cycle beyond this differentiation. They are not associated with women's tambaran, and thus fear nothing from the tambaran of men. They may see its paraphernalia with no detriment to the principle of differentiation through gender. The penalty for fertile women 'seeing the tambaran', it is told though, is swift and sure death for the whole hamlet group.

At each completed stage of the preparation, slit-gongs are beaten with signals announcing the achievement. Thus when the coconut mast is raised, the beat for coconut is repeated many times, the beat for taro when the taro is lined around the *wising wimbing*, that for pig when the pig is caught and tied up, and all of the above again in sequence when the construction is finished. Thus affines and receivers are made aware of the progress of the hamlet's tambaran, and are reminded of their obligation to come and receive the payment.

During all this the man who leads the construction of the palem (*nawang narwung*, 'foods father')[8] is taught the names (*paru*) of *patuki* and ancestors who allow the successful completion of each stage of the production, by older men. From the very outset in the garden, it is a man's knowledge of local names, myths, and animating spirits which allows him to grow the 'body' which is finally given away; and it is the ability of this man to call on the aid of his tambaran, or the spirits of his ancestors and the land in which he lives, which allows the production to take place.

Hirsch describes how Fuyuge people of Central Province construct ritual villages (*gab*) in which important life-cycle events take place.

> For the duration of the *gab*, the hosts, their supporters and the invited guests reside either inside the village, or outside in the vicinity. At any one time, only one *gab* is performed in the valleys of the Fuyuge. It thus becomes the focus of attention…. This is made visible by the many roads which are traversed and those which are opened up as the *gab* concentrates hundreds and even thousands of people within its space. (Hirsch 1994: 701)

Hirsch focuses on the roads (*enamb*) which bring the participants, wealth, and observers to the event, emphasising that 'each *gab* attempts to maximise the number of roads concentrating on its village space'. The Fuyuge chief 'facilitates an axis of centrality; the "holding together" strength manifest at the ritual centre' (ibid.: 702) in a way similar to the bringing together of spirits, people, produce, and exchange partners achieved in a palem production. Hirsch describes roads as idioms for 'denoting social action and agency' (ibid.: 698), emphasising the effect of drawing the Fuyuge social landscape together into a ritual space.

Reite people achieve the effect of drawing their productivity, their achieve-ments of growth, control over land and spirits, and their connectedness as kin, into a moment of revelation. This moment of 'holding together' is when husband and wife finally welcome their affines into their hamlet to receive payment, displayed as a palem. It is also the moment when the *nawang narwung* is aware how the pro-ductive unit he is part of is received. The man who organises the payment is the visible head of the persons and spirits which have produced this display. This is also a moment in which divisions between places are crystallised.

Ann Chowning, writing about Molima on Fergusson Island in the Massim, analyses funerary payments made between kin. She suggests that important divi-sions in Molima society are made operative through ideas of those who may handle the body of a kinsman on death, and those who may not. Those who may handle the body are paid for this service. Thus, in this cognatic society, despite the fact that

> [a]ll those with whom one regularly interacts, including one's spouse, are likely to be consanguineal kin… social divisions exist: affines do form a distinct group, though their distinctiveness may be modified by consanguineal links; the father's side is differentiated from the mother's side; the village is composed of exogamous hamlets; and above all, death brings about a rearrangement of all kin into two unlike categories. (Chowning 1989: 99)

There is a suggestion in Chowning's analysis that what is paid for by *valevaleta* (mourners) in making prestations to *geyawuna* (workers) is in recompense for help these people (who are also kin to the deceased) gave in producing the deceased as a person (as well as burying them). They cannot benefit from this work in any other context because of their consanguineal links to that person. In other words, though these kin helped that person reproduce, they cannot reproduce down this route themselves. Funerary exchanges in Molima thus make apparent differences between kin which do not appear in other contexts. Chownings' suggestions are pertinent for Reite (also described as 'cognatic'). The feasts a *nawang narwung* pre-pares for his supporters and kaapu recompense them for labour which does not open up new routes of exchange or affinity for them, but is reproductive for the palem as a whole, with him at the head.

Making One Body

In the hamlet of Sarangama a palem presentation was made to two separate groups of affines on a single day in 1994. Although it was more usual for a single presen-tation to be made by a hamlet, and a single palem to be constructed at one time, the payments made on this occasion provide illustrative evidence of the sociology of such exchanges. Both palem were prepared as payments for/by children to their maternal kin. The two men staging the payments were co-resident in the hamlet of Sarangama. One of the men, Palota, originated from a palem group called

Kumundung, physically proximate to Sarangama. Kumundung had come under the protection of Sarangama at some time early in the twentieth century when its population had been decimated. At this time they had moved from their own land to the hamlet occupied by Sarangama.[9] In 1994 there were only two adult brothers and their one sister who cited Kumundung as their origin. The elder of these brothers had recently returned to live on Kumundung land, while the younger of the brothers was resident in the hamlet of Sarangama. This younger brother (Palota) was the man making one of the palem that day (he was *nawang narwung*). It was not 'his' palem, however, but was made in payment for a young man long-resident in Sarangama (the *nawang saporung*). This young man, the eldest son of a Kumundung man who had died long ago, had been brought to live with the protectors of his father's kin – among them, Winedum – at Sarangama, following his father's death. Palota 'made' the palem in the sense of taking responsibility for the production, and organising the gathering of wealth and garden food on behalf of this younger Kumundung man, and his deceased father.

The other man responsible for a payment on this particular day was Nangu, the eldest surviving child of Winedum, one of the two old men who claimed Sarangama as their origin. He was making a payment for his third child, to a brother of his wife. The relation of the two men was distant. Along one route of reckoning, Palota was connected to Nangu as FMFBSDS; along another cited by Palota, Nangu was his MMFBSS. They practised name avoidance appropriate to cross-cousins. Yet the preparation for the palem they were to display was made together, pooling the resources of their lands and tambaran. Nangu's father, brother-in-law (by his sister's marriage), sister, and other members of Sarangama hamlet (his siblings) helped Palota with food, labour, and, in the case of the old man Winedum, invaluable advice about the procedure for palem construction. In parallel, Palota and his wife and brother rendered assistance to Nangu.

The receivers in this case were from two different *yating* (villages) – Sorang and Asang. The affines receiving these two payments, which were made on separate beds on either side of the *passae*, were distinct. They were not in any way considered 'the same' simply because of sharing the day of receiving a payment from Sarangama.

Now it was said that there was one tambaran (i.e., collection of men and spirits) responsible for the presentation of both palem and for 'pulling' the receivers to the exchange. This was the combined male labour and spirits of Sarangama and Kumundung. Though the presentation came from different kin within the hamlet of Sarangama, and though subsequent to the presentation, Nangu and Palota continued to practise name avoidance, their relationship from this time forward was as 'one door', one palem, *'palem konaki'*. To the receivers of the payments, their destination was the hamlet 'Sarangama', and they brought *pununung* (meat) to present to the Sarangama tambaran. Sharing the *passae* on this occasion intensified the kin connection between Nangu and Palota, and made them 'one door', joint-producers of the palem at Sarangama. It should be noted that they were also friends prior to this day, having grown up in close proximity.

In her description of *malangan* ceremonies in New Ireland, Suzanne Küchler describes how the 'ritual confederations' which arise through sharing land and sharing the memory of a carved image (*malangan*) do not depend on clan affiliation.

> The regulation of relationships over land, labour and loyalty is virtually independent of clan identity and marriage. It is articulated rather with participation in the mortuary ceremonies which climax in the production of sculptures. (Küchler 1992: 96)

People who share the memory of a carved image, presented on the death of a person, 'purchase' this right from the kin of the deceased. This occurs at a ceremony named after the generic term for the carved images themselves: *malangan*. Sharing the rights over reproduction of an image (that purchased at a *malangan* ceremony) gives rights over the land of the deceased. The confederation of persons with rights to reproduce this image share the land of which the image is the 'skin' (*tak*). Sharing land is the determining criteria for membership of these federations, as joint work on the land implies joint work for the dead, and is thus 'articulated' by the joint memory of the image which is produced at this time.

> The imitate relation between land and sculptured image is highlighted by the indigenous term for skin (*tak*) which applies to both…. Those who share land on account of sharing the memory of an image call each other 'of one skin' (*namam retak*). (Küchler 1992: 96)

Sharing land in Reite, and sharing the site from which payments (bodies) generated by this land are given away, make persons 'one door' to one another; one palem. There is a perception of a single source for the offspring of a place – a single container from which they emerge as they appear at the same door. This means that those who share a palem also share land – that is, substance. Palem are more than ritual confederations, they are confederations of a process in which connections to co-residents and supporters are dramatised through sharing of labour, food, and name, and separations from other places (affines) are demonstrated through the removal of a payment from an (apparently) singular source.

In both the Massim (Molima) and New Ireland cases cited above, death brings about a recognition of the placement of the living in terms of realignments and exchanges focusing on the deceased. In Molima, this is articulated through the avoidance of the hamlet and fruiting trees of the deceased by all those who mourn them. In New Ireland, confederations of those who share land are articulated by their rights to use a single image on the death of a kinsman.

In Reite, payments are made during life which *anticipate* the placement of the person on their death. Buying bodies and bones through the construction of a palem thus makes distinctions between affinal groups visible while persons themselves are still alive. These distinctions between kin become distinctions between places on the death of the person. Their remains can only be kept in one place. The kin connection that comes through sharing one place is deferred to the next generation (of persons who are siblings to one another through sharing the same source, substance, or placement).

One might say that the alignments of kin made in palem construction have future consequences which are 'articulated' (to use Küchler's term) by the placement of bones after death. Adding to a place through the power of bones makes the source of the offspring of that place all the more singular.

The Distribution of a Palem

People in Reite tell of how they used to remember important appointments by tying a series of knots in a piece of string (*gnalo*). A knotted string would be presented to the prospective receivers of a palem, and each night and each morning, they would untie one knot. Today, people do not bother with knotted ropes, but anticipation on both sides still builds to a crescendo. Affines enter the hamlet of the *nawang narwung* as a group, bearing their *kaiyung* (return payment). They are fed with garden food, and sit listening to the voices of the kaapu *simang* ('child spirits') from inside the *passae*. After preparation of the payments by the hosts, the man or woman named in the payment stands beside the palem and calls the names of each recipient in turn, placing their item of wealth – a wooden plate or bowl, dogs' teeth, pigs' tusks, bark cloth, clay pots, cash, cotton cloth, steel tools, aluminium pots – in their hands. In all the cases I witnessed, there was consultation between the two sides about how many receivers had arrived and who was to be given wealth items. As many of the donor's side in the exchange (those resident elsewhere) only arrive on the morning itself, their contributions to the payment are added to the pile at this point, and calculations are made as to who is to receive which items. Amounts to be given and the names to receive payment are now written in the backs of exercise books, where they remain as a record. The final name called is that of the principal recipient – the maternal uncle who has or will initiate a child, or the eldest brother of a woman given in marriage. The principal recipient is also handed wealth, but this time along with the rope of the pig, surrounded by shooting coconuts and branches of betel nut (*rawirawi*). In Reite it is usual for the principal recipient, at this point, to give some items of wealth they have brought themselves back into the hand of the donor, proclaiming loudly that they make a return for what they have received.[10]

Next the affinal visitors strip the palem of its garden food, women filling their string bags, while men tie the pig to a pole and strip the mast of its coconuts. It is vital for the recipient to strip the coconut mast with great vigour. In Kerimang's narrative in the Chapter 5, he was required to scale a tree in the Pomo *mundutor* to prove his ability in making ceremonial food. When stripping a palem as receivers, rising quickly up the mast, and rapidly removing the coconuts from the top downwards shows that one will not be bowed by the weight of what is received. Holding the name of the ancestor who parried a falling tree in *te tangaring patuki* in his head,[11] the recipient shows by his speed and strength that he will

Photograph 15 *Palota Strips the Mast of its Flesh*

not be crushed and will continue to achieve status through making palem in the future. The host hamlet gives an enormous roll on their slit-gongs, by which the recipients are 'chased' out. They run from the hamlet, whooping and shouting as they carry the pig, as if in a race, back to their hamlet. Women follow more slowly, with heavy bags of coconuts and tubers.

Next comes dancing (*sare*, or *sare'keiting*). Both sides cook their pigs, the donors feed their tambaran with plates of pork, while the recipients deal the food raw to all who have a claim to the body that has been replaced. Then the donors prepare themselves to take their tambaran and follow the recipients to their homelands and *te singap wanget* ('tread on the ashes': a reference to the cooking of their pig in the receiver's hamlet).

Although women move in marriage, men stay on the land of their fathers. Like the post of the coconut mast, or the backbone of the taro pile, they are stripped of their produce, of the bodies of sisters and children that have been grown on their lands and through their agency. The power to grow bodies, however, is not removed – the spirits of the *mundutor* (sacred groves) and *tupong ting* (spring pools), the voices of these spirits, the designs they inspire men to carve on their house posts and dancing head-dresses – remain. In certain circumstances permission to use these things may be given out; however they cannot be alienated from the land on which they originate. They are not consumable. As the strength of a place itself, they remain identified with that place and its people. It is men's ability to control and utilise this strength that they evince in the build-up to, and execution of, a palem construction. Knowledge of *patuki*, of *paru*, of *mundutor* and kaapu are how people demonstrate they belong to places, how they make connections between land itself and the substance it produces and grows. One conclusion we might draw from this ethnography is that bones *remain*. What is grown is partible; an aspect of it is always lost. Men move and are active, but they are anchored in places. Beyond the human lifespan something remains, and this is bones – and the bones of a place are its spirits and myths. They are a palem's potential to grow things and persons, and to attract others to this product. It is this final act, that of attracting others, which I describe below, and which brings us full circle to the gendering of persons and hamlet groups which I began describing in Chapter 3. I described the effect of emotions, and their quintessential moment, at the end of the previous chapter.

Spirit Voices and Dancing

[In what follows, the activities described are performed exclusively by initiated men, unless otherwise stated.]

The general designation kaap – spirit or ghost – covers the spirits which are called upon for aid in the construction of garamut, in the initiation of young men and women, and in the construction of a palem. These beings provide accompaniment (their voices) for *sare'keiting* (rhythmic movement of decorated dancers).

They also inspire words (in dreams or normal consciousness) to go with the tunes that are their voices, and designs to decorate each spirit's manifestation. Their most common manifestation is in the form of their voices, the production of which is the secret of the male cult. However, their influence may also be felt in sickness and death, and in crop growth or failure. Some even appear as actors in myth – the spirit in the taro myth of Samat Matakaring, for example, is 'tambaran'.

Such spirits are summoned from pools formed where a spring rises. They are known as *kaapu tupong yara* – tambaran of the water. Their voices are mystical presences, the basis for a kind of sacred music for Nekgini people. Thus they are central to the night-time performances in which these hamlets are adept.[12] Some of these spirits inhabit *tupong ting* (lit. water-eye) – spring pools – and are fetched from these pools when they are required by the men who control them.[13] Others 'reside' in other places: the sites of mythic happenings, or places where human bones are placed. All spirit places are called *mundutor*. Those specifically housing tambaran are called *kaap kung* (spirit hole). Pools formed by springs are called *tupong ting*, and it is from these pools that the kaapu are always summoned. All *mundutor* are perilous to enter unless you are 'known' to the spirits; one of what is sometimes referred to in Tok Pisin as their *bisnis* (which I translate as issue, or concern).

While there are other categories of spirit (*kaap sawing*, wild or bad spirit, *aignu kaap*, man's ghost, for example), within the designation *kaap* there are three principal *kaap tupong yarung* (water spirits) which are musical.[14] The first is *kaapu simang* – the 'tambaran child' – an eerie and resonant voice which can be heard many miles away. *Kaapu simang* are hidden within the *passae* or in forest clearings during initiation and garamut construction. They are not mobile, other than in the journey between the site of their pool, and the place where they are fed and housed for the duration of the time they stay with people.

The second musical spirit is *kaapu neng*, the 'tambaran mother'. This kaapu has a deeper, although also highly resonant, voice, with the quality of a drone. This kaapu is mobile, and is the tambaran used for dancing together with women, and for trips to other hamlets. As a mobile spirit, it can be concealed by a group of men in their midst, and thus not risk exposure. The third spirit, called *pfangaap kaap* (*pfakung*), has a breathy voice and is used inside the *passae* and in forest clearings. It was traded from kin to the west within living memory and is the only genre of kaapu which is owned exclusively by a particular palem.

Meat (or other *pununung* such as fish or eggs) must be provided when kaapu are called to come from their *tupong ting*. Not to provide adequate food for the tambaran invites sickness and rancour. The presence of the tambaran is judged by the quality and resonance of the music produced. It is a matter of shame on the part of a hamlet, and particularly its initiated men, if a tambaran performance goes badly. The possibility that the tambaran has not eaten well enough will be investigated first in such a case.

Kaapu tupong yara are brought from a spirit pool to the hamlet where they will perform only when they are required. Feeding the tambaran is a costly business in local terms. Men collect the *maal* (the loin cloth)[15] of the required tambaran from the *passae* (where they are ordinarily stored) at night, and set off carrying hourglass drums, green coconuts and betel nut branches. They also take red paint and variegated croton leaves to decorate the tambaran. Arriving at the pool, a senior man cuts a coconut open, leaves betel nut around it, and chews a little piece of an aromatic root (*manieng*)[16] known locally as 'fragrant ginger', which he spits over the pool. He calls the names of each tambaran that he wants to attend. The *maal* of each tambaran (mother, child and/or *pfakung*)[17] is washed in the spirit pool, and water is collected in a bamboo tube to keep the *maal* clean and refreshed throughout the performance. The *maal* is then decorated with the croton leaves and flowers. The betel nut provided for the tambaran is chewed by the men who are present, and a red mist blown from their mouths over the shells of the coconut and betel. The voices of the spirits are asked to make themselves present, each in turn, and over the next few hours all will declare their presence by a rendition of their voice. The group then sets off back to the site where the tambaran is required, keeping one or another of the tambaran crying out as they go. 'Child tambaran' will go straight into the *passae*, or forest clearing, until it is time for their return to their pools, while 'tambaran mothers' are usually taken straight to the hamlet in which they are to be performed. It is also possible to keep all kinds of tambaran in a *passae*.

Performing Places. People and Spirits as Land Made Mobile

Other preparations are made for the presence of the tambaran. When there is to be an outside performance of *kaapu neng*, particularly one in which the tambaran travels to another hamlet, perfume and special decorations are prepared for the event. This occurs in the *mundutor* of the spirits which are to accompany the men. It is these places, and the dreams or imaginings they are said to cause in those who spend time in them, which inspire the forms of the carved decorations called *torr*, and endow them, along with the perfumes prepared, with the power over those who see and smell them. In some cases, men are adept at hearing what is called in Tok Pisin *tok bilong graun* – the speech of the ground – and it is something akin to this which inspires designs and skill in the minds and hands of the men of this place (*nala kaaping* – earth spirit). As with the words or phrases that people sing to accompany a spirit voice, designs are not direct revelations in the understanding of Reite people, rather they are things people see in the lands they traverse each day, or in places which they enter to find spirits, things which they associate with the voices and power of each tambaran spirit. Thus *torr* carry designs such as a snake, often seen lying on the rocks near one spirit pool, or a blue-tailed lizard, named in the words of one tambaran song and known to frequent the *mundutor* of the spirit involved.

Perfume is made by cooking together certain barks, vines and flowers, gingers, and most potently, the secretion glands of a male cuscus. The vegetable matter is shredded into a piece of palm bark, the gland added, and the whole is then heated over a fire. Some plants have an effect as love-magic, and at times, perfumes will be made especially to be spat over the body of a man who has identified a desirable woman in the hamlet to be visited. Perfume in this case is an aspect of love-magic. Other perfumes are prepared merely to add an extra dimension to the performance to be staged by the hamlet and its spirits. Smell is thought important in many 'magical' endeavours undertaken by Reite people, including *sare* where the object is to 'move' people.[18]

Torr are carved posts, anything up to three metres long, which a single man carries on his head during the night of a *kaapu neng* performance. They are supported by an ingenious structure called a *mangmang*. This is made from a bamboo pole, split at one end to open like an umbrella, under which a frame is lashed, and which the dancer mounts on his back and shoulders. The base of the *torr* rests in the unsplit end of the bamboo tube and is thus supported vertically.

Photograph 16 *Sarangama Dancing Group Lit by a Flaming Torch, 2000*

Torr carry relief images of snakes, lizards, birds, fish, or in some cases items such as canoes or ships.[19] Under these raised carvings (cut from one piece of wood as in sculpture) are cut abstract designs, owned by men of the dancing group. The post is usually charred black as a base, onto which colours are added (white from calcinated lime, yellow from mango bark, red from clay or seed pods, green from leaves). The overall effect is striking, with lifelike images of forest animals against a background of complex and coloured patterns.

Only the *nawang narwung* (the one with the responsibility to feed the guests) has the right to put light near these carvings, and expose them for the first time during the night's performance. A good *torr* will bring the comment *kaaping garring* (it has a spirit), and *kaaping ruri'renae* (spirit is attached). It is an extraordinary spectacle to witness the dancing group lit with a flaming firebrand for the first time during the night. Dancers decorate extensively, covering their backs with flowers and coloured leaves (the sheer volume of foliage is used to hide the tambaran paraphernalia), red paint shining on their skin, white feather head-dresses bobbing as they dance, and rising above them all, tall posts with intricate and lifelike carved animals hung from them.

Innovation in the designs of these posts is expected – they are newly inspired for each occasion – and thus are eagerly anticipated, especially from a group of hamlets such as Reite which have a tradition of making *torr*. After the night's dancing, *torr* are never used again. Occasionally they may be left to decorate the hamlet in which they have been carried. Usually they are removed to the *mundutor* in which they were carved, and left to rot by the spirit pool of the tambaran they decorate.

It is usual, in making a palem, for the tambaran to be brought to the hamlet of those staging the payment some days before the day of presentation. Several of the tambaran children (*kaap simang*) available to the men involved are brought and housed in the *passae*. After the palem has been stripped, the affinal group departed, and the *kaiyung* (return present) cooked for these tambaran, they will be sent back to their spirit pools as soon as is practical. Sending kaapu back is accomplished after they have been fed by pointing them in the direction of their home pools. While it is possible to call for a range of spirits from a single pool,[20] it is essential that they are sent back to their own *mundutor*. It is said that were they sent off all together, and not put on exactly the right path, they might well hang around and cause sickness. Men hold the memory of the spirit place in mind while that particular spirit sings for the last time, and, as the dancing group stands at the entrance to the path in question, the spirit is sent off. This is always done as soon as their work is completed. While the tambaran is present it must be fed.[21] Thus during the night of a *kaapu neng* performance, towards dawn, the group of men surrounding the tambaran will move to the edge of the dancing ground in the direction of the path to a tambaran's home pool, and send back one by one all but a final spirit voice which accompanies the men home.

In order, then, to collect *kaapu neng* on the night they are to visit the receiving hamlet, the men from the place which has staged the palem presentation will return to a spirit pool and call for their *kaap* to join them on a journey to the hamlet of the receivers. If *kaapu tangawakating* (Chapter 5) or love-magic is to be performed, it will be prepared here before the journey. Women from the performing hamlet make their own way, and both men and women find a suitable place outside the hamlet they are to dance in to finish preparations, cover their skins in paint, apply perfume and decorative valuables. Thus it is often not until after midnight that a performance begins.

Once decorated and ready, the performers announce their presence with a roll on the hourglass drums used in accompaniment of the *kaapu neng* voices. They move as a fairly tight knot of men into the hamlet they are visiting. Concealing in their midst the paraphernalia of the tambaran they shuffle to the centre of the dancing ground. All viable hamlets have an open space in front of their *passae* and palem which can be swept and cleaned as a dancing area.

There a lead man (*maning saporing* – base of the song, the man who owns the spirit voice) will take what is called the 'eye/shoot of the song' (*maningting*) to begin a rendition of a particular tambaran tune. He is said to 'get the tambaran up', leading, as it were, the growth of its 'shoot' (*ting*). In Chapter 4 I discussed the uses of the word '*ting*' in connection with the 'eye' of the garden. In tambaran activity this word recurs – as the description of a water spring, which is also the generation of a *kaap* spirit, and as the leading words which draw out and raise into song the voice of the spirit. The use of the concept is unsurprising; the tambaran embodies the power of growth. In this case, the words (*maningting*) relating to the particular spirit in some way draw forth its voice, its presence. Each 'verse' is only one phrase, usually two words, repeated back and forth with vocables surrounding the words, giving rhythm to the sung phrases. The voice of each spirit has a cycle of rising and falling which last between two and four minutes, and a specific drum beat. At the end of each short section, the *maning saporing* takes the next word or words and leads the voice into life again. Each tambaran 'song' may last anything from fifteen minutes to several hours. I was told that the tambaran sounds good when a spirit takes the lead of the men and 'lifts' their voices into its own (cf. Feld 1982). The women of the dancing group circle the tambaran group in pairs, keeping rhythmically in step and lifting their own voices in accompaniment. The women enclose, physically and acoustically, the tambaran.

The host hamlet may form a group of their own with their own tambaran, or they may join in the dancing led by the visitors. Many sit around fires made at the edge of the dancing ground, chewing betel and smoking tobacco, waiting for the dawn.

I give below the words of one series of *maningting*, those for a tambaran belonging to, and dreamed by, Siriman Kumbukau of Reite Sisawilkin palem. When I asked how such words were composed, the most consistent answer I received was that things people see in their own lands, things that make them feel emotion or connection with those places or with other people in those places, are used as *maningting*. Thus one may *saating* something – literally 'sing something' that you have seen. To make this into a *maningting* for a tambaran is *saatingdet*. I quote from Porer Nombo: 'They sing these things, and about these things, with their names, to make others empathetic when they hear them. People feel emotion for their own land, their own forest; for the things that look good, and for those that look slack or dry. It is of these that they sing if they feel they are able to.'

I have highlighted in **bold** text the words in each round (verse) of Siriman Kumbukau's *maningting*, and give a direct translation and then, as appropriate, a brief (native) exegesis beneath. Much of the text is said to evoke a feel of place, thus line three ('lizard noise') was explained as evoking the noise a lizard makes as it walks through a dry garden, gently crushing and moving leaf debris). The text presented is a mixture of recognisable words and other vocables to give an impression of the rhythm of the words as sung.

Aisir – Blue-Tailed Lizard

*Eehoo, ehoo, ohho-a **Arararai, Aisir** oo ararai Aisir oo, Aisir, aisiir arawoh arawoh*
walking (ararai) – blue-tailed lizard (Aisir)
[blue-tailed lizard crawls through the garden in the sun]

*Kelooh, kelokelo **aisir** oh **kelo** aisiir aisiir oh, kelo keloh*
turns lizard turns
[turns his head and looks (*kelonkit*) with one eye, as lizards do]

***Orei** oroh, **Aisir orei** arai aisiir ohohohoh*
noise lizard noise
[makes a noise on leaves as it walks]

***melmelmel** melmelmel, mel mel mel, **Aisir** ohho, melmelmelmel, Aisir yeh, aihoaiho hoo-o hoo-o*
comes to eye – blue-tailed lizard
[*mel yokat* – you come, Aisir comes into view and is seen]

***Nareng** narengnareng eh, **siung nareng** nareng eh, **so nareng** siung nareng yeh, ahio ahio..,*
arm decoration
[*Nareng* – decoration, *siung nereng, so nereng* – perfumed plant that is cooked, tied up into bundle, and put in the armbands of dancers]

***Nana yong** eh **kaka yong** eh, kaka yong eh nana yong eh, aiho aiho...*
my shady spot, your shaded place
[*yong* – place with shade to sit and rest, also a hidden area where *torr* may be carved or boys initiated]

*Kekekekeke, **tiak kekekeke**. Kekekek, tiak kekekek, aiho aiho...*
song (*kekeke*) of (*tiak*) Regiana bird of paradise [found on Reite lands]

*Totei, **dotei, aisir** eh totei dotei dotei, hehoo, oh*
sits sits down Aisir
[Aisir stops]

***Alo** aloo weh **nana ya** neh alloo aloo weh, nana yano*
go up (*alo*) (to) my house/place (*nana ya*)
[Aisir goes to his house – end of tambaran.]

Aisir is the name of the tambaran. This does not mean that the spirit is that of a blue-tailed lizard. Like the carvings carried on *torr*, what is sung of in the *maningting* is related in some way to the spirit – to the place in which it resides, or to something that happened there. There may also be words referring to previous performances involving this tambaran. Most often, however, things carved and sung are things which appear in and around the place of this spirit, the kind of flowers that grow by a spirit pool, the kinds of fauna found in a *mundutor*, or the happenings of a myth in the place where the spirit can now be found. Aisir is said to be the 'child' of another spirit. The tune (its voice) was dreamed by Siriman after spending time in the *mundutor* of this parent spirit, where he watched a lizard.

In Aisir we have the appearance of a beautiful lizard walking through a garden in the sun. Next the lizard is seen turning and observing the watcher. It makes a noise and pushes leaf debris from its path as it walks. The words then turn to the smell created by the bundles of perfumed leaves in the armbands of a dancing group; to the highly valued shady places where people sit and rest, chatting and chewing betel nut, and to the places where the tambaran grows boys into men. The *mundutor* of the parent tambaran is one such a place. Above these places can be heard the call of birds of paradise. Then we are back with the lizard, sitting now in one place. It may be reading too much into the words, but one might almost imagine the lizard encompasses in its gaze these human activities, and the forest birds. Then the lizard returns to its hole, and the tambaran is sent back to its pool.

Each spirit voice is distinctive, and is from a particular place, owned by a particular palem or group of palem. Hamlets guard rigidly against 'theft', by imitation, of spirit voices. They are treated as valuables, and may be purchased by others who wish to use them, or more often given as part of a woman's dowry, or as part of other exchanges between affines. Spirits, one could say, are part of the body of a palem, and thus may be transacted as part of the make-up of a body.

The purpose of all the preparation for a *kaapu neng* performance is to cause emotion on the part of the audience. A successful performance is judged by the effect it has on others. The anticipation is for people, especially women, to follow the dancers and their kaapu home, falling in love with the smell, sight, and most of all, the resonant voices of the men and women of the visiting hamlet singing together with their animating spirits. The songs they sing speak of the land from which the dancers come, of the process of life in that land. The dancers sing of things which move the people who live there. They are a metaphoric recall of past events and movements, a singing of places by those familiar with them, full of emotion for the place in which they reside. Spirit voices are the sounds of places themselves, and of relationships associated with, made in, or out of, these places. Women enjoy and feel the evocative nature of these voices as strongly as men. Although barred from the paraphernalia of men's tambaran, women participate fully in, and take great pleasure in their contribution to, a kaapu performance. Their participation is through decoration, through dancing, and their singing which fills out and completes the vocal depth and resonance of the spirit voices. Women occasionally add *maningting* they have composed to a tambaran. Both men and women hum their tunes as they go about their daily tasks. Memories of kinsmen who have used, and who are associated with, particular spirits and places are conjured by the voices of that spirit. Thus tunes and voices act as mnemonics for kin relations and past activities. In his book on Foi poetics, Weiner writes:

> Language and place are a unity. The manner in which human action and purposive appropriation inscribes itself upon the earth is an iconography of human intentions. Its mirror image is speech itself, which, in the act of naming, memorialises these intentions, makes them a history-in-dialogue.... For the Foi, speech, *me* – saying – creates the world, but it also brings forth the earth as a collection of human places, as the grounding of that world. (Weiner 1991: 50)

Spirit voices exist as an 'iconography' of places and peoples' movements. As they are a part of peoples' daily activities, they become associated with their owners, with the places of their generation and residence, and with these peoples' memories of one another. Memory of spirit voices also encompasses past performances. Thus people weep in memory of a deceased kinsman or affine when they are reminded of his or her participation in *sare*. Such reminders are most powerful, it seems, in the presence of a *kaap* associated with the deceased through their daily use of it, or their participation in past performances. Spirit voices are also connected at a less quotidian level with knowledge and places.

Tunes and Names

Tunes, words, and spirits are tied into the land, into places and palem histories. *Kanine'ing kete* is singing names in the tune of a spirit voice to effect growth or change in an object. It will be recalled that when a Reite man plants taro in his garden, he hums the tune of the *patuki* Samat Matakaring, the voice of the taro *patuki*, and in doing so, follows this deity's instructions as to the correct procedure for planting taro. Now within the *maningting* of the Samat Matakaring *kaap* are named certain items which are to be used in the planting of taro. Thus when a man has handed onto him the correct procedure for, and the names of, the *patuki* and kaapu for taro, he also learns the tune of the spirit's voice. Knowledge, revelation, place, and performance (the elements of *patuki*, or 'stories') are brought together in kaapu.

I have not yet done more than touch upon spells (*paru* – secret names) and power. When a man plants taro, he hums (*kanine'ing*) the name of the man who discovered taro. This is one of the things he learns from whoever teaches him garden magic. When knowledge of power is passed on, it is in the form of names, and of tunes which accompany those names. There is a conjunction between names of people, and the voices of the spirits.

Kaapu are located in the land. They have homes (*kaap kung*) in *mundutor* which are specifically the concern of groups of land-owning men. As owners of the land, they are able to enter these places without risk of sickness, and gain the aid of the spirits. People who own the lands on which spirits are resident also know the *paru* which are associated with the particular provenance of the spirits that dwell there. It is this kind of knowledge of land that allows successful hunting, pig-rearing, and garden production – the basis of palem. Knowledge allows people to gain the aid of the kaapu in more than singing and dancing. They are able to call on that tambaran for aid in the endeavours they undertake on their lands. These are placed spirits with a history of relationships with humans. *Paru* recall and bring into the present these past relationships, naming the people who had productive relationships in the past, and thus legitimate their users' place on the land, and their calls for the aid of these land-based spirits. As I pointed out in Chapter 4, men take the names of their grandfathers, and thus names stay on land. Recalling the names of the past is an act of placement in itself. The history of revelation and accomplishment which produced one's predecessors is made present by the use of hidden names. This is kastom, for Reite people. I give an example below.

There is a kaapu which Reite hamlets may call upon, known as Pomo. It is a tambaran which is used sometimes in dancing performances, but its principal use is to aid the construction of a fine palem. The myth of Pomo speaks of a fight over a woman between two brothers. Now there is a place in Reite lands where a limestone reef is said to be the palem of the household which remained in the Pomo myth. When Reite people want to construct a palem, they take valuables (*palieng*) to the *tupong ting* of this *kaap*, and singing the name (*paru*) of the characters in the tune of the tambaran's voice, they hang their valuables by the water. They collect flowers around the edge of the pool, and then take their valuables and remove to the *mundutor* where the Pomo palem is situated. As Kerimang described, the man who is staging the palem scales a tree there, and taking leaves from as high as he can, places them with the flowers in the hollow base of the *wising wimbing* – the taro body's backbone.

The relationship of exchange is emphasised through what is done with the name and tune of this *kaap*. It is said that this procedure makes the taro pile stand tall and strong, ensures the man will have plenty of pigs and exchange partners in his subsequent life, and attract exchange valuables to himself. His performance in collecting leaves from the *mundutor* of this *patuki*/kaapu anticipates his future prowess. The form of productive relations instigated by the characters in Pomo Patuki is brought into the present; it is the separation which allows productive exchange.

While many know the tune which is the voice of the Pomo tambaran, only Reite people know the name, and are able to enter the spirit place without fear of retribution. Thus the place 'Pomo' has a *kaap* which aids the construction of palem by Reite people. The knowledge necessary for gaining the aid of this spirit is contained in the combination of voice (*punging*), name (*paru*) and words (*mangting*) that those with a history in this place recall. Kaapu are musical, but their voices, and the power to evoke response in others, arise in a real conjunction of the history of human relationality, knowledge (as revelation to specific people), and the potential growth which they embody (albeit as disembodied voices.)

Kaapu are about places. People are moved by their voices and songs in recollection of the beauty of places as they have been known, and in recognition that this beauty is a power which lies within people from there. Hearing the voice reminds them of the deceased, it is in fact the reappearance of an aspect of all the deceased from that place, and also the generation of new people there. Thus kaapu speak of past and future, of places and relationships which are tangible, which are known to their hearers. The power of places is to generate the conditions, we might say, to produce persons. Tambaran performances are a concentration of the history of kin relations as they are remembered through places themselves. The very processes of generation become kinship and placement at the moment of performance.

I suggest that what we see in the text of Aisir above, and in the Pomo *kaap*, is a concentrated image of places. 'Place' here refers to an enfolded history of land and kinship. The presentation takes the form of dancing and singing, decorating and perfuming, growing crops and animals, and presenting them for exchange. Thus the presentation has a form. Within a genre, each form is unique. This form presents the land and its inhabitants as dual. It is a body of a kind, one differentiated into 'bones', and 'skin' or 'flesh'. The receivers make this differentiation in their activity of stripping the palem. Thus they separate the partible, or the produce of a place, from the place itself. Much the same process occurs in the division of a sibling set into a marriageable (mobile) woman and her brothers. Palem construction and *sare* are, in a sense, performances, of Reite lands, of the power of places, of the history of their generation of persons, and thus of kinship itself.

This presentation takes the form of a body in two ways: firstly as the palem itself, and secondly as the body of the tambaran dancing group, endowed with the voices of the land. Their affines' acceptance of the body of a palem is an acceptance of the donors' placement in the land, an acknowledgement of where they have come from. When a body is taken, it assumes a set of 'bones' from which this body has been removed. After the construction of a palem, the donors are named as the people of the land which they have used. Kinship through shared substance (siblingship) is recognised in this process. Thus the offspring of Palota and Nangu in Sarangama will be siblings, sharing their residence, land and also their tambaran.

When women follow the tambaran home from the hamlet in which it has performed, they come to a place – that place is the source of what has been shown in its decoration, smell, and sound. Bringing in new wives as the culmination of making a payment for a body begins the cycle of growth and presentation again, maintaining the productive separation, and thus the relationships, that Reite people look for.

Persons are aspects of places, and places are animated by persons. Incorporated in places are the activities of the people who have resided in them; persons are given identity through the generative power of the land in which they are 'grown': thus the palem is named after the land on which it is constructed, and the people are identified with this constructed entity. I have shown how the ungendered identity of a group of persons living in a place (kinsmen through the substance of the land they share) is split into its component aspects by the action of affines. A palem is not in fact one body, but it is the product of one place, and thus appears as such. It requires the attentions of outsiders to separate the siblings of this place, the brothers from the sisters, and, removing the latter, to keep the former productive (in relationship). In Reite understanding, it is land which is fundamental to creative process. In fact calling it land is hardly enough. Land here is the enfolded space of human history. Bearing testimony to this history are the spirit places and bones that are kept there.

Death and Bones

By making a payment of the kind described above, a hamlet group buys the rights to dispose of the body of a person at the time of their death. As we might expect by now, the affines of the person in question are brought in to handle the body, and this work is paid for. However, the matter of where the body will be kept should now be beyond dispute. This is the outcome of making a payment as a palem – belonging to the place where it was constructed. Placement of the dead is extremely important to Nekgini speakers. A married woman who has not bought her body from her brothers will be brought back to her natal land at her death unless huge payments, *ukung suoririe* 'covering the body' of the woman, are paid. Thus on the death of a young Reite woman married into a Serieng hamlet in 1994 for whom no palem had been completed, her body was buried in Reite lands. At this time her husband was put under a number of taboos, including one on future marriage, by the kin of his deceased wife. His grief was ignored, and his wife's body taken from his care, because he had not made the payment for her. In another case, a large payment was received from another Serieng hamlet for the 'body' of an old woman, near to death. Although she had made a palem on her marriage, Reite 'brothers' had somehow been overlooked in the distribution, as the palem was made for Ngaing-speaking kin to the east. Reite people were compensated for this, and the loss of a sister, before her death in order that no claim could be made for her body when she died.

Just as a frame is stripped of flesh in a palem payment, traditional disposal of bodies for Nekgini speakers was a process in which family members watched the flesh slough off from the bones. It was a sister's son who attended this process. A variety of methods were used to support and contain the body of the deceased. In each case, the newly deceased person was placed in a foetal position before rigor mortis set in. The body was covered with the *kulung* leaves used to wrap processed sago, and supported by a bamboo pole at the back (another *wisung wimbing*); in a large split bamboo tube with a hole in the base for the liquids produced by decomposition to drain into the ground; in a large plate (for women) and again covered with leaves; or finally, on occasion for a man, in his own split garamut. The covered body – often with the jaw left uncovered and a tube protruding from the fontanel – was placed sitting upright in the deceased person's own house. Close family sat with the body as it decayed, unable to work, cook, wash, or move about.[22] A specific person (usually a classificatory sister's child) was nominated to collect the insect larvae which emerged from the rotting flesh, placing them in a small covered bamboo tube. I was told that another bamboo tube, pushed through the deceased's cranium, facilitated the collection of these insect larvae in the case of bodies which were wholly covered in leaves. When the insects in the tube hatched and flew off, it was thought the body was fully free of life. I should draw attention here to the role of a sister's child in assisting the removal of flesh, and thus the removal of the 'form' of the person, from the bones. It is also important to note how the house acts as a container for the concealment of the process of death, just as it was a container concealing the process of birth, and from which the child was 'born'.

Everyone I spoke to about this, including those who were old enough to have seen it practised, spoke of it as a terrible ordeal. No family member could be excused. The work of watching for and collecting maggots (which would have been paid for with important valuables) was said to be particularly unpleasant. Yet the respect given to a body was also emphasised. Any disruption of decorum around a body brought swift and stinging anger from its kin.[23]

Bones prepared in this way are thought to give 'power' to those who keep them and look after them. They are described as 'hot', as are men who have contact with them. It was common practice for a man to keep the skeleton of his father or grandfather at the head of his sleeping place inside the house, and eventually to take the jawbone to carry with him when the other bones fell apart. Such bones would make a man powerful – in sorcery, in warfare, in hunting and in love-magic – all the activities in which 'heat' is required in Nekgini understanding.

Women's bones were as good to 'watch over' their keepers as were men's. However the bones of men of particular prowess or skill in weather-working would be placed with the remains of, and in the same place as, previous weather-workers. There is a tradition, still regarded as important in Reite, of 'joining bones' of the deceased. This is a way of keeping a place's continuity, and means simply placing newly uncovered bones with older bones of people from the same place. Bones were sometimes stored in tambaran houses, but mostly placed in *mundutor*. The *mundutor* which house bones are all on high ridges in Reite land, away from water. They are spoken of as hot and dry places themselves. The proximity of the 'traditional' hamlets such as Reite Yasing (discussed in Chapter 2) to these places locates them far from sources of running water.

Buying bodies has a future in Reite hamlets. As I argued in Chapter 4, bodies are not a mixture of substance, they belong in one place. They arise from it, and go back into it, being the hot dry power of a place. As I have shown with the palem, bodies are viewed as grown by particular places. The strength for this growth lies in the 'bones' of that place. These bones remain after the form of life has been removed (just as it was given, by maternal/affinal kin). While the body on death is *samu* (dirty/rubbish), the bones are thought to have power.

Scattered then throughout Reite lands are *mundutor*, places where human bones are kept. Each hamlet site has a *mundutor*. Women and outsiders do not enter such places; men visit them only rarely. These places are called upon in name by men when they seek assistance from spirits and ancestors. A man performing a healing ceremony will name the *mundutor* and surrounding high places in his land, as he asks for assistance in driving out the poison or ill will of another place. The bones of weather-workers are spoken to by their descendants, ensuring good harvests or retribution for enemies. These places are centres of the character and history of each landholding. One might say they are wholly themselves: that is, they are places whose singularity of character or history is maintained without being given form through current relationships. In certain circumstances, men imitate the source of power in these places by giving their bodies the form of the bones of their ancestors. This involves removal from relationships with 'others'. The power men gain by making this transformation produces a form of interaction detrimental to others, as it is destructive of the products of relationality (persons).

For the undertakings of sorcery and poison, weather-magic, hunting, warfare, love-magic, and initiation, men in Reite hamlets are *kundeing* – tabooed from water. These enterprises require 'hot blood'. Men go into seclusion, avoiding women completely, and roast their own dry food on the ashes of a fire (cf. Mosko 1985: 41–5). They do not wash, eat 'cool' or 'wet' foods, or drink liquid of any kind.

It was explained to me that healthy people have a layer of fat or water beneath the skin. It is this which makes them appear fleshy, and which is stimulated by the power of a mother's brother's kaapu during initiation. The wet layer 'grows' the skin, giving form and making a body attractive. This appearance, dependent on matrilateral relations, is produced by eating many kinds of food that come from different places (*nawang palangpalang net*), and food prepared by women, who boil it in water and coconut grease. Eating food prepared by women, and eating food from more than one place, implies conjugal relations, and therefore affinal relations. Wet foods (those boiled in pots) are said to be 'cold' by men in states of ritual preparation. They are associated with water, flow, and movement. These are also 'female' characteristics for Nekgini speakers. Too much contact with women is said to make a man 'cold' and 'weak' in the sense of spiritually inept. Particular emphasis is thus placed by men who are *kundeing* on limiting the intake of foods to those produced by a man himself or his close male kin. By this method, water in the body is lost (*matek tupuyung wiyung wakatkin*). This water is 'bad' (*wiyung*) in the context of performing sorcery or initiation.

Mosko reports a regime undertaken by married men among the Mekeo of Central Province in order to 'close' their bodies to the war sorcery of neighbouring groups, and to protect against the ingredients of a man's own sorcery preparations. In this case 'the groom's body is viewed as thin, light and dry' (Mosko 1983: 26). The opposite of this state, as it is conceived among the Mekeo, is to have an 'open body' through which substances flow easily. While in an open state, a man is 'procreatively hot', but cannot partake in war sorcery due to the risk he would pose to himself and his wife and children. It is when he is in a closed, dry state, by contrast, that a Mekeo man can practice *mefu* (poisoning) (Mosko 1985: 54). Then he is said to be 'hot' contraceptively (Mosko 1985: 94), and also 'hot' for sorcery. The contrasts between a cold, wet, open (reproductive state), and a hot, dry, closed (destructive state), are very similar to those imagined in Reite for the same purposes. Thus when a Reite man is 'close to' (eats the food of, has conjugal relations with) women, he becomes 'cold' and 'weak' for sorcery and hunting. His attentions being on productive relations with people (procreative, affinal), he loses his singular power as wholly constituted by a single place. However, when he gives up productive relations (and substitutes for them for the destructive power of sorcery), he moves away from the company of those from other places, those who produce flow and who move (women).

Men who are *kunding* become thin and emaciated, they sit huddled in tambaran houses, not washing or eating, and thus imitate very old people who are near to death. In fact in extreme cases, people in *kundeing* are described as 'just bones'. It is in this singularly constituted state (the form of the body is not dependent on outside inputs) that transformations occur, or sorcery is performed. The inverse of a fat and healthy wet life (given form in essential affinal and conjugal relations) is dry, emaciated death.

* * *

This final ethnographic chapter has examined the ritual constructions around which the social organisation and the residence patterns I have reported are formed. I have shown that every such construction amounts to a body, made from substance and power provided by a particular place. Affines remove 'flesh' (wealth) from this construction in payment for their loss of a bride, and then her child, in marriage. The construction involves the total effort of a place and its group of landowners to produce, and this group of persons become 'kin' – they have a social identity and demonstrate constructive use of the potential resources in the land – through the ritual production and performance. I examined the role of spirits in this process. I made the suggestion that people are performing their land – making the relations they have with spirits and ancestors (those that strengthen and grow them) present – for other places to see or experience. This anticipates future relations with those who experience the generative and aesthetic power of that place. A discussion of funerary rites, bones, and the placement of the dead on the land has been included to confirm the argument about substance and power as aspects of places, while the form of bodies is the outcome of relationships.

In the concluding chapters of this book, I shall look at recent theoretical work on landscape and place in the light of the ethnography presented here. My discussion moves from landscape to place, and then to kinship, where I discuss the genealogical model of kinship in contrast to the model I have developed throughout this work. Unlike in the genealogical model, I maintain that Nekgini understandings of kinship and personhood are intimately bound up with land and placement, not as a backdrop to people's lives, but as mutually entailed in the process which is life and death.

Notes

1. At other times, food is piled on the ground on newly cut banana leaves and coconut leaf mats (Photograph 9 in Chapter 5).
2. Of four brothers living in Ririnbung and Saruk hamlets during 1994, I accompanied two to a presentation of bride payment in the village of Sorang. They went to collect payment for a sister who had married there. The eldest of the brothers however had been called on by the husband of this woman to pay back help he had given when this elder brother himself married years previously. As the eldest brother could not attend, he sent one of the remaining younger siblings to the presentation with the wealth he was to contribute. His emissary was happy in this role, and added wealth of his own to his eldest brother's, thereby placing them both firmly in the camp of the hamlet paying for a wife. This eldest brother explained to me that it was acceptable if at least one person from their hamlet (sibling group) ate pig for the woman, and he had his own interests in finishing his obligation; he was happy to forego his share. Reite people often said it is unacceptable to eat one's own pigs, or marry one's own sisters. One might say that at a certain distance, such ideals are subsumed by practicality. I examined this in Chapter 3.
3. Here and in what follows, unless stated differently, the tambaran refers to the men of a hamlet group in conjunction with kaapu (spirits) of the kind whose voices lead the sacred music performed whenever they are present. This whole is referred to locally as 'the tambaran', blurring the distinction between men and spirits. ('Avatip men impersonate cult spirits in ritual, and claim ... to have really become the spirits,..' (Harrison 1993: 113). To achieve a measure of descriptive clarity, 'kaapu' in this chapter is used to refer to the spirits in abstract, and the Tok Pisin term tambaran to the spirits and men of the palem engaged in joint activity.
4. Winedum remembers as a teenage boy the time when white people were heard of, seen on the coast, and then later when the first native mission workers came through the area. It is thought the latter occurred in the mid 1930s (Lawrence 1964, Reiner 1986).
5. *Matapo* is the name for body payments given by a child to their MB (Chapter 5).
6. Winedum told a myth for the origin of coconut at this point: 'In this, an elder brother became coconuts and the younger became a pig. Thus they stand up the elder and tie his younger (brother) to his base. Taro is the same, a woman bore it, so they make a woman and put it in her belly' [I think 'they' here refers to ancestors, or everyone who makes a palem. [The myth is as follows:]

    Two brothers lived together. The elder would cook but not give his younger brother any of the food. He alone would eat. At one time, the younger ate his elder's faeces because he was so hungry and wanted his elder to feel sorry for him. But the elder thought his brother must be a pig, and taking his bow and arrows, he chased the younger brother. He called to his younger brother to come and help him catch the pig, but the pig itself came to him instead. Then he understood that by not giving his brother food, he had caused him to turn his body into that of a pig. He was distraught. He put his stone axe in his belt and became a coconut palm standing upright where he was. He said, 'when they make food they will stand me there first. They can tie my little brother to my leg'. [The stone axe seems to be a reference to the fruit of the palm.]

The theme of separation, through violence, of a sibling pair, and the loss of one through this violence, can be seen here to mirror the theme of Pomo reported in Chapter 3. In this case the separation facilitates or provides a model for the separation of a 'body' of produce from a hamlet group.

7. (de Coppet 1994) reports that 'Are'are marriage payments consist of the three parts which correspond to the make up a person in 'Are'are cosmology. These parts are 'body' (garden food), 'breath' (pigs) and 'image' (shell money). Shell money (image), as what is left after death and displayed in funerary rites, amounts to a 'stopping' of the woman's body and breath, and her demise as a person in the clan of her origin (cf. Gillison 1993). 'For the clan of origin, the two monetary presentations "stop" her body and breath by converting them into money. From their standpoint, her marriage is the funeral of her body and breath – while for the husband's family it is – not the advent of a new ancestor, but – the confirmation that the bride's body and breath belong henceforth to them' (60). On marriage, a woman is converted into an ancestor image for those who lose her life's productivity. Yet as I am suggesting here for Reite people, those who lose this body do not part with creativity itself. The shell money is transactable for other women in marriage, and thus the 'power' of the clan's ancestors, as images of that power displayed in partible shell money, remains with the wife-givers. 'Since the woman's side is always responsible for converting the money into the three "living" "species" [taro, pigs, ancestors], affinity relations often bear the burden of these opposite ritual tasks, which are alike submitted to the authority of the ancestor money' (59).

8. The man who makes a palem may be called *nawang saporung*. *Saporung* means roots, and *nawang*, food. However, in the context of palem construction there are two *nawang saporung*. The man who organises the construction, *and* the man who is principle recipient. In fact those who help make the palem will say that they cannot eat from it as *ne newang saporung* (we are the base of the food). To avoid confusion, I distinguish the principle donor as 'father' of the food (*nawang narwung*).

9. See Chapter 2.

10. In one such transaction I witnessed, the maternal uncle involved had no wealth to hand over at this point, and shouted, as if in anger, that he would not return (*bekim* [T.P.]) this payment. It was explained to me afterwards that although this hid his shame at not having a return to make, it meant exactly the opposite.

11. The *patuki* which tells of how wealth items came to be distributed over the Rai Coast. For more on *te tangaring patuki* and its significance see Leach (2002).

12. Reite won first prize for their *singsing* in the first annual show in the district headquarters of Saidor in 1995.

13. Reigle (1995) states that music 'functioned as the embodiment, symbol and reminder of the system of spiritual beliefs of many Rai Coast cultures. This system is characterised by male dominance based on control of the spirit voices' (2). Spirits 'can cause sickness, restore health, ensure good crops and assist with love magic' (4).

14. The following description applies to differences between the three kinds of musical kaapu. The differences are due to differences in the paraphernalia associated with each spirit (i.e., mobility of the spirit is dependent on the size of the ritual paraphernalia needed to 'house' it, the voice on the shape and materials of the objects, etc.).

15. The accepted euphemism for paraphernalia. The *maal* of the tambaran gives shape to the spirit when it comes among humans. In doing so, in a sense, it clothes the spirit. Men use these ways of talking among themselves.

16. *Manieng* is used in all spirit-related activities, including healing and weather-working. It was explained that the pungent, musty aroma of this root when crushed in the mouth attracts the attention of entities and beings beyond human sight.

17. The paraphernalia of each of three 'types' of tambaran.

18. 'The phenomenon of magic confronts us with a situation in which matter and meaning become miscible fluids, a scandal, of course, from the standpoint of scientific method. Looking at this from the angle just indicated – the olfactory dimension which is both part of, and reference to, the world – assists us not only in coming to grips with magical techniques which make direct use of odiferous substances, but also in understanding, in a more general way, how this paradoxical "mixing" takes place' (Gell 1977: 27).

19. Things that are sung in the words accompanying particular kaapu are available for display as *torr* posts. As there is innovation in this artistic form, and new kaapu are dreamed by certain accomplished men, the images sung are sometimes surprising for an 'ancestor cult', which is the way tambaran is usually understood (Niles, personal communication). One tambaran speaks of canoes and ships, referring to the history of the *mundutor* in which this spirit resides; the place in which the events of the Pomo myth, related in Chapter 3, took place.

20. Although green coconut ought to be cut, and *manieng* spat, at the *mundutor* of each and every kaap to be called.

21. Shifts between singular and plural pronouns in describing the tambaran is an effect of what is described. While there are many kaapu (individually named spirit voices), and many ritual items (also called kaapu), when there are spirits gathered in a *passae*, or a dancing group is performing, it is always spoken of as a singular entity. This is clear in Tok Pisin. People say 'the tambaran is present', or 'we took the tambaran to [another hamlet]', however many individual spirits might be present. Thus one fetches 'the tambaran' to a hamlet, not 'tambarans'. As stated before, a group of initiated men in the presence of spirits are also called 'the tambaran'.

22. Although now all bodies are buried in the village graveyard, a period of mourning is still undertaken by all close kin of the deceased. For one or two days, the body is watched over by family members while others come to view the body and grieve. After the burial kinsmen are prohibited from working, cooking, and washing for a month or so.

23. People cry in mourning using the tune of the voice of a tambaran spirit that belongs to them. Crying is judged by the relatives of the deceased for authenticity, and for composure. It is still the case that a poor performance in mourning, or disrespect in some other form, would bring accusations of malice against the deceased, and of sorcery against them. In the past, retribution was instantaneous in such cases.

Chapter Seven
Places and Bodies, Landscape and Perception

As André Marchand says, after Klee: 'In a forest, I have felt many times over that it was not I who looked at the forest. Some days I felt the trees were looking at me, were speaking to me... I was listening... I think that the painter must be penetrated by the universe and not want to penetrate it... I expect to be inwardly submerged, buried'. (Merleau-Ponty 1964: 167)

Water, which is principally what men avoid while under the self-imposed restrictions of *kundeing*, animates the land. The places of rising water (*tupongting*) generate the kaapu which animate growth, the palem, and *sare*. These in turn are the basis for relations with other places. Water in the body makes it swell and take on a shiny, healthy appearance. However, in *kundeing*, men imitate their dead ancestors, the singular source of a place's power. Separated from existing definitions, their efforts are not in the mode of generation. They may in fact be turned to destruction. In *kundeing*, men take on the form of their ancestors as they exist in *mundutor*. Reite people say that through *kundeing*, 'the breath of your ancestors comes to you'; you take on their power. When thunderstorms threaten a Reite hamlet, one might see an old man running from his house, shaking a spear at the sky and shouting *asik wimbing ereiting gna* 'bones of ancestors here!' to move the storm on.

Ancestral bones, while the outcome of previous affinal relations, exist outside them. In their stillness and their and dusty-dryness, bones are an image of the power which has shaped the unique history of a place. They are its character. This character could not be known without human relationships to constitute place. Spirits (kaapu), landforms (nala, patuki), and ancestral bones (wimbing) are similar in this way. Men deliberately oscillate between states of singular constitution (power) and multiple constitution (growth). While *kundeing*, they imitate the form of ancestral bones and are momentarily removed from the obligations of relationality. Power for 'magic', for sorcery, or for transformation is only effective when hidden (Chapter 4). Outside affinal and conjugal relations, men in kundeing, like bones, are not 'visible'. It is this power, the basis of the growth, which is also the basis of the power of the tambaran over others. Because they are integral to place, bones and spirits are not alienable. They are the basic strength or support for the life in a place. The paradox is that although 'hot' and 'dangerous' (antithetical to life), bones are also the basis on which relationships-in-life are formed. That is, encompassed by relationships, they provide the power from which new relationships are fashioned. They are also the ultimate outcome of those relationships.

The final act of recognition by matrilateral kin in these hamlets is to assist the removal of flesh from the bones of a mother's brother. This reverses the order of payments made by this child to his mother's brother. Formation and differentiation are aspects of affinity, of human existence as established by Pomo (Chapter 3). Thus the sister's child who was given form by their MB assists in the removal of form from their MB. The obligations of affinity, of relations based on gender difference, are finished. The MB's bones are free to 'join' the singular line of bones in one place. His MB's bones belong to the land on which he has lived, but the sister's child has bones of his own; he belongs to, and draws substance from, another place. The differences between persons are differences between places. When people decorate and dance, they show themselves to be a part of a particular place. The form of their appearance is given by the relations they have to their affines, and so the bodies they grow are claimed by their affines. However, the bones of a place – its spirits, its ancestors, the history of its production of people (kinship) – are maintained as images of a specific, emplaced, power for generation.

* * *

The rest of this chapter contrasts somewhat with what has gone before. I turn briefly to the concept of landscape, and to understandings of perception, as they appear in some selected recent writings in anthropology. There is a slight disjuncture between this discussion, and the ethnographic writing and analysis already presented. The concepts are extraneous to the material in some ways. Yet I consider this 'lack of fit' itself to be illuminating. In fact, my task here is to try and determine whether there is a language in (albeit a limited selection of) anthropological writings on landscape to describe Nekgini understandings of land. This is a potentially jarring transition. The issue seems to turn on where representation (that is, the use of a token-event which stands for, or re-presents, something else) figures in our theorising.

Much of the problem with the genealogical model is that it separates term from referent. Language then is representational in this model. Kin terms relate to a more concrete reality – positions within a genealogically specified series of biogenetic relations. As noted, it is this conceptual construction which makes 'incest' a problem. The idea that sexual relations can occur between people who are 'too close' is possible because people's identity is thought to be pre-specified. Terminology describes or represents this underlying reality. I have argued to the contrary that terminological use is an aspect of what constitutes the person. It is not a description, or representational token for something else, but elicits the form of relation in which definition is constituted. This process is not separate from sare or palem construction. My argument about how sare and palem performances relate to our understanding of land and landscape is a direct development of my description of kinship and relatedness among Nekgini speakers.

In his philosophical writings, Merleau-Ponty reminds us of the presence of our own bodies in our perceptions of self and world, and of the meeting of the two in the intersection of the consciousness of spatial relations and of the meaning of things. His effort is to reintroduce a human scale to the philosophy of space and time, grounding both in the movements people make: movements between everyday tasks, between kinsmen, and between places. His argument seems helpful to my intention of describing the generation of Reite places:

> Scientific thinking, a thinking which looks on from above, and thinks of the object in general, must return to the 'there is' which underlies it; to the site, the soil of the sensible and opened world such as it is in our life and for our body – not that possible body which we may legitimately think of as our information machine but that actual body I call mine, this sentinel standing quietly at the command of my words and my acts. Further *associated bodies* must be brought forward along with my body – the 'others', not merely as my congeners, as the zoologist says, but the others who haunt me and whom I haunt; the 'others' along *with* whom I haunt a single present, and actual Being as no animal ever haunted those beings of his own species, locale or habitat. (Merleau-Ponty 1964: 160–61, original emphasis)

Starting from the spatiality generated by bodily dispositions and potential, Merleau-Ponty moves outward into the significant aspects of the human world, and lights upon sociality – the way that human others 'haunt us' by entering our consciousness and forming it – and the situated nature of human sociality in places redolent with meaning.

Landscape as a vista, or as a backdrop, as I mentioned early on, is of little interest to Reite villagers. However, a situated understanding of their surroundings, its history, and the people who have been generated by this history, is something Reite people are deeply interested in. An exhilarating moment during my first few days in Reite was sitting with Gayap after he brought me a welcome gift of tobacco and betelnut. He baffled but excited me by his knowledge of old and new gardens and their owners, of places, of mundutor, and of the names of surrounding hills and landforms. Of course, at that moment, Gayap was using language to represent his knowledge to an outsider, and observing the land as if from without. I focus in what follows on moments when Reite people do things with their knowledge of land which are not representational. I believe these moments (of sare and palem construction) constitute how places come to have meaning for Nekgini speakers.

In what follows, I draw some theoretical points from the ethnographic material which will turn on understandings of land, and the possibility of using the term 'landscape' in a way which would make sense in the indigenous context; that is 'the composite formed out of the body in its perceptual environment...' (Gell 1995: 252). While my intention here is not to enter into a debate about the status and history of the concept of 'landscape' as art work or cultural resource, I attempt to come to a sense of the term which would tally with the practices and understandings of Reite people. The work necessary to achieve any kind of 'fit' between a concept of landscape, and Nekgini perceptions of their lifeworld, while involved, is illuminating. This is because the difference between representational understandings of landscape, and Reite understanding of places mirrors a parallel difference between terminology (language) as primarily representational, and terminology as primarily constitutive, which I outlined in Chapter 3. I begin by drawing on some recent anthropological literature on landscape which discusses representation and vision. Noting a plausible philosophical challenge in the writing of Merleau-Ponty to the usual contrast between vision as objectifying, and hearing as experiential perception, I explore whether there is a way in which we might keep hold of the notion of landscape while applying it to the Nekgini lifeworld. This suggestion goes against the grain in interesting ways, as their practices and performances involving land, place, and spirits, are not primarily representations. The focus on landscape helps to make this clear.

The Concept of Landscape in Anthropology

In a useful book, Thomas (1984) documents the development of the term 'landscape' from a late sixteenth century technical term used by painters: 'landskip'. For the developing middle classes of cities (such as eighteenth- and nineteenth-century Paris), 'the initial appeal of rural scenery was that it reminded the spectator of landscape pictures. Indeed the scene was only called a "landscape" because it was reminiscent of a painted "landskip"; it was "picturesque" because it looked like a picture' (Thomas 1984: 265). Thomas emphasises the historical nature of the concept of landscape, the emergence of which ran parallel to the development of an urban bourgeois class.

Agreeing with Thomas's understanding of the development of the term, Ton Lemaire argues that the defining aspect of 'landscape' is the distanciation of the viewer from the object viewed. He writes,

> The environment could only manifest itself as a landscape when the perceiving subject withdrew from his involvement in it and when he had the power and desire to know and to embrace the totality of his world by a distanced and disengaged look. (Lemaire 1997: 6)

As such, the meaning of the word landscape arose from the development of perspective, a fifteenth-century 'invention' which made possible the representation of the world in this form, and went hand in hand with other developments in Europe at the time, including growing urban populations.

Lemaire traces the movement, in European thought and culture, from a 'mythical' ordering of space (such as that understood by Australian Aborigines), in which the subject was involved and present, as were other powers and deities, to a modern view of the observer as removed from and giving meaning *to* space. Space came to be seen as a 'neutral separate realm' (7). Instead of man existing at the centre of relationships to deities and places given in a meaningful world, the blank space of the earth was given meaning by man's perceptual, and actual, ordering of it. It was partly in this movement, Lemaire argues, that 'European man' discovered himself in his own autonomy and subjectivity. Thus the world beyond man came to be seen as under his control, and that control was manifest in the ordering of space and nature. As creativity was transferred from the land and its mythological figures to the autonomous subject, so the latter was removed from the object of his gaze. Land became, to recall the argument presented here about genealogical kinship, the inanimate substrate upon which animate beings played out their lives. These lives involved creating the landscape, as if from without. Lemaire lays the blame (he sees the position as objectionable) for this removal of the person from the land, and its attendant consequences (as he sees them) of alienation and environmental degradation, firmly at the door of Descartes, whose conception of the 'Cogito' went together with a will to control and dominate nature.

> Nature is reduced to a mechanism, the world is 'mechanised' and refined, while the source of all meaning, symbolism and morals is contracted and concentrated in man himself.
>
> As a matter of fact, the landscape as a picture is affected by these conditions. On the one hand, it reflects the modern will to dominate nature, the distance taken by an outside observer. But on the other hand, one of the functions of landscape painting was to offer to the eyes of modern man, compelled to live in a disenchanted world, an aesthetic compensation for the narrowing of the perception by the modern sciences. In short, it reminded modern man – whose freedom and autonomy are built on the control of an objectified and reified nature – of the world in its completeness... (Lemaire 1997: 8).

Lemaire, then, outlines the genesis of the modern understanding of landscape, and of the consequences of this removal from the thing to be ordered, represented, and looked at, for art, science, and philosophy. 'A good deal of the work in the nineteenth and twentieth century philosophy and the social sciences is meant to counter and compensate the effects of these separations' (ibid.).

Introducing a volume of papers dealing with the concept of 'landscape' in anthropology, Hirsch also describes the development of the concept, from its beginnings in Dutch painting in the sixteenth century, to the present. As far as anthropological use of the concept is concerned, he notes that despite the landscape appearing as a backdrop to anthropological description, the concept itself has received little treatment. In anthropological texts, landscape figures in two main ways – as a picturesque backdrop, the scenery against which cultural events take place, or as a resource from which cultural symbols are taken. 'There is thus the landscape we initially see and a second landscape which is produced through local practice and which we come to recognise and understand through fieldwork and through ethnographic description and interpretation' (Hirsch 1995b: 2). This is a widely applicable characterisation of two kinds of understanding an anthropologist might experience – an initial appraisal of a place as seen for the first few times, and a second understanding based on the meanings attributed to physical features by local people. I think that both these uses of 'landscape' by anthropologists could be accommodated under Lemaire's portrayal of the way the term has come to imply the separation of the observer (be she ethnographer or native) from the thing observed. Thus representation, a central feature in the development of the concept of landscape in art, is preserved in both of these two senses. The landscape is represented by a description of something picturesque, or perhaps degraded, yet always present. It is a backdrop to the real action, which takes place in social life or culture. Even the nuanced understanding of the long term fieldworker makes it appear that their ethnographic subjects construct the meaning of their landscape within the symbolic operations of cultural representation. Meaning lies outside the actual relations with the land. While ethnography itself is a form of representation, landscape often appears within it as if it were something at a remove from social life – as if the subjects themselves considered it outside sociality.

In essence, my argument is as follows. The way in which representation figures in ethnographic accounts of landscape relies upon the distance of the observer from the thing observed. Ethnographers are apt to imagine that their own analytic distance from the action they observe is replicated by the distance people have from the landscape. (There are notable exceptions, see Weiner 1991, Basso and Feld 1996, for example.) In other words, they organise understanding about it through representation of it in ritual or artistic form. Understanding lies at the level of representation rather than engagement. I do not object to representation on any grounds other than that it is inappropriate to Reite people's practice. Just as a representational model of language appeared inappropriate in the specific instance of Reite kin terminology (Chapter 3) understanding Reite *sare* and *palem* as representation – a token event with a referent elsewhere – is unhelpful.

Hirsch develops his own model of landscape in order to move away from the paramount significance attached to representation, and instead produces a series of contrasts: between image and representation, foregrounded actuality and background potentiality, place and space, and inside and outside. He argues that it is in the process by which these things are related, particularly foregrounded image and background potential, that landscape emerges. One might situate a cross-cultural study of landscape as attending to this process, he suggests. 'The argument presented here suggests that the Western convention of landscape representation is a particular expression of a more general foreground/background relationship that is found cross-culturally' (1995b: 3).

Landscape, for Hirsch, covers a process whereby background potential – space, outside, or a representational overview – is drawn into everyday human activity as known places, situated images, the 'inside' of human experience. He tells us that landscape painting and design rest on

> a relationship between an ordinary workaday life and an ideal, imagined existence, vaguely connected to, but still separate from, that of the everyday. We can consider the first as 'foregrounded' in order to suggest the concrete actuality of everyday social life ('the way we are now'). The second we can consider as 'background', in order to suggest the perceived potentiality thrown into relief by the foregrounded existence ('the way we might be').... (Hirsch 1995b: 3)

Hirsch hopes to find a comparative tool in the concept of landscape by thinking of the relationship between foreground and background, between image (situated) and representation (abstract), as applicable cross-culturally.

When we imagine persons, buildings, or places, as emerging from the background of their connection to the land, is not this an outcome of having a perspective from which to view the emergence of places from spaces, or foregrounded actuality from background potential? Our imagination plays on the distance between the viewer and the objects viewed, and similarly between the object viewed and its context. Hence the apparent relevance of a description of Nekgini speakers' 'landscape' as a context and background to their peculiar form of social life. It is this distancing, of viewer and analyst from those studied, and then of these peoples' everyday lives from their 'cultural background' as possibly inscribed in the landscape, which leads us to think we can discern the relation between context and event, or image and background, for those whom we study.[1] The outcome of representation such as landscape art, or the movement that Hirsch describes between foreground actuality and background potentiality, is to draw the viewer or analyst into making connections between background and foreground – this is the aesthetic work that framing things within their contexts does. It is a particular (perspectival) mode of understanding, and relies on the perspective of the viewer or analyst. It also imagines those represented operate, as cultural actors, on something outside them. But if human substance is drawn from the land – persons are land in another form – one might ask where background, image, and land converge?

Hirsch's argument is, then, that 'landscape' might come into being through the relationship between the 'two poles' of human experience: everyday quotidian existence and the background of potentiality from which the positioning and form of this existence are drawn. Referring to Parkin (1991), Hirsch gives the example of the Kaya – an empty ritual capital of the East African Giriama – as a place of potential and restorative power which

> has long been vacated and is divorced from the everyday experience of most Giriama. Parkin describes how an analogous method of animal sacrifice is performed both in the homestead and at the Kaya. When performed in the homestead, the background potential of the Kaya is foregrounded into everyday experience. And when performed at the

Kaya, the diverse experiences of foregrounded place are channelled towards this sacred centre as if to achieve, momentarily, the experience of potentiality, of life as independent and powerful like the Kaya, only to recede into the background and return the Giriama to their fragmented, quotidian existence. What is being defined as landscape here is the relationship seen to exist between these two poles of experience... (1995b: 5).

Landscape inheres in the relation between foregrounded quotidian experience and its background in religion, or space, or culture.

With the ethnography in mind, my question thus becomes that of how Reite people can achieve the production of persons (kinship and exchange), which includes a performance of things in the land, without this 'performance' implying representation as I think it does in Hirsch's argument above. That is, something which stands for something else in its absence. The work of the analyst, it seems, is to make the connections between foregrounded image and background apparent. The performance of sacrifice in the homestead is a token event, re-presenting a more real, or ontologically distinct, level of existence/meaning and importing it to re-animate the proceedings at hand. Implicit in 'performance' is the relation between token event and that which it enacts. Reite people *present* place, rather than re-present it in another form. Performance then does not capture what I describe. Instead I turn to J.L. Austin's definition of the 'performative'. As mentioned, my question is: Can a Reite conception (how persons produce themselves for others to view) replace something more familiar, such as representations of modified space, or something specifically understood as foreground from background potential, as a 'landscape'? I am after a description which would capture the 'performative' nature of what Reite people do in *sare*. Words which are performative do not represent an action, they *achieve* the effect they describe.

Here we come back to the notion of 'view', and to Hirsch's positioning of the analyst as able to account for a 'landscape' by drawing out the significance of foregrounding things against their background. The objectifying and distanciating properties of vision as it is often understood, and of the privileging of vision as a sensory modality in Western language and perception – particularly in relation to concepts of land and nature – need to be examined closely if we are to use 'landscape' in the Nekgini context. That is to say, the palem/sare complex is performative in that it results from distance in *relationships* – from the active separation of kin in marriage which creates different places to be viewed, and viewers to recognise their distinctiveness. It does not result from distance between viewers (humans) and viewed (landscape). Distance is between people and places. In the relationship of dancer and audience, places understood as complex combinations of persons, spirits, history and power have their effect. This in turn relies upon a notion of 'visibility' (Chapter 5) rather than 'vision'.

In Reite, when things are open to inspection, they may be demanded. Seeing can effect transformation by gendering persons in respect to one another. While hiddenness is essential to growth, revelation is essential to the recognition that change and growth have occurred. 'Visibility', then, is what I have argued Reite people seek to achieve in the social world (and see Strathern 1988: 255–6). To have a name is to be visible and to be taken account of in others rationale for action; to be gendered is to be seen and desired by another. People take account of those significant others within their horizons of action. There are multiple perspectives, but no 'outside' perspective.

Hearing and Vision as Sensory Modalities

In his book *The Taste of Ethnographic Things* (1989), Paul Stoller considers the possibilities of theorising personal experience itself as a legitimate anthropological mode of data collection. The distance usually adopted by an anthropologist-as-analyst, he argues, is a result of imagining the world full of discrete and already given objects-of-analysis. For an alternative approach, Stoller draws on ideas set out by Merleau-Ponty in his essay 'Eye and Mind'. In examining the philosophy of vision and seeing, Merleau-Ponty uses the writings of artists such as Cézanne to show how some painters have no interest in 'objects-in-general', but rather in the felt, the experienced qualities of light and shade, colour and texture, which are available to a human body as a situated perceptual entity. 'Merleau-Ponty believed that we lose much of the life-in-the-world by thinking operationally, by defining rather than experiencing the reality of things' (Stoller 1989: 37). This kind of thinking is attributed in part to the way our discourse privileges vision as an activity internal to the perceiver whereby stimuli are ordered into a meaningful set of perceptions.[2]

This put me in mind of the form and effect of *kaapu* as described in this book. Tambaran is about experience – about sound, fragrance, emotion – and as we have seen, it is also about substance, the growth and generation of bodies from places. Now we might say, following Weiner (1995), that in tambaran activity, and the creation of significant bodies and places through its presence, '[i]nsofar as time and space are being demarcated in these practices, they are a specifically embodied time and space, which convey the limits and capacities of the intentionality, the forward-lookingness of human consciousness and of the human body, the shape and contours of the body's productive movement and sexual and intersexual configurations' (Weiner 1995: 56).

Stoller himself was concerned with understanding his experience of sorcery among the Songhay of Niger. He reports that the Songhay stress the direct effect of sounds on people, and that sorcery works through this effect. The Songhay experience of sorcery is an experience of the medium of the sorcerer's power – his control over words, over sound. In a similar vein, Jackson (1989: 140) writes of how, through metaphor and analogy, 'the world of *things* is merged with the world of *Being*', effecting 'magically' the status of both for the perceiving subject.

However, Merleau-Ponty's essay on painting describes the predilection in Aristotelian and Cartesian thought to understand the world as a set of given objects, as things *beyond* the perceiver. This is a result of a particular theory of vision. He writes, 'the Cartesian concept of vision is modelled after the sense of touch' (Merleau-Ponty 1964: 170) – in other words for Descartes and his followers, vision, like touch, was understood as a connection, internal to the perceiver, between bodily sensation and mental representation, and had nothing to do with the experience of light as such. Against this, Merleau-Ponty argued for a relational view of the process of sight born out of an understanding of the painter's art as experience – experience of the medium of sight – which is light: 'For henceforth, as Klee said, the line no longer imitates the visible; it "renders visible", it is the blueprint of a genesis of things' (183).

For my argument it is important to be clear that there are two traditions of thought here – phenomenological and Cartesian. Broadly, phenomenologists argue that we perceive the world through the reality of our experiential engagement. Thus light and sound themselves are our medium for knowing. Cartesian philosophy and psychology, on the other hand, thinks perception occurs indirectly, by the ordering of stimuli that the body registers in the brain.

Cézanne was trying to put into paintings, and Merleau-Ponty into words, what we may all experience, even though we are disinclined to recognise this experience in our dominant (visualist) discourse. It is the discourse of visualism, argues Merleau-Ponty, not the experience of vision, that constitutes seeing as the intellectual representation of distant objects. The medium of their appearance within our minds, within our experience and bodily spatiality, escapes much Cartesian- and Aristotelian-inspired theorising about how we experience things, as Cartesian understandings of perception are not based on the experience of light or sound as such, but on the interpretation of bodily indices by the brain.

Yet there are also differences within the phenomenological tradition. Stoller, for example, follows Merleau-Ponty in arguing that Songhay sorcery works through the direct experience of the texture and power of words; it is the sound itself that is experienced by, and moves, the hearer. For Stoller, sound is the basis of Songhay sorcery because it does not distance the hearer from what is heard – sound is the means and the object of the experience. Yet in this regard, Stoller draws a sharp distinction between hearing and vision. For him, vision is a distancing modality, it *does* separate the experiencer from the object regarded: there is no contact with the things seen. Merleau-Ponty, by contrast, argues that we do, in fact, *see light*, and that vision is therefore not that different from hearing. For him, in both cases, it is direct experience of the medium of knowing that allows the perceiving subject to experience the thing itself.

The contrast, in short, is between those who claim that we do not see light as we hear sound, and those who claim that we do. The former position is exemplified in the work of the ecological psychologist, J.J. Gibson, whose position is in many other ways close to Merleau-Ponty. He insists that we do not see light, we only see things (Gibson 1979: 54); that is, we see only the surfaces which reflect light so as to reach the eye. It is remarkable that Gibson's view of light – as something that is not experienced as such, but serves only to specify the properties of environmental objects,[3] is not far removed from the position taken by Descartes, and to which Merleau-Ponty took explicit exception.

We do not see light, says Gibson – but do we hear sound? On the basis of his Songhay ethnography, Stoller answers unequivocally in the affirmative: 'sound is a dimension of experience in and of itself' (1989: 112). This is a point upon which many Western analysts and ethnographers seem to agree. Writing about the West Sepik Umeda, Gell tells us, 'Hearing is (relatively) intimate, concrete, and tactile, whereas vision promotes abstraction' (Gell 1995: 235). It seems to be an orthodoxy of a kind that we see things (rather than light) and that we hear sounds (rather than things which emit sounds, or off which it echoes). Likewise the idea that vision is objectifying and distancing, whereas sound is subjective, immediate and experiential, is quite familiar to Western sensibility. Many ethnographers, including Stoller and perhaps Gell, have imposed this contrast on their non-Western ethnography as though it was simply given, a direct contrast in the functioning of alternative sensory modalities.

But perhaps what Merleau-Ponty conveys to us is that this is only one possibility. Vision may not always work as a sensory mode which relies on extracting data about objects from a neutral medium, and re-organising this data into meaningful representations within the brain of the observer. In many ways the philosophical credibility of his alternative is established in relation to the ethnography I have presented. Many ethnographers (such as Gell and Stoller) have achieved brilliant analyses working with an idea of vision as ultimately distancing and sound as a contrasting, direct modality. Following from my arguments about terminology and representation in Chapter 3, I try the alternative presented by Merleau-Ponty. Merleau-Ponty argues we *do* see and experience light as such, and that we are moved by this experience. For him, vision is not so different from hearing after all. We can see light just as we can hear sound. This point is also implicit in the statement, attributed to Klee, which heads this chapter, and which also came from Merleau-Ponty. One moment Klee is talking about looking and being looked at, but the next moment he says 'I was listening'. Looking and listening are treated as self-evidently interchangeable – we scarcely even notice the difference. If, then, one follows Merleau-Ponty, contra Gibson, vision is an experience of light, lighting, shadows, colours, reflections, and so forth. This means our having to reject the appeals made by Stoller, and by Steven Feld in his work on Kaluli song, among others, to sound experience as a *contrastive* modality to that of vision (i.e., one that is more intimate, bodily, emotional, and energetic).

Now, as I have described, in Reite we have *sound* as the manifestation of power, and the effects of the voices of the tambaran spirits are tangible in the wealth and wives they draw to their performers. That the palem/sare complex could constitute a landscape – a presentation of land for others to experience – could make sense if one looks at the way it is experienced.

Whereas Reite people privilege sight and revelation for the presentation of grown and changed objects (of regard, of desire, of exchange),[4] the performance of their land, of places themselves, appears to be a more energetic experience (mainly through sound) of the relationships which constitute places as 'loci of kinship'. As Feld would have it, 'sound, hearing, and voice mark a special bodily nexus for sensation and emotion because of their co-ordination of brain, nervous system, head, ear, chest, muscles, respiration and breathing' (Feld 1996: 94). In one sense we could argue that the presentation of places is made through sound (music, song, spirit voices) as this provides a more genuine experience of place (meaning the field of relations which produce persons) than vision could. Yet, as we have seen, this conclusion rests on a distinction, which is at least questionable, between sight and hearing as essentially different ways of knowing things. Against the argument that places are presented through sound, sight and light are not totally absent from the power and performance of a dancing group.

My assertion that Reite people perform places, that they are in effect showing their landscape for others to see, is absurd in one sense: the very essence and substance of the performance – the *kaapu* – are not only invisible, but are only there as the combined efforts of the men of a place to produce themselves as an entity of regard. Their landscape is not a 'soundscape' (Feld 1996: 114), if by that is meant a representation in sound of the contours of the land; rather the presentation of places is through all the energetic media of relationship – movement, sound, smell[5] *and* luminosity.

I believe the resolution of this issue lies in following Merleau-Ponty and therefore refusing to endorse the separation ethnographers such as Stoller and Feld make between hearing and sight in all instances. Vision need not always be distancing, as Merleau-Ponty proves through specific reference to the work of great painters. If the concept of visibility, of which I seem to make so much, refers essentially to an energetic presentation of places – the forms of the carvings, of the dancers' decorations, and of the dancing group as a whole appearing in the light of dawn – then it would encompass both the luminous and the sonic aspects of that presentation. This then resolves the paradox that while the *kaapu* are *invisible* (in the sense that they are hidden from view), they are nevertheless central to the process whereby places are rendered socially *visible* in people's experience – that is to the presentation of place. At this moment of presentation, the reason that the master idiom is a sonic one has nothing to do with an ontological or perceptual a-priori difference between vision and hearing, but has everything to do with the Nekgini idiom of hiddenness in relation to potency (Chapter 4). Many aspects of sare/palem performances are visible. The animating potency is not. Strength is given by bones.

If by 'seeing' we mean the kind of immediate, poetic involvement of the perceiver and the world that Merleau-Ponty was delineating when he contrasts the 'see-er' and the 'spectator' (1964: 162), then *kaapu*, in the presentation of place, are *seen* even though they remain invisible; and this conclusion also accommodates the conception of agency which I have argued for in this book. Rather than being outside spectators of the performance, the people of the host hamlet to a *sare* performance provide recognition. Their response is integral to the performance and the perception the performers have of themselves. The perspective they have on the performance is not that of outsiders, but that of constituting their effect, their perception of their power, through what the hosts feel has been elicited from them by the form which the land-as-presented, takes.

What Merleau-Ponty calls for in Western science and philosophy, drawn from art, Reite people in their way already practise as an experiential art/ritual/exchange form. Reite places, like the mountain in Merleau-Ponty's description which I cite below, are interrogated for their relationality, and this relationality is presented in media which connect rather than distantiate. These include light, if not direct sight of any 'object'.

> It is the mountain itself which from out there makes itself seen by the painter; it is the mountain which he interrogates with his gaze.
>
> What exactly does he ask of it? To unveil the means, visible and not otherwise, by which it makes itself a mountain before his eyes. Light, lighting, shadows, reflections, colour, all the objects of his quest are not altogether real objects; like ghosts they have only virtual existence. In fact they exist only at the threshold of profane vision; they are not seen by everyone. The painter's gaze asks them what they do to suddenly cause something to be and to be *this* thing, what they do to compose this worldly talisman and make it visible. (166, original emphasis)

I might similarly ask, in a Nekgini epistemology, what makes a place? What makes it known, significant, present? What is it about places that gives growth, names, beauty, satisfaction, longing, and belonging? If Merleau-Ponty's painter interrogates the mountain for its light, he interrogates it to discover the means by which it makes itself visible before his eyes. These means are 'not altogether real objects' – as with 'ghosts' (or spirits, I might say, thinking of Reite ethnography), it is his *relation* with the thing, with the world, which he interrogates and which is his medium for knowing. In attending to the medium, the subject opens him- or herself to experience, to light, sound, and smell as relational media, not to the object *sui generis* or distant from him or her as a represented landscape might be thought to be. Producing bodies and persons makes places for Reite people. This process of production is dramatised in the form of *sare* and palem, whereby relations and powers are made present for others to experience. If landscape is about relationships (i.e., the history of places is a history of kin groups and growth/production), then the presentation of the landscape is a presentation of these relationships.

It is in this sense that we would have to use 'landscape' – as the presentation of the relational and energetic media of knowing, and of evidence of the outcome of this knowing (bodies) – to make it have relevance for Nekgini practices in relation to land. Many readers may think this is pushing the word beyond what is reasonable. I make no apology however. Whether we call sare performances a 'landscape', or a 'presentation of place', or something in between, at least we are now aware of the issues involved in doing so.

Landscape in the Nekgini Lifeworld

As I have described them, the activities of Reite people are largely concerned with the anticipated outcomes of presenting places for others to experience. This is why kastom has such salience in their eyes. Kastom specifies the correct way of 'gathering everything together' (*turum maliemung*) which makes palem-based sociality possible. In making a palem and preparing for a night of *sare* people are not seeking to *represent* a place – and thus to produce a landscape in the sense of a static picture (Cosgrove 1988; cf. Ingold 1994a) – but rather to *present* themselves as aspects of a particular place by way of a dramatic and sensory production of what a place is, or can be made to be, in Nekgini understanding. In these performative moments there is no outside position to view them from, no absolute removal from the thing presented. Land is made mobile, and thus appears 'in' other places, while encompassing those 'within' it.

My position here is inspired by Werbner's (1989) analysis of the Umeda *ida* ritual reported by Gell (1975). There, he describes how Umeda contrast territory and women, the former as immovable, and the latter as mobile. Both are containers of a kind. When Reite palem perform sare, women and men combine as a single entity which like 'territory' contains people. It is their containment by the mobile body of the palem's tambaran which masks internal differentiation and *externalises* relations of gender. Movement on the part of the audience is what a palem seeks to achieve, paradoxically, as it were, eliciting movement in another while the mobile embodiment of a fixed place. The play on gender principle, the nesting of one encompassment in another, means that although mobile, out of their own territory, their appearance as a single and undifferentiated whole invokes the placement on which their effect is based. This place encompasses its audience, produces movement in their audience which reverses the movement of one group coming onto another's land. In their image of wholeness, they evoke a fixity in another place which is made to have its effect in separating persons from the host's hamlet. They are moved, as I outlined in Chapter 5, and thus gender is re-established as an external relation produced by the performing palem. One could say this is why it is the *male* tambaran which is musical and mobile. It is what extracts or dislodges persons from places and thus appears fixed in relation to their movement, even though it 'travels' to have this effect. The mobile men's tambaran (*aignu kaap*) is called *kaapu neng* (mother spirit). As a mobile entity, like a woman, its movement elicits future relations.

We could not call these processes representation. Nor could we call them 'symbolic', any more than we could regard the funerary procedures reported in the previous chapter as primarily 'symbolic'. In both, there is an experiential and bodily involvement in the process whereby persons and places come into being, and in the case of funerary practices, in the process by which the form of life dissolves.

The question is whether for such people, who do not privilege representation, their perception of the lifeworld is so far removed from what is entailed in our concept of landscape, as to make the concept irrelevant. Against this, I have, after all, described their endeavour as one of 'presenting' the enfolding of persons and land. For Peter Gow, writing about the Piro of Western Amazonia, the fact that these people 'do not create representations of their land', does not mean they cannot be described as having a 'landscape':

> I do not argue that Native Amazonian people have some sort of immediate relationship to their land… particular people have densely mediated relationships to particular places: this is what makes Amazonia a lived human landscape. But I am arguing that these medi-ations do not, on the whole, take the form of *representations*. (Gow 1995: 44, original emphasis).

Gow's point here about mediation brings me to my final point about landscape and performance. Knowledge of the land is not generated and mediated through representations, but through the work of generating other people.

For land to be seen, to be experienced, Reite people work very hard. This work is the work of growing people, it is the provision of the conditions under which people grow, and through labour and knowledge, the culmination of such effort in a particular *form*. I have dwelt on the creation of one aspect of this form (that of a palem) and its relation to the growing of other kinds of bodies. Here, I take a comparative example from elsewhere in Melanesia to bring together the points I have made about the character of mediation in the creation of an appropriate form for bodies to take.

Nancy Munn (1986: 139) reports a myth from the island of Gawa in the Massim. In the story, men of Gawa tried to hack a canoe from the earth itself, and failed. Then a woman revealed to the men the right trees from which to carve a canoe by smearing their trunks with her body fluids. Strathern (1991: 66–7) finds this a striking image. She relates how a canoe is the medium of relationships, moving away from its source on trading voyages – always to return to its point of departure – the land on which the trees of the canoe's hull, grew. While the outside of the canoe is decorated with white paint to look like a young man, it is essentially formed from the land of the maternal clan, from maternal blood. The work of men gives this substance form. Thus one might say that men's relations to one another (in trade) in which they win renown, are mediated by the container in which they arrive – that of their maternal origin. The mediated form that relationships take produce a form of their own, and that form embodies the relationality of the home place, the maternal lands, as a body moving in trading relations (men in a male canoe formed of female substance). 'Thus the carving and decorating of the canoe is done so that the canoe will travel away from the land where the trees grew, in order to effect exchanges with persons from other lands' (Strathern 1991: 66). Male creativity and renown are made possible by their relations to maternal kin and land. Male relations are mediated through relations to women. Female relations are mediated by men who travel. The form these mediated relations produce (the canoe as a container for men) allows other relationships to be generated. Thus one might say that one set of relations produces a form which elicits other relationships.

What does the form of a palem elicit? The right to dance at the place of another group, defined as such in the transaction itself. As Hirsch points out in an article on aesthetic 'coercion' in Melanesian ritual,

> such an aesthetically interested focus on the object (the *gab* village [the palem]) would privilege one aspect of this complex ritual and ignore a more fundamental aesthetic issue: what the object makes possible or facilitates. I argue that it allows the person, as mind or body, to be in a position of eliciting an effect from another. (Hirsch 1995a: 67)

And the effect that presenting an affinal payment elicits is both a separation from the receivers, and also an indebtedness which can only be compensated by reciprocation of the chance to come into a hamlet as visitors, and elicit a body from them in return. Thus land is given form both as bodies (persons), and also as the performance which detaches these persons from their source.

I have described how Reite people perform places, how they turn what Hirsch would describe as the background potentiality of land itself into voices, movement, fragrance and produce – bodies and persons. This is not representation, 'something that stands for something else in its absence' (Gow 1995: 44). What is produced from land are persons, and because they are exchangeable, they are neither tokens of something else, nor does something else stand for them. What is performed is what is present, and what is present always has a partible aspect and an origin. Reite places are produced for a purpose – that of moving specific people. 'Landscape' might be a term for this – as the presentation draws together elements of the land and produces a place as an aesthetic experience for others to behold. It has a form (bodies, designs, songs) which is appropriate for others to view. Thus relations to land are mediated through social others, it is social bodies that give form to the land, and thus produce it as 'landscape'.

The difference between Reite 'landscape' in this sense, and a Western understanding of a 'landscape', or perhaps Hirsch's cross-cultural concept, is that it is not up to the viewer to make the connections between foreground and background, nor to take up a position separate from, or outside, the thing regarded. The experience of the receiver of the attentions of a place, in this regard, is both to encompass (by consuming) the produce of a place, that is to internalise part of that place, and, in turn, to be encompassed by the place – by its voices, fragrances, words, and movement. This encompassment is experienced as emotion, as sympathy for those performing.

Not all landscape is representational. Gow describes the Piro landscape as kinship: 'The production and circulation of food produces people, who respond with memory of these acts of caring. But equally, these productive activities create the mosaic of vegetation zones around the village', which are not 'detritus' but a source of ongoing food production, and the 'loci of kinship' (1995: 49).

Notes

1. This perspective is also apparent in studies which relate 'culture' to environmental factors – Steward (1955); Rappaport (1971).
2. As Feld puts it, introducing his discussion of Kaluli 'place' perception, 'by and large, ethnographic and cultural-geographic work on senses of place has been dominated by the visualism deeply rooted in the European concept of landscape' (Feld 1996: 94).
3. It is on these grounds that Gibson distinguishes between 'energetic stimulation' and 'stimulus information' (1979: 53).
4. Recall Gillison's assertion that for Gimi people, seeing is tantamount to possession (Gillison 1993; Weiner 1995).
5. Umeda magical practices (as reported by Gell) centre around another ambiguous medium – olfaction – to take advantage, as he describes it, of the ambiguous status of smells as neither objects in themselves nor thoughts, but something reminiscent of both (Gell 1977).

Chapter Eight
Creative Land

Land, Place, and Person

Tim Ingold writes that 'while places have centres – indeed it would be more appropriate to say that they *are* centres – they have no boundaries' (Ingold 1994b). Boundaries do not exist in space, or between places, unless they are generated as such in purposeful activity. As with places, for Nekgini speakers, so with persons. Nekgini speakers' identity is crucially bound, not to genealogy, but to place. As Casey writes on the concept of place, 'we find that porousness of boundaries is essential to place. A place could not gather bodies in the diverse spatiotemporal ways it does without permeability of its own limits' (Casey 1996: 42). The gathering of relations shows that a person's make-up is also porous. It depends on sharing the relations by which places come into being. It depends also on what is implicated in the process of a place's recognition as such: in this case that is the production of persons. One cannot then specify the relations of kinship without reference to exchange; that is, to place.

There is no general relation of kinship, only specific ones, only a social world of others who are cognates, affines, or aliens. As Gow writes:

> in so far as kinship is only about direct social relations, and in so far as these relations implicate direct landscape modifications [for the Piro], native people must be able to perceive kinship in the landscape. It is of course true that each native person must be socialised into doing so, but this is already given in the relations of kinship. (1995: 56)

The issue that Lawrence faced in his Garia ethnography was one of how to describe the workings of a society where the limits of kinship, therefore of social organisation, institutions, ritual confederations, or territorial groups, were similarly porous. The model through which Lawrence analysed his Garia material posited closed groups in which persons are individuals, specified in advance, and gain identity by virtue of their genealogical position. Now we have seen that the openness of places is mirrored in Reite understanding by the openness of the body itself. Thus, far from being specified in advance, the person can be said to be defined within a field of social relations which they progressively embody as moments in an unfolding process. Each person is a node or point in this field of relations. Their definition and agency is crucially bound up with what other people do. This process is the generation or continual creation of the Nekgini 'lived world' (Gow 2001). As places enter directly into the constitution of persons, and as places gather those implicated in the labour of producing persons, we can say that places are themselves like persons. In parallel, people take their name and identity from the place in which they are thus grown.

I asked (Chapter 3) what role *asurung* (blood) plays in Reite understandings of kinship. The answer was a reiteration of my description of creative processes among Nekgini speakers. Persons, specified by the relations they have to other persons who nurture them, and to the place in which this nurture occurs, are connected through sharing the source of the nurture itself – placement. The land, as a continuous field, is in fact very similar in this way to kinship for Reite people. Thus separations are needed between kin (specified as such through sharing land) to produce difference. These differences are embodied in the differences between places themselves. Land as a continuous field, and relatedness as a continuous field, must be separated into places, and into different social bodies. *Asurung*, then, cannot mean genealogically transferred substance, but must refer to the shared history of relations and growth by which persons are understood to come into being.

This undermines the idea of an 'ego-centred' set of relationships as Lawrence describes the basis of Garia organisation. Relationships based on individuality see persons initially specified by genealogical substance at the moment of conception, then related to one another by society. Reite relationships, however, are based on accumulation (history) through sharing either the labour of others in creating the conditions for growth, or through creating the conditions under which others may grow. Substance, far from being given immutably at birth, is an outcome of the relations which produce the person. Thus a person may be in a position to apprehend the relationships he or she embodies, and will act on, or because of, these connections. Kinship is, in a sense, geography, as the constitution of persons and of places, and of the separations between them, is mutually entailed.

The associations Reite people make between men, land, and bones, and between women, movement, and flow, do not consign us to a view of either land or persons as singularly constituted (for example that men come from land, or that land is male), nor to the view that persons are gendered by their attributes. Nekgini understanding of persons is that they are the outcome of cross-sex relationships. Persons are not simply identified as either 'male' productions or 'female' productions. The wealth given in a palem exchange, or as a daughter in marriage, is not the product of an individual, but of a reified history of relations between persons which appear as a whole entity. Wealth is generated by dividual social entities (palem) – by the combination of male and female into a whole which produces wealth because it is internally gendered. In a body, or in a palem, to quote Strathern: '[u]nity only partially conceals an anticipated dual or multiple identity. And it is only appropriate for certain stages in the development of the child/food. Thus the ... woman's claims to the growing crops [or children] she has planted depend for their effectiveness on the fact that her work is also part of the joint work of the spouses, and it is conceived as separate only in relation to her husband's' (1988: 253). Likewise, Reite men who claim status through palem production mirror their wives' pride at having paid for themselves in the same transaction. In their productivity, neither can claim pre-eminence. Production is elicited in the relationship which brings them together.

What is interesting about the Reite material is the transparency of the mechanisms by which persons may be detached from one whole and integrated into another (the porous boundaries of places). This is a result of the centrality of land and places to Nekgini notions of identity and substance. Strathern (1988: 254) describes a similar conceptual link to the one I have reported for Reite between land and substance in Mount Hagen. She writes, '[w]hether a woman resides with her husband or is back at home with her brothers, the very territory is conceptually agnatic. Her partaking of its products (via the food she grows) invests her own body with its strength'. Where the Paiela husband is said to have planted his wife in the centre of his garden (Biersack 1984: 126) and thus to have enclosed her in clan substance, newcomers to Reite lands are bought so that they might contribute their substance to the land itself on their death. Women's bones are as coveted as men's, and not only her progeny, but also her own body, become identified through her particular contribution to a place's multiple constitution. People become different depending on their location. Thus all kin are specific kin *because* they are all spatially located in a pattern of places which provide the substance of difference.

A palem, like a person, is internally differentiated for the purposes of production, but externally appears as whole. In constructing a palem, a couple mask their cross-sex relation as internal to the body of the hamlet group which is produced. However, when affines take their pay, they do not take the bones supporting the growth of that wealth, and thus both accept the inclusion of their child into the land and identity of their exchange partners – it is her body or bones which are replaced and thus remain – while simultaneously creating asymmetry between themselves and the donors. The receivers are 'female' on the land of the donors.

In contexts where land is at issue in Reite, it is said to be under men's control. Men stay on land, they can allow others to use it, they have knowledge of, and relationships with, the spirits of places. But this is balanced by other contexts in which connections through women are emphasised: the necessity for exchange, the rights maternal kin claim over growing a child. Then there are contexts in which palem, married units, or sibling sets, have equal rights to use and produce from land. Women are as much 'persons' in this sense as are men. This comes from their incorporation into the places through the same complimentary mechanism as their husband's siblings.

Complexity in describing and analysing a land-based kinship system rests not on the principles people hold about ownership (Lawrence 1955, 1984). Ownership is multiple because people trace multiple connections within any one reification. There are multiple aspects any person or place can present, or be forced to yield, to another. Rights and obligations are difficult to trace into coherent wholes other than persons (Strathern 1992b) or palem as wider configurations of a 'bodily' kind because agency may be located outside of any single person, any single place. Knowledge of kastom gives authority to palem leaders because kastom is the particular mode of effective practice which differentiates one place from another: its patuki, kaapu and so forth. Take the example of love-magic. In coercing a woman to follow him home, the performer of love-magic becomes the agent in enforcing a gender on not only the woman, but also all her other siblings. Thus their personhood, their substance, is impinged upon by another person, another place upon which they are subsequently obliged to make claims and from which they receive wealth. (Male and female siblings receive wealth for a bride.) Yet their identity, or position with regard to their affines in this case of marriage, may not alter the form of their internal relationships. In other contexts, they may be the agents of their own (garden) activity (thus appearing whole again) or they may have relations to other places in which they detach women. The position forced upon them by the activities of the love-magician on one of their palem will not be the position they adopt with regard to other palem, to other persons. Places, made up of kin groups who may each have separate obligations, desires, intentions, and most fundamentally, history (i.e. embody particular past relations), and who pursue these or are affected by them, are no more individual or bounded than are persons themselves. Nor are they exclusive. Küchler writes illuminatingly of another Papua New Guinea location, Northern New Ireland:

> the land which serves for gardening and for habitation is thus conceptualised as a body: the communally shared land or 'skin' associated with affinal relationships surrounds the houses or 'womb' which are the domain of the women and the matriline.
>
> However, this physiological structure imposed on the social landscape is not fixed, but is blurred and made indistinguishable in the process of restructuring house sites and garden areas.... (Küchler 1993: 97)

I have suggested that we can approach an answer to the question of why kinship looks as it does here through an understanding of what land and landscape might mean for Nekgini speakers. This involves rethinking the basis of our understanding of kinship in a genealogical model. Places themselves, as socially significant and created through people's incorporative projects in the land, are relationally constituted and thus communally or socially present. If people are grown by places, and places are non-bounded, non-exclusive, and open to motivation and discovery, open to the incorporation of any number of persons, Reite personhood and Reite landscapes come together as more than mere analogies of one another. They are consubstantial. 'It is impossible to talk about place, or to talk about how people talk about place, without encompassing biography, including one's own at points of social interaction' (Kahn 1996). Hence the story of arrival with which I began.

Simple Principles, Complex Process

Persons (male or female) are parts of places. Places are constituted by the field of relationships which produce persons, and thus implicate kinship. The sharing of substance comes from the sharing of land. The aspect of personhood which could be termed placement is a 'male' constituent in certain contexts, as when wealth or flesh is stripped from bones in an exchange or death, or when a woman leaves her brothers in marriage. But land itself could be said to have both male and female components, as do its products. Things which move from the place they were grown become female due to their movement, and are eventually included in another place. (It is the movement which is gendering, not that which moves.)

The principles that I have laid out in this work can be simplified as follows. Nekgini speakers imagine persons moving between the following modes of being, and their appearance as one or another, or as more than one simultaneously, depends upon which relations with others (including spirits) are paramount to their project in any given endeavour. First, there are ungendered persons (sibling sets, hamlet groups, mythic beings prior to differentiation). Secondly, there are internally gendered persons (married couples, palem at the moment of production, gardens). Thirdly, there are male persons (persons who detach wealth from others, or have wealth detached from them; both men and women achieve this in palem construction, thus both earn the right to be buried in the place from which wealth is taken [males stay on land]); and fourthly, there are female persons (detached from places and incorporated into new places). From these four principles are generated the intricacies of a Nekgini lived world. Any single person or place may evince one or all of these modes during a lifetime.

Simple as these principles appear, they are tied into a complex of differing perspectives where persons, like places, are at once parts of others (constituted in relation to them and through incorporation into them), and whole in themselves. That is why the palem is the crucial point at which to enter into Nekgini sociality – it is at once one body and the product of one place, dual in its construction as both a partible body and a non-partible set of 'bones', and divisible in its make-up as multiple persons, the outcome of productive cross-sex relationships. It is a truly 'dividual' (Clay 1986: 4, quoting Mariott [1976]; Strathern 1992b) entity; and in marriage, it is divided and thus an archetypal image of a Nekgini person. Claims over persons in their different aspects (labour, body, reproductive potential, relations with land and spirits, knowledge, animating spirit, names, social appearance) are drawn out differently in different moments, as indeed are claims over land.

Here is the source of the 'complexity' of kin relations, residence, and sociality which I discussed in Chapter 2. There I pointed to the inadequacies of a mode of analysis that sees persons as specified by genealogy, and growing due to this specification, and not due to their relations to other people. Thus relations to other people have to be explained (by appeal to society).

I have demonstrated in this book that while the discovery of principles plays a part in the analysis and understanding of Reite sociality, these principles do not need to be highly complex in order to produce the complex patterns of Nekgini social life, or 'cognatic kinship'. The production of persons and therefore relatedness turn out to be the result of fairly simple principles which are nevertheless responsible for the generation of a complex process (Rubin 1988). I have been unable to avoid complexity in my account. The lifeworld of Nekgini speakers, what they take for granted, does not translate without contextualisation and exegesis. There is processual complexity in any 'lived world'.

Creativity

Recently, creativity has been described as a preoccupation of modernism (Leip 2001). The idea that unique combinations produce novelty, and that such an understanding of individuality is integral to Euro-American self-perception and self-valuation is hard to deny. That this is an aspect of our history is demonstrated by looking only as far as kinship and models of the person. Kinship, for the English at least, became a matter of unique combinations producing ever more differentiation (Strathern 1992a). The genealogical model of biological relatedness and differentiation bequeaths each person a unique identity because they combine and recombine substance in a unique form. The assumption of incest interdiction works as a prohibition on combinations of 'the same' substance. The imagined consequences amount to cosmological speculation. Health and human vitality are understood to depend on (following the dictates of nature) proliferating new kinds of entity (creation). Individuals, unique and biologically self-contained, are the result. It is not people that are primarily inventive. 'Nature' brings existing elements together in novel ways. The incest prohibition is a visceral reaction against the unnatural (Edwards 1993); and creative people are thought to be, in essence, different from the rest of us. Like biogenetic substance, genius is internal to a person, not an aspect of relationships.

Yet I have used creativity as a way of describing a generative process of another kind. Combination is part of this process, but the dualism between society and nature is not. Creativity is something that, like all other attributes and definitions, exists as a relationship with other people. When Nekgini people make claims to ownership, they claim control of, or centrality to, a particular set of relations. These processes of generation are predicated on the viability of entities which maintain their multiple, (not dualistic) character. Unique appearance is thought of as a manufactured outcome, a reification.

Recently, Gow has argued that Lévi-Strauss has been misinterpreted in his view of myth (2001: 10–14). Rather than the perception of primitive society as unchanging in comparison to modern societies (which cumulatively add differentiation by multiplying entities) Gow argues that Lévi-Strauss's analysis was in fact aimed at capturing an in-built principle of change in primitive society. Everything that has power and effect can be seen at once as contemporary, and as a version of the past. If the creation of the world *was* autopoetic, the creation of the world is *still* autopoetic. That is, people achieve it through following the principles which make a productive process out of human endeavour. In Reite, they follow the particular kastom germane to each place. Through the production of people – bodies, gender, ideas, objects, places – human life is made to appear as exactly that (Mimica 1991).

There may well then be alternatives to the 'creativity' described by modernity. For Euro-Americans, creativity is first and foremost that which transcends the everyday. That it intrudes upon human possibility and may be partially held or captured by artists, or innovators, makes these people seem special – creative individuals – geniuses, as psychologists among others have called them. They have a 'divine spark'. Whether it is nature or divinity that is creative, humans have the ability to touch this creative power, and thus momentarily elevate themselves. We are back to a dualism between the individual and an entity which exists separate to or beyond them. Leip adheres to this contrast as one between general creativity going on all the time (the background to human existence) – procreation, social formation, culture – and specific creativity in which human beings have radical effects – the work of the genius. This is a contrast between 'distributed' or 'conventional' creativity, and 'true' creativity. 'If "conventional creativity" spreads like an ocean on the surface of the world, "true" creativity rises like an island here and there' (2001: 12).

Creative engagement, the expectation of novel combination and innovation is something I have described as 'conventional' for Reite people. Its power lies in its connection to the project of making human existence as established in myth and kastom. Does this mean the creative land I describe is similar to Leip's ocean? It is tempting to acquiesce to the power of such metaphors, particularly as I have made so much of the continuity in relatedness which has its basis in the continuity of the terrain. On the other hand, if Leip's description is of the creativity valued and accessed by modernity (with its assumptions about the intrinsic difference between entities) then we must proceed with caution. I have described a field of specific relations for each person. In Reite, Leip's 'true' creative moments (the 'restructuring' of experience) are integral to the autopoetic existence which is the Nekgini lifeworld. Recreating the conditions for human existence through everyday activities of gardening, growing and gendering persons, and creating places, shows us that the notion of creativity as *extraordinary* is not their understanding. The appearance of Reite people and places exhibits 'transcendence' (Mimica 1991) as the condition of human being itself. Restructuring experience and making fundamental knowledge is what Reite people do by following *patuki*.

For Reite people, I have argued, creativity is something that is fully human. Humans do not touch on a creativity beyond them for moments of genius. By being the process and outcome of creation, separating persons, making new persons, generating and regenerating places, inventing designs and spirit songs, incorporating novelty, they *are* the patuki of their landscape. Kastom is adhered to as the ultimate source of power. Theirs is an existence in which creativity is the inherent principle. It is the human condition, and thus persons and myths, garden produce and designs, are commensurate. All that is produced is part of the production of humanity itself. Land as known places is integral to personhood. It is generated in the same process.

In the opening chapter, I pointed out some dangers with the notion of process. In what I have described, entities are not pre-specified, and *process is not process* either. It is *already* gardening, growing people, making separation in the mode of gender difference, death, and dissolution of the body. That means the palem is indeed a coming into being. Its description and the description of its formation are one and the same (Whitehead 1929). What things 'are' depends upon their 'process' of generation, the relationships in which they appear as entities, and their dissolution. It is creative endeavour that animates *both* people and things. Individual creativity is not the model I have discovered or uncovered in the Reite lived world. Instead I have tried to capture objects in their making – in their coming into being. Process is already places and persons. Process is a creative land.

Glossary

Nekgini

ai yakaapu	– men's sprit cult (tambaran)
asurung	– blood
gnalo	– knotted vine, each knot indicating a sunrise or sunset, for remembering dates
kaapu	– spirit/ghost/spirit voice/ritual paraphernalia/group of initiated men and spirits combined
kaapu neng	– spirit mother (a category of spirit secret to men's cult; spirit voice used in performances in the open, controlled by men, and this type of spirit's secret paraphernalia or *maal*)
kaapu tupong yara	– water spirits (musical male tambaran spirits)
kaap sawing	– wild spirit/bad spirit. Used when constructing slit-gongs and drums
kaap simang	– spirit child (a category of spirit secret to men; a spirit voice used in performances inside closed spaces by men, and this type of spirit's secret paraphernalia or *maal*)
kaapya tangawakting	– spirit cult causes wailing and crying (by the beauty of, or memories evoked by, their performance)
kiramung	– slit-gong drum
luhu	– *Zingiberaceae hornstreditia scottiana.* Gorogor (gorgor) in Tok Pisin. A 'cold' plant. Wards off malice, brings healing, a sign of peace
maal	– loincloth, also, euphemism for secret paraphernalia which are necessary to the appearance of each type of spirit voice
mangmang	– structure worn on the shoulders to support a *torr* post
maning'ting	– words of a sacred song

mernung	– homicidal sorcery through adulteration of something discarded by the victim
mundutor	– spirit place/sacred site
munsing	– dangerous person/enemy/marriageable person
palem	– refers to a social grouping, and also a bed on which food is piled in affinal exchanges, and the meeting house where visitors are welcomed into a hamlet
parieng yara kaapu	– women's spirit cult (tambaran)
paru	– spells (secret names)
passae	– (male) cult house, in which paraphernalia of the men's spirit cult (*kaapu*) is kept. Called *haus tambaran* in Tok Pisin
patuki	– stories, myths, knowledge, characters in myth.
pfakung	– type of spirit voice controlled by men and this spirit's secret paraphernalia (*maal*)
pununung	– possum or cuscus; generic for protein foods.
rauang	– 'women's play'. While the male cult is present in any hamlet, women indulge in raucous and lewd behaviour
Sare (Sare'keting)-	– decorated men and women dancing together with spirit voices
ting	– eye/shoot/point of growth
torr	– decorated head-post, carried in *sare*
tupong ting	– spirit pool, formed by a rising spring ('water eye/shoot')
wating	– eye/shoot (central) planting in a garden

Tok Pisin

bilum	– knotted string bag
birua	– dangerous person/marriageable person (to specified other) accident/enemy
garamut	– slit-gong drum
gorogor (gorgor)	– see *luhu* above
haus tambaran	– (male) cult house called *passae* in Nekgini
kandere	– a relative, connection traced through a female (MB, MBS, FZS)
tambaran	– spirits, cult objects and paraphernalia, combination of men and spirits
tambaran singsing	– decorated dancers perform with the spirit cult as accompaniment

References

Astuti, R. 1995. *People of the Sea. Identity and Descent among the Vezo of Madagascar.* Cambridge: Cambridge University Press.

Austin, J.L. 1976. *How to Do Things With Words: The William James Lectures Delivered at Harvard University in 1955.* Oxford: Oxford University Press.

Barnes, J.A. 1962. 'African Models in the New Guinea Highlands.' *Man* 62: 5–9.

Bateson, G. 1958. [1936]. *Naven. A Survey of the Problems Suggested by a Composite Picture of the Culture of a New Guinea Tribe Drawn from Three Points of View.* Stanford, California: Stanford University Press.

Bentinkt, R. 1949/50. 'Saidor/Madang Patrol Report.' 6 – 27/7, Australian Trusteeship Administration.

Biersack, A. 1982. 'Ginger Gardens for the Ginger Woman: Rites and Passages in a Melanesian Society.' *Man (N.S.)* 17: 239–58.

———, 1984 'Paiela 'Women-Men': The Reflexive Foundations of Gender Ideology.' *American Ethnologist* 10: 110–38.

Böck, M. and A. Rao. (eds) 2000. *Culture Creation and Procreation: Concepts of Kinship in South Asian Practice.* New York and Oxford: Berghahn Books.

Bolton, L. 1999. 'Women, Place and Practice in Vanuatu: A View from Ambae.' *Oceania* 70:1 (Special Issue) 43–55.

———, 2002. *Unfolding the Moon: The Recognition of Women's Kastom in Vanuatu.* Honolulu: University of Hawai'i Press.

Burton, J. 1998. 'Yaganon People of the Rai Coast.' Report prepared for Highlands Pacific Limited. Pacific Social Mapping: Canberra.

Carsten, J. 1995. 'The Substance of Kinship and the Heat of the Hearth: Feeding, Personhood and Relatedness among Malays in Pulau Langkawi.' *American Ethnologist* 22: 223–41.

———, 1997. *The Heat of the Hearth: The Process of Kinship in a Malay Fishing Community.* Oxford: Clarendon Press.

———, 2000. (ed.) *Cultures of Relatedness. New Approaches to the Study of Kinship.* Cambridge: Cambridge University Press.

Casey, E.S. 1996. 'How to Get from Space to Place in a Fairly Short Stretch of Time: Phenomenological Prolegomena.' In *Senses of Place,* (eds) S. Feld and K.H. Basso. Santa Fe: School of American Research Press.

Chowning, A. 1989. 'Death and Kinship in Molima.' In *Death and Life in the Societies of the Kula Ring*, (eds) F.H. Damon and R. Wagner. DeKalb: Northern Illinois University Press.

Clay, B.J. 1977. *Pinikindu. Maternal Nurture, Paternal Substance*. Chicago and London: University of Chicago Press.

———, 1986. *Mandak Realities. Person and Power in Central New Ireland*. New Brunswick, New Jersey: Rutgers University Press.

Corbin, H. 1969. *Creative Imagination in the Sufism of Ibn Arabi*. Princeton: Princeton University Press.

Cosgrove, D. and Daniels, S. 1988. 'Introduction: Iconography and Landscape.' In *The Iconography of Landscape: Essays on the Symbolic Representation, Design and Use of Past Environments*, (eds.) D. Cosgrove and S. Daniels. Cambridge: Cambridge University Press.

Dalton, D. 1992. From Shells to Money: Symbolic Transformations in a Highland New Guinea Economy. In *Abschied von der Vergangenheit*, (ed.) J. Wassmann. Berlin: Deitrich Reimer.

Damon, F. 1989. 'Introduction.' In *Death Rituals and Life in the Societies of the Kula Ring*, (eds) F. Damon and R. Wagner, Dekalb: Northern Illinois University Press.

de Coppet, D. 1994. 'Are'are.' In *Of Relations and the Dead: Four Societies Viewed from the Angle of their Exchanges*, (eds) D. de Coppet, C. Barraud, A. Iteanu and R. Jamous (Trans.) S. Suffern. Oxford: Berg.

Dyer, K.W. 1969/70. 'Saidor/Madang Patrol Report.' Australian Trusteeship Administration.

Edwards, J. 1993. 'Explicit Connections: Ethnographic Enquiry in North-West England.' In *Technologies of Procreation. Kinship in the Age of Assisted Conception*, (eds) J. Edwards, S. Franklin, E. Hirsch, F. Price, and M. Strathern. Manchester: Manchester University Press.

———, 2000. *Born and Bred. Idioms of Kinship and New Reproductive Technologies in England*. Oxford: Oxford University Press.

Englund, H. and Leach, J. 2000. 'Ethnography and the Meta-Narratives of Modernity', *Current Anthropology* 41(2): 225–48.

Eggan, F. 1937. 'Historical Change in the Choctaw Kinship System.' *American Anthropologist* 24: 34–52.

Feld, S. 1982. *Sound and Sentiment: Birds, Weeping, Poetics, and Song in Kaluli Expression*. Philadeliphia: University of Philadelphia Press.

———, 1996. 'Waterfalls of Song: An Acoustemology of Place Resounding in Bosavi, Papua New Guinea.' In *Senses of Place*, (eds) S. Feld and K.H. Basso. Santa Fe: School of American Research Press.

Feld, S. and Basso K. (eds) 1996. *Senses of Place*. Santa Fe: School of American Research Press.

Finsch, O. 1996. *Archipelago of the Contented People? Madang (Freidrich Wilhelmshafen) in 1884*, (trans.) Christine Harding. Madang: Kristen Press.

Fortes, M. 1953. The Structure of Unilineal Descent Groups. *American Anthropologist* 55, 17–41.

———, 1984. 'Foreword.' In *The Garia* by P. Lawrence. Melbourne: Melbourne University Press.

Foster, R.J. 1995. *Social Reproduction and History in Melanesia. Mortuary Ritual, Gift Exchange and Custom in the Tanga Islands*. Cambridge: Cambridge University Press.

Fox, R. 1967. *Kinship and Marriage. An Anthropological Perspective*. Harmondsworth, Middlesex: Pelican.

Gardi, R. 1960. *Tambaran. An Encounter with Cultures in Decline in New Guinea*, (trans.) E. Northcott. London: Constable.

Gell, A. 1975. *Metamorphosis of the Cassawories: Umeda Language, Society and Ritual*. London: The Athalone Press.

——, 1977. 'Magic, Perfume, Dream…' In *Symbols and Sentiments,* (ed.) I.M. Lewis. London: Academic Press.

——, 1995. 'The Language of the Forest: Landscape and Phonological Iconism in Umeda.' In *The Anthropology of Landscape. Perspectives on Place and Space,* (eds) E. Hirsch and M. O'Hanlon. Oxford: Oxford University Press.

——, 1998. *Art and Agency: an anthropological theory.* Oxford: Oxford University Press.

Gibson, J.J. 1979. *The Ecological Approach to Visual Perception.* Boston: Houghton Mifflin.

Gillison, G. 1987. 'Incest and the Atom of Kinship. The Role of the Mother's Brother in a New Guinea Highlands Society.' *Ethos* 15 (2): 166–202.

——, 1993. *Between Culture and Fantasy. A New Guinea Highlands Mythology.* Chicago: The University of Chicago Press.

Goodale, J.C. 1981. 'Siblings as Spouses: The Reproduction and Replacement of Kaulong Society.' In *Siblingship in Oceania. Studies in Kin Relations,* (ed.) Mac Marshall. Ann Arbor: The University of Michigan Press.

Goody, J. 1969. 'The Mother's Brother and the Sister's Son in West Africa.' In *Comparative Studies in Kinship,* (ed.) Jack Goody. London: Routledge & Kegan Paul.

Gourlay, K.A. 1975. *Sound Producing Instruments in Traditional Society: A Study of Esoteric Instruments and Their Role in Male-Female Relations.* (New Guinea Research Bulletin 60). Canberra: Australian National University.

Gow, P. 1991. *Of Mixed Blood: Kinship and History in Peruvian Amazonia.* Oxford: Oxford University Press.

——, 1995. 'Land, People, and Paper in Western Amazonia.' In *The Anthropology of Landscape,* (eds) E. Hirsch and M. O'Hanlon. Oxford: Clarendon Press.

——, 2001. *An Amazonian Myth and its History.* Oxford: Oxford University Press.

Harding, T.G. 1967. *Voyagers of the Vitiaz Strait: A Study of a New Guinea Trade System.* Seattle: University of Washington Press.

——, 1985. *Kunai Men: Horticultural Systems of a Papua New Guinea Society.* (University of California Publications in Anthropology, 16). Berkeley and Los Angeles, California: University of California Press.

Harding, T.G., Counts, D.R and Pomponio, A. 1994. 'Introduction'. In 'Children of Kilobob.' *Pacific Studies* 17 (Special Issue No. 4) December 1994.

Harrison, S. 1990. *Stealing People's Names.* Cambridge: Cambridge University Press.

——, 1992. 'Ritual as Intellectual Property.' *Man (N.S.)* 27: 225–44.

——, 1993. *The Mask of War. Violence, Ritual and Self in Melanesia.* Manchester: Manchester University Press.

Herdt, G. 1999. *Sambia Sexual Culture: Essays from the Field.* Chicago: Chicago University Press.

Hermann, E. 1992. 'The Yali Movement in Retrospect: Rewriting History, Redefining "Cargo Cult".' *Oceania* 63 (Special Issue [1]): 55–71.

Hirsch, E. 1994. 'Between Mission and Market: Events and Images in a Melanesian Society.' *Man (N.S.)* 29: 689–711.

——, 1995a. 'The Coercive Strategies of Aesthetics: Reflections on Wealth, Ritual and Landscape in Melanesia.' *Social Analysis* 38: 64–75.

——, 1995b. 'Landscape: Between Space and Place.' In *The Anthropology of Landscape,* (eds) E. Hirsch and M. O'Hanlon. Oxford: Oxford University Press.

Holy, L. 1996. *Anthropological Perspectives on Kinship.* London: Pluto Press.

Ingold, T. 1992. 'Culture and the Perception of the Environment.' In *Bush Base; Forest Farm. Culture Environment and Development,* (eds) E. Croal and D. Parkin. London: Routledge.

———, 1994a. 'Hunting and Gathering as Ways of Perceiving the Environment', In *Beyond Nature and Culture*, (eds) R. Ellen and K. Fukui. Oxford: Berg.

———, 1994b. 'Introduction to Social Life.' In *Companion Encyclopedia of Anthropolgy: Humanity, Culture and Social Life*, (ed.) T. Ingold. London: Routledge.

———, 1994c. 'The Temporality of the Landscape.' *World Archaeology* (Special Issue: Conceptions of Time in Ancient Society).

———, 1996. 'Growing Plants and Raising Animals: An Anthropological Perspective on Domestication.' In *The Origins and Spread of Agriculture and Pastoralism*, (ed.) D.R. Harris. London: UCL Press.

———, 2000. *The Perception of the Environment. Essays on Livelihood, Dwelling and Skill*. London: Routledge.

Jackson, M. 1989. *Paths Towards a Clearing*. Bloomington and Indianapolis: Indiana University Press.

Jolly, M. and Thomas, N. 1992. 'Introduction.' *Oceania* 62, 241–48.

Kahn, M. 1996. 'Your Place and Mine: Sharing Emotional Landscapes in Wamira, Papua New Guinea.' In *Senses of Place*, (eds) S. Feld and K.H. Basso. Santa Fe: School of American Research Press.

Keesing, R.M. 1992. *Custom and Confrontation*. Chicago: Chicago University Press.

Keesing, R.M. and Tonkinson R. (eds) 1982. 'Reinventing Traditional Culture: The Politics of Kastom in Island Melanesia.' *Mankind* (Special Issue) 13.

Kempf, W. 1992. 'Time and Chronology.' *Oceania* 63 (1): 72–96.

———, 1996. *Das Innere des Ausseren: Ritual, Macht und Historische Praxis bei den Ngaing in Papua New Guinea*. Berlin: Reimer.

Kocher Schmidt, C. 1991. *Of People and Plants. A Botanical Ethnography of Nokopo Village, Madang and Morobe Provices, Papua New Guinea*. Basel: Ethnologishes Seminar der Universität und Museum für Volkerkunde.

Küchler, S. 1987. 'Malangan: Art and Memory in a Melanesian Society.' *Man (N.S.)* 22: 238–55.

———, 1992. 'Making Skins: Malangan and the Idiom of Kinship in Northern New Ireland.' In *Anthropology, Art and Aesthetics*, (eds) J. Coote and A. Shelton, *Anthropology, Art and Aesthetics*. Oxford: Clarendon.

———, 1993. 'Landscape as Memory: The Mapping of Process and its Representation in a Melanesian Society.' In *Landscape: Politics and Perspectives*, (ed.) B. Bender. Oxford: Berg.

Lambert, H. 2000. 'How Karembola Men Become Mothers.' In *Cultures of Relatedness: New Approaches to the Study of Kinship*, (ed.) J. Carsten. Cambridge: Cambridge University Press.

Lane, R. 1971. 'The New Hebrides. Land Tenure without Land Policy.' In *Land Tenure in the Pacific*, (ed.) R. Crocombe. Melbourne: Oxford University Press.

Latour, B. 1993. *We Have Never Been Modern*, (trans.) C. Porter. London: Harvester Wheatsheaf.

Lawrence, P. 1955. *Land Tenure among the Garia. (The Traditional System of a New Guinea People.)* Social Science Monographs, No. 4. Canberra: Australian National University.

———, 1964. *Road Belong Cargo*. Melbourne: Oxford University Press.

———, 1965. 'The Ngaing of the Rai Coast.' In *Gods, Ghosts and Men in Melanesia*, (eds) P. Lawrence and M. Meggitt. Melbourne: Oxford University Press.

———, 1967. (1955) 'Land Tenure among the Garia.' In *Studies in New Guinea Land Tenure*, (eds) P. Lawrence and I. Hogbin. Sydney: Sydney University Press.

———, 1984. *The Garia. The Ethnography of a Traditional Cosmological System in Papua New Guinea*. Singapore: Melbourne University Press.

Lawrence, P. and Hogbin, I. (eds) 1967. *Studies in New Guinea Land Tenure. Three Papers by Ian Hogbin and Peter Lawrence.* Sydney: Sydney University Press.

Leach, E.R. 1956. 'Review of Lawrence (1955).' *Man* 56 (32): 33.

Leach, J. 1997. 'The Creative Land. Kinship and Landscape in Madang Province, Papua New Guinea.' Unpublished Ph.D. thesis. University of Manchester.

———, 1999. 'Singing the Forest. Spirit, Place and Evocation among Reite Villagers of Papua New Guinea.' *Resonance* (Journal of the London Musician's Collective) 7: 24–8.

———, 2002. 'Drum and Voice: Aesthetics and Social Process on the Rai Coast of Papua New Guinea.' (J.B. Donne Prize Essay, Royal Anthropological Institute, 1999). *Journal of the Royal Anthropological Institute* 8: 713–34.

———, n.d.(a) (forthcoming) 'Livers and Lives. Organ extraction narratives on the Rai Coast of Papua New Guinea.' In *Commodities and Identities: The Social Life of Things Revisited*, (eds) P. Geschiere and W. Van Binsbergen. Oklahoma: Duke University Press.

———, n.d.(b) 'Multiple Expectations of Ownership.' Conference presentation: Tradition, Ownership and Knowledge: Transaction and Protection, Motopure Island, Port Moresby, November 2000.

Leavitt, G. 1990. 'Sociobiological Explanations of Incest Avoidance: A Critical Review of Evidential Claims.' *American Anthropologist* 92: 971–93.

Leip, J. 2001. 'Introduction.' In *Locating Cultural Creativity*, (ed.) J. Leip. London: Pluto Press

Lemaire, T. 1997. 'Archaeology Between the Invention and the Destruction of the Landscape.' *Archaeological Dialogues* 4 (1): 5–38.

Lévi-Strauss, C. 1969. *The Elementary Structures of Kinship.* Boston: Beacon Press.

Lindstrom, L. 1993. *Cargo Cult: Strange Stories of Desire from Melanesia and Beyond.* Honolulu: University of Hawai'i Press.

———, 1999. Mambu Phone Home. *Anthropological Forum* 9: 99–106.

Mackenzie, M. 1992. *Androgynous Objects.* Canberra: Gordon & Breech.

Malinowski, B. 1965 [1935]. *Coral Gardens and Their Magic, 1. Soil Tilling and Agricultural Rites in the Trobriand Islands.* London: George Allen & Unwin Ltd.

Mariott, M. 1976. 'Hindu Transactions: Diversity without Dualism.' In *Transaction and Meaning*, (ed.) B. Kapferer. Philadelphia: Philadelphia Institute for the Study of Human Issues.

McAlpine, J.R. 1953/4. 'Saidor/Madang Patrol Report.' Australian Trusteeship Administration.

McSwain, R. 1977. *The Past and Future People. Tradition and Change on a New Guinea Island.* Melbourne: Oxford University Press.

Merleau-Ponty, M. 1964. 'Eye and Mind.' In *The Primacy of Perception, and Other Essays on Phenomenological Psychology, the Philosophy of Art, History and Politics*, (ed.) J.M. Edie, (trans.) C. Dallery. Evanston Ill.: Northwestern University Press.

Mihalic, F. 1971. *The Jacaranda Dictionary and Grammar of Melanesian Pidgin.* Milton, Queensland: Jacaranda Press.

Mimica, J. 1988. *Intimations of Infinity.* London: Berg.

———, 1991. 'The Incest Passions: An Outline of the Logic of Iqwaye Social Organisation.' *Oceania* 62 (1+2): 34–57, 81–113.

Morauta, L. 1974. *Beyond the Village. Local Politics in Madang, Papua New Guinea.* London: Athalone Press.

Morgan, L.H. 1970. *Systems of Consanguinity and Affinity in the Human Family.* Washington, DC: Smithsonian Institution Press.

Mosko, M.S. 1983. 'Conception, Deconception and Social Structure in Bush Mekeo Culture.' *Mankind* 14 (1): 24–32.

————, 1985. *Quadripartite Structures. Categories, Relations and Homologies in Bush Mekeo Culture.* Cambridge: Cambridge University Press.

Munn, N.D. 1986. *The Fame of Gawa. A Symbolic Study Value Transformation in a Massim (Papua New Guinea) Society.* Cambridge: Cambridge University Press.

Murdock, G.P. 1949. *Social Structure.* New York: Macmillan.

Niles, D. 1992. 'Konggap, Kap and Tambaran: Music of the Yupno/Nankina Area in Relation to Neighbouring Groups.' In *Abschied von der Vergangenheit*, (ed.) Jurg Wassmann. Berlin: Deitrich Reimer.

————, 1997. 'Editor's Introduction.' In *Songs of Spirits: An Ethnography of Sounds in a Papua New Guinea Society*, Y. Yamada. Boroko: Institute of Papua New Guinea Studies.

Nombo, P. and Leach, J. 2000. 'Reite Plants. Medicinal and Ritual Plants Used by Nekgini Speaking People of the Rai Coast of Papua New Guinea.' Cambridge mss.

Parkin, D. 1991. *Sacred Void: Spatial Images of Work and Ritual among the Girama of Kenya.* Cambridge: Cambridge University Press.

Parkin, R. 1997. *Kinship: An Introduction to the Basic Concepts.* Oxford: Blackwell.

Peletz, M. 1995. Kinship Studies in Late Twentieth Century Anthropology. *Annual Review of Anthropology* 24: 343–372.

Pomponio, A. 1992. *Seagulls Don't Fly into the Bush. Cultural Identity and Development in Melanesia.* Wadsworth Modern Anthropology Library. Belmont, California: Wadsworth.

————, 1994. 'Namor's Odyssey: Mythical Metaphors in Siassi.' *Pacific Studies* 17: 53–91.

Radcliffe-Brown, A.R. 1922. *The Andaman Islanders.* Cambridge: Cambridge University Press.

————, 1952a. *Structure and Function in Primitive Society.* London: Routledge & Kegan Paul.

————, 1952b. 'The Mother's Brother in Southern Africa.' In *Structure and Function Primitive Society*, (ed.) A.R. Radcliffe-Brown. London: Routledge & Kegan Paul.

Rappaport, R.A. 1971. 'Nature, Culture and Ecological Anthropology.' In *Man, Culture and Society*, (ed.) H.L. Shapiro. Oxford: Oxford University Press.

Rapport, N. 2000. '"Criminals by Instinct": On the "Tragedy" of Social Stucture and the "Violence" of Individual Creativity', in *Meanings of Violence* (eds) G. Aijmer and J. Abbink. Oxford: Berg.

Reigle, R. 1995. 'Sound of the Spirits, Song of the Myna.' In 'New Guinea Ethnomusicology Conference: Proceedings', (ed.) Robert Reigle, *Occasional Papers in Pacific Ethnomusicology* 4: Auckland.

Reiner, H. and Wagner, H. (eds) 1986. *The Lutheran Church in Papua New Guinea. The First Hundred Years 1886–1986.* Adelaide: Lutheran Publishing House.

Rodman, M. 1992. 'Empowering Place: Multilocality and Multivocality.' *American Anthropologist* 94(3): 640–56.

Rubin, D.C. 1988. 'Go for the Skill.' In *Remembering Reconsidered: Ecological and Traditional Approaches to the Study of Memory*, (eds) U. Neisser and E. Winograd. Cambridge: Cambridge University Press.

Schieffelin, E. 1976. *The Sorrow of the Lonely and the Burning of the Dancers.* New York: St. Martin's Press.

Schneider, D.M. 1968. *American Kinship: A Cultural Account.* Englewood Cliffs, New Jersey: Prentice Hall.

————, 1984. *A Critique of the Study of Kinship.* Ann Arbor: University of Michigan Press.

Schweitzer, P. (ed.) 2000. *Dividends of Kinship. Meanings and Uses of Social Relatedness.* London: Routledge.

Stafford, C. 2000. 'Chinese Patriliny and the Cycles of *Yang* and *Laiwang*.' In *Cultures of Relatedness*, (ed.) J. Carsten. Cambridge: Cambridge University Press.

Steward, J.H. 1955. *Theory of Culture Change*. Urbana: University of Illinois Press.

Stoller, P. 1989. *The Taste of Ethnographic Things. The Senses in Anthropology*. Philadelphia: University of Pennsylvania Press.

Strathern, A. 1972. *One Father, One Blood*. Canberra: Australian National University Press.

———, 1973. 'Kinship, Descent and Locality: Some New Guinea Examples.' In *The Character of Kinship*, (ed.) Jack Goody. Cambridge: Cambridge University Press.

Strathern, M. 1972. *Women in Between: Female Roles in a Male World*. London: Seminar [Academic] Press.

———, 1980. 'No Nature, No Culture: The Hagen Case.' In *Nature, Culture, Gender* (eds) C. MacCormack and M. Strathern. Cambridge: Cambridge University Press.

———, 1984. 'Marriage Exchanges: A Melanesian Comment.' *Annual Review of Anthropology* 13: 41–73.

———, 1988. *The Gender of the Gift. Problems with Women and Problems with Society in Melanesia*. Berkeley and Los Angeles: University of California Press.

———, 1991. *Partial Connections*, ASAO Special Publication 3. Savage, Maryland: Rowman & Littlefield.

———, 1992a. *After Nature: English Kinship in the Late Twentieth Century*. (Lewis Henry Morgan Lecture Series). Cambridge: Cambridge University Press.

———, 1992b. 'Parts and Wholes. Refiguring Relationships in a Post-Plural World.' In *Conceptualising Society*, (ed.) A. Kuper. London: Routledge.

———, 1998. 'Divisions of Interest and Languages of Ownership.' In *Property Relations. Renewing the Anthropological Tradition*, (ed.) C. Hann. Cambridge: Cambridge University Press.

———, 2001. 'Money Appearing and Disappearing.' Paper presented at 'The Commodity and its Alternatives' Girton College, Cambridge.

Stürtzenhofecker, G. 1998. *Times Enmeshed: Gender, Space and History among the Duna of Papua New Guinea*. Stanford: Stanford University Press.

Telban, B. 1998. *Dancing Through Time. A Sepik Cosmology*. Oxford: Clarendon Press.

Thomas, K. 1984. *Man and the Natural World: Changing Attitudes in England 1500–1800*. Harmondsworth: Penguin Books.

Tilley, C. 1994. *A Phenomenology of Landscape: Places, Paths and Monuments*. Oxford: Berg.

Tuzin, D.F. 1980. *The Voice of the Tambaran. Truth and Illusion in Ilahita Arapesh Religion*. Berkeley: University of California Press.

———, 1991. 'The Cryptic Brotherhood of Big Men and Great Men in Ilahita.' In *Big Men and Great Men. Personifications of Power in Melanesia*, (eds) M. Godellier and M. Strathern. Cambridge: Cambridge University Press.

Van Trease, H. 1987. *The Politics of Land in Vanuatu from Colony to Independence*. Fiji: Institute of Pacific Studies of the University of the South Pacific.

Vivieros de Castro, E. 2001. 'GUT Feelings about Amazonia: Potential Affinity and the Construction of Kinship.' In L. Rival & N. Whitehead (eds), *Beyond the Visible and the Material: The Ameridianization of Society in the Work of Peter Rivière*. Oxford: Oxford University Press.

Wagner, R. 1967. *The Curse of Souw*. Chicago: Chicago University Press.

———, 1972. 'Incest and Identity: A Critique and Theory on the Subject of Exogamy and Incest Prohibition.' *Man (N.S.)* 7: 601–13.

———, 1974. 'Are There Social Groups in the New Guinea Highlands?' In *Frontiers of Anthropology*, (ed.) M. J. Leaf. New York: D. van Nostrand Company.

——, 1975. *The Invention of Culture*. Englewood Cliffs: Prentice Hall.

——, 1977a. 'Analogic Kinship: A Daribi Example.' *American Ethnologist* 4: 623–42.

——, 1977b. 'Scientific and Indigenous Papuan Conceptions of the Innate: A Semiotic Critique of the Ecological Perspective.' In *Subsistence and Survival*, (eds) T. Bayliss-Smith and R. Feacham. London: Academic Press.

——, 1986a. *Asiwinarong*. Princetown: Princetown University Press.

——, 1986b. *Symbols that Stand for Themselves*. Chicago: University of Chicago Press.

——, 1987. 'Figure-Ground Reversal among the Barok.' In *Assemblage of Spirits: Idea and Image in New Ireland*, (ed.) L. Lincoln. New York: Geo Braziller with The Minneapolis Institute of Arts.

——, 2001. 'Condensed Mapping: Myth and the Folding of Space/Space and the Folding of Myth.' In *Emplaced Myth: Space, Narrative and Knowledge in Aboriginal Australia and Papua New Guinea*, (eds) A. Rumsey and J.F. Weiner. Honolulu: University of Hawai'i Press.

Wassmann, J. 1993. 'Worlds in Mind. The Experience of the Outside World in a Community of the Finisterre Range in Papua New Guinea.' *Oceania* 63: 117–45.

Webster, S. 1982. 'Dialogue and Fiction in Ethnography.' *Dialectical Anthropology* 7(2): 91–114.

Weiner, J.F. 1985. 'Affinity and Cross Cousin Terminology Among the Foi.' *Social Analysis* 17: 93–112.

——, 1988. *The Heart of the Pearl Shell. The Mythological Dimensions of Foi Sociality*. Berkeley and Los Angeles: University of California Press.

——, 1991. *The Empty Place: Poetry, Space and Being among the Foi of Papua New Guinea*. Bloomington: Indiana University Press.

——, 1994. 'Myth.' In *Companion Encyclopedia of Anthropology: Humanity, Culture and Social Life*, (ed.) T. Ingold. London: Routledge.

——, 1995. *The Lost Drum. The Myth of Sexuality in Papua New Guinea and Beyond*. Madison, Wisconsin: The University of Wisconsin Press.

Werbner, R.P. 1989. *Ritual Passage, Sacred Journey. The Process and Organisation of Religious Movement*. Washington: Smithsonian Institution Press.

Whitehead, A.N. 1929. *Process and Reality*. New York: Macmillan.

——, 1938. *Modes of Thought*. New York: Macmillan.

Worsley, P. 1957. *And the Trumpet Shall Sound: A Study of 'Cargo Cults' in Melanesia*. London: McGibbon & Kee.

Wurm, S. and Hattori, S. 1981. *Language Atlas, Pacific Area*, Pacific Linguistics Series C, 66. Canberra: Pacific Linguistics.

Index

A

affiliation, 147–8, 155

affines/affinity, 54n3, 97–99, 128–30, 145–55, 194

agency, xviii, 23, 40, 79–80, 86, 145, 169–70, 204–5, 212–4

and structure, 25

and growth, 95, 99–100

agnation, 46–51, 117–8, 213

agricultural development, 15–16, 42

aibika (and garden magic), 106, 121

Aisir (tambaran) 181–2

analogy between taro and children, 104–6, 115, 118

analytic domains, 23, 28–30, 53, 71, 93–95

ancestor, 22, 40, 43, 77, 94, 118–9, 169, 188–9, 191n7, 192n19, 193–4

ancestry, 30, 48, 117

Apirella Mt., 8

Asang (Village), 8, 39, 103, 119, 160

Astrolabe Bay, 3, 13

atom of kinship, 149

audience, 98, 153–4, 182, 206

Austin, J. L., 25, 200

Australian administration, *see* colonial administration

autopoeisis/autopoetic, 75–77, 79, 217

B

backbone, 133, 137, 162–5, 184

Bagasin Hills, 26, 36

Bateson, G., 33, 96

betel nut/areca palm, 6, 16, 18n8, 81, 96, 129, 138, 163, 177, 195

Biliau, 13

bilum, (men's), 121, 137: (women's), 96, 108

biological/social dichotomy, 22–24, 28, 49–53, 69–73

and incest, 84, 85–87

biological theory, 29, 89n4, 216

birth, 115, 131–3, 135, 138, 147, 156n5

and death, 187

of social group, 43

of taro/yam, 107, 165

birua, 44, 68, 153

bisnis and kastom, 8, 100–101

(tok pisin for issue, children, concern), 176

blood (*asurung*), 46, 50, 87, 91, 115, 117–8, 132, 146, 188, 212

body

and place, 208, 211–5

and sorcery, 188–9, 193–4

decoration of, 133–6, 148

internal differentiation of, 28, 115, 128, 147–50, 185–6, 206, 212–3, 215

palem as, 25, 31, 135, 159–68, 186

payments, 88n6, 98, 128–9, 135, 139–40, 166–7, 191n7, 208

rights over, 157n19, 186

social, 101, 115, 147, 170

transformation of, 123, *see* initiation, growth, *see also* palem

bones 21, 132, 135, 137, 185–9, 171, 187–8

and custom 184–5
and heat, 54n11
and power, 125n19, 187–9, 193–4
and wealth, 117, 134–5, 137, 148–9, 194
of palem, 21, 162–8, 185, 215
of places, 22, 123, 165–8, 175, 188, 213
placement of, 67, 172–3, 175–6, 186–8
British Museum, 11, 125n14
bridewealth, 64–68, 149–51, *see also* palem,
wealth

C
cargo cult, xvii, xix, 15, 26–27, 76
Carsten, J., 22–24, 51
cash/money, 8–11, 16, 19n14, 41
cash crops, *see* agricultural development
Catholic church, 5, 14, 19n9, 42
Cézanne, P., 201–2
childbirth, 66, 94, 115, 131–2, 134, 148–9
children, 14, 18, 47–48, 60–61, 82, 128–43, 213
    and growth, 29–30, 94, 96, 99, 115–6,
        128, 144, 148, 155–6
    and substance, 117–8, 128, 157n19
    and taro, 91, 93, 103–4, 106–8, 111–13,
        120–3, 165
    first born, 128–31, 138, 139, 156n1
    payments for, 98, 117, 127–143, 148–9,
        151, 154–5, 166, 170–73, 190n5
    spirit children (*kaapu simang*) 182
Chinese taro, 110
Chowning, A., 170
classification, 85–86
climate 3–4, 103
    winds, 4, 102
coconut, 190n6
cognatic kinship, 24–5, 27, 48–51, 170, 216
cold (spiritual state), 124n10, 131, 187–9
colonial administration, 12–16, 26, 34, 36–7,
        39–40, 45
community school (Ambuling), 8, 11
community work, 10–11, 34, 54n1, 101
complexity, 33, 49–53, 127, 214–6
composition of songs, 180–3
conception, 29–30, 99, 115, 149, 212
container/containment, 30, 98–100, 115–6,
        123, 147, 151, 155–6, 166, 206–8
    body, 93–4, 119, 128, 186–7

environment, 29–30, 127
    house as, 151–3, 172
cosmology, 73–7, 84
creativity, xvii–xix, 22–26, 67, 75–77, 84,
        93–5, 211–2
    and palem, 53, 122, 159, 207
    and place, 117–9, 186, 191n7, 197
cross-cousin, 62–67
crustaceans (*kindam*), 17, 124n10, 133
crying (*tangawakating*), 152–4, 192n23

D
dancing (*sare*), 122, 151–4, 157n21, 168,
        175–80, 182–3, 192n21, 194, 200 *see
        also* Sare'keiting
Daribi (PNG people), 91, 159
death, 172, 186–8
decomposition of body, 187–8, 192n22
Descartes, R., 197, 202–3
descent, 27–28, 30, 44–52, 91, 117, 128, *see
        also* lineality
destructive power, 188–9, 194
dividual, 28, 115, 161, 211–2, 215, *see also*
        individual and society
doors, importance of, 43, 47, 101, 115, 122,
        147, 161, 167, *see also* 'one door'
dowry, 182
dry, *see* wet/dry contrast
dual sexed productivity, 82–84, 87n1, 93–95,
        108–9, 114–5, 144, 212–3

E
education, 97, 117
elders authority, 10, 45, 66–8, 88n4
emergence, 25, 127–142, 145–146
    and growth/after seclusion, 96–97, 115–7,
        148
    of social person/group, 43, 45, 133–4,
        139–40, 145–8, 151
emotion, 21, 70–1, 152–4, 180–3
energetic stimuli, 203
environment, 27, 29–31, 53, 196–7, 203
essence, 25, 29–30, *see also* substance
ethnography, 26, 29, 198, 201
exchange, 66–67, 91, 116, 122–3, 127–156,
        160–1, 169–70, 172–3, 184, 211–2
    and marriage, xviii, 21, 74–5, 160–1

competitive, 134
of like-for-like in initiation, 133–5, 137, 148
of perspectives, 38, 146–8, 151, 155
return payment (*kaiyung*), 173
sociology of, 149, 170–72

F
father, 29, 98, 116–8, 132–3, 136–8, 149–50, 187
and lineality, 30, 45–48, 117–8
and mother, 25, 62, 139, 147, 156n5
Feld, S., 180, 198, 203–4, 209n2
field of nurture/relations, 30–31, 106, 116–7, 127, 212, 215
fieldwork, 8–12, 26
relations with hosts, 9–12
flesh, 21, 159–177, 215
foetal, 138, 187
Foi (PNG people), 79, 147–9, 154, 183
food taboos, 96–7, 106, 111, 114, 129, 133, 168, 188
form (of person), 145–9, 151, 156, 187–8, 207–8
Fortes, M., 26–28, 51
Foster, R., 100–101
Fox, R., 72–73
fragrance, 135, 177, 201, 208
Freud, S., 73
funeral/mourning, 135, 170, 186–7, 192nn22–23
Fuyuge (PNG people), 169

G
garden, 7, 12, 91–95, 99–125, 128, 132, 136–7, 162, 214, 218
year, 102–4, 114
myths, 107–8, 119–23, 124n2
ritual, 104–114
wating, 104–8
produce, 21, 24, 101–2, 110, 144, 168–9
Garia (PNG people), 26–29, 36, 39–40, 49–53, 91, 101, 117–8, 211–2
garamut, 97–99
Gawa (PNG people), 207–8
Gayap Makon, 107–8, 153, 195
Gell, A., 154, 192n18, 196, 203, 206, 209n5

gender, 21, 57, 62, 70–71, 86, 87n1, 93–115, 118–124, 124n8, 149–51, 169, 175, 194, 212–5, 217–8
differentiation, 66, 82–85, 167, 186, 194, 200–1
roles, 60–61, *see also* initiation, love-magic, marriage, movement, tambaran
genealogical model, 23–25, 29–31, 46, 49–53, 62–64, 68, 71, 85–7, 91, 117–8, 127–8, 145, 155, 190, 194, 211–2, 214–6
and kinship terminology, 46–7, 85–86, 71–72, 75, 194
generation, 24, 53, 57, 70–71, 76–77, 93–94, 116, 138, 185–6, 194–5, 207–8, 215–6
of persons, xiii–xix, 21, 30–31, 117, 122–3, 201
of villages, 38–39, 43
of places, 116, 193–5
generations (differentiation of), 62, 66, 75, 138, 144, 150–1
generative model, 38–39, 44
German traders, planters, 12
ghosts, 10, 94, 195–6, 205–6
Gibson J.J., 202–3, 209n3
Gillison, G., 93, 144, 149–51
Gimi (PNG people),149–51, 156n7
Goody, J., 143–5
Gorogor (*luhu*), 67, 88n6, 93, 104–6, 124n6
Gow, P., 76, 80, 207–8, 211–2, 217
growth, 91–102, 106–7, 115–6, 122–3, 180, 193–4, 212–3
and identity, 101, 116–8, 144, 188
and recognition, 148, 155–6, 175
and spirits, 95–7, 104, 106–9, 119–22, 168–9, 175–6, 180, 183–6
of name/renown, 151, 170, 201
of people, 29–31, 127–8, 132–3, 138–9, 146, 148, 156n2, 188–9, 207
of plants, 101–113, 118–9, 124n3, *see also* seclusion, *ting*

H
hair (see also severance), 129, 132, 134–5, 148, 220
hamlet groups, 39–42, 44–45, 59–61
Harding, T., 4, 77–78, 124n3

haus tambaran (*passae*), 38, 41–43, 47,
     54n3n14, 97, 121, 137, 167–9, 171–5,
     177, 179–80
harvest, 114
hearing and vision, 196, 201–5
heat (in sorcery), 187–9, 194, *see also* cold
heavy foods, 97, 132, *see also* food taboos
Hirsch, E., 169
     on landscape, 197–200
     on aesthetics, 208
houses/dwellings, 8–9, 16, 38
     female seclusion in, 96–7
     and bush, 115, 131–2, 146–7
     as container, 187
households, 100–101, 109–10, 115, 146, *see
     also* door, 'one door'
Hungeme, 104–6, 128

I

identity, 82–3, 186, 211–4, *see also* growth,
     visibility, place, and gender
incest, 68–85, 88n8, 194
independence (national), xix, 15, 19n12, 36
individual and society, 27–9, 49–53, 72, 84,
     86–7, 100, 217–8
inheritance
     of land, 45–66
     of substance, 91, 118
initiation, 61, 64, 93–94, 98–99, 129, 143,
     156n8, 169, 188
     concealment, 99, 134, 148
     education during, 93, 97, 117, 135–8
     female, 88n3, 96–7
     male, 44, 96, 134–8, 146, 175–6
influenza, 13, 54n6
Ingold, T., 23, 116, 206, 211
inspiration, 83, 140, 175–180, 183–4
intergenerational obligations, 138–40, 150
internal differentiation, 144, 157n18, 215
     of palem, 144, 206, 212–4
     of marriage partners, 115, 144
     of person, 28, 147, 155

J

Japanese occupation, 14
jawbone, 187

K

kaapu, 94–99, 176, 184–6, *see also* initiation,
     music and *patuki*, 176, 183
kastom, 7–12, 64, 68–9, 162, 206, 214, 217–8
     bisnis and, 100–101
     definition of, xviii–xix
Kerimang Nombo, 135–9
kinship terminology, 46, 71–75, 85–87, 194–5
     Nekgini, 47–49, 57–67
     see also, agnation, affinity, gender,
         genealogical model, descent, sex
Klee, P., 202–203
knowledge (*patuki*), 76–7
     of plants, 104–5
     of spirits, 95, 168–9, 183–5 *see also* initiation
     representational compared to Nekgini,
         195–209, 86–7
Küchler, S., 172–3, 214

L

labour migration, 12–13
Lagap plantation, 3, 5, 16–17
land, 207–8, 212, *see also* place
     and kinship, 28–31, 49
     and spirits, 177, 184–6
     and substance, 114–8, 213, 215

landscape, 194–201
     and representation, 86, 196, 198, 206, 208
language, 8, 54n9
     and representation, 85–86, 194 – 6
Lawrence, P., 26–29, 49–53, 211–2
     on myth, 77–8
Leach, E., 26, 145
leaders, 18n3, 34, 44, 66
Leip, J., 216–7
Lemaire, T., 196–8
Lévi-Strauss, C., 72–4, 128, 144–5, 217
life-cycle, 23, 131–43, 186–7
     payments, 127–30
     puberty, 61
lime gourd (*koro*), 156n4
lineality, 46–52, 117, 127–8, 145, 149, *see also*
     father, descent, Unilineal descent
     group model
local government council, 10–11, 15, 34

loss, 79
  in marriage, 22, 83–4
  of knowledge/power, 13
love-magic (*marila*), 21–2, 44, 61, 70–71,
    83–84, 178, 214
Lutheran mission/Rhenish mission, 13

M
magic, 152–3, 184, 192n18, *see also* love
    magic
Mai'anderi (taro mother), 106–8, 113, 118–9,
    123–4, 163, 165
Maibang, 6, 8, 40
malangan, 98, 172
male cult (*aignu'kaapu*), 14, 98, 122–3,
    168–9, *see also* haus tambaran, initia-
    tion, *kaapu*, garamut
Manambu, 44
Manup/Kilibob myth (*pomo*), 77–85, 131,
    184
marila, *see* love-magic
marriage, *see* Chapter 3, *see also* love magic,
    palem, internal differentiation
  and burial, 151, 186
  and gender, 21, 26, 67, 84–5
  arrangement, 66–67
mediation, 207–8
memory of deceased, 154, 172, 182–3
menopause, 169
menstruation, 96–7
Merleau-Ponty, M., 195–6, 201–5
millenarian, 15, 34, *see also* cargo cult
Mimica, J., 73–6, 217
mission/missionary influence, 12–14, 41–42,
    190n4
missionisation, 8, 12–14
modernity, 54n8, 78
  and creativity, 217–8
  and conception of space, 197
Molima (PNG people), 170, 172
Morgan, L.H., 23, 85
Mosko, M., 188–9
mother, 82, 131–2
  payment to, 139, 143
  tambaran (*kaapu neng*), 176, 206
  taro, 93, 103–4, *see also* Mai'anderi
mother's brother, 25, 127–52, 194

  and growth, 148, 188
  duties towards, 97, 133–40
  in anthropological literature, 127–8, 143–5
mourning 135, 186–7, 192n3
movement 45, 91–2, 154, 206
  importance of to gender/kinship,
    118–119, 167, 175, 206
  metaphor for emotion, 70, 152–5
multiplication (of entities), 53, 217
Munn, N., 207
Murdock, G.P., 57
museum collection, 10, 11, 125n14
music, 176, 191n13, *see also* sound
musical spirits 151–3, 176
myth, 76–85, 107–8, 118–123, 217–8
mythopoeisis, 76

N
Nalasis palem, 39, 45, 47, 135
names, 117, 138–9, 151
  and tunes, 183–6
  as spells/*paru*, 124n2, 169, 184
  avoidance, 59, 55n18, 62, 171
  of places, 33–34, 39, 41–43
naming and palem, 47–48
Nangu Wineduma, 171–2
N'dau language, 8
Nekgini epistemology, 86–7, 205–7
Ngaing language, 8
Niles, D., 94–5, 159, 192n19

O
observer, 197–200, *see also* audience
'one door', 101, 115, 161–2, 171–2
  and death and placement, 172
origin
  myth, 78–85
  of landforms, 38–40
  of taro and yam, 92–93, 118–122
ownership, 214, 216
  of land, 49

P
palem, 20–21, 31, 45–9, 156n9, 159–86, 195,
    206–7, 213
  and person, 115, 118, 128, 213
  and settlement patterns, 34–49

and yating, 43–4
as sibling groups/bodies of kin, 60, 60–65,
    70, 130–1, 134–5, 143–4, 150–1,
    170–73
construction of, 77, 123, 159–170
definition of, 53n3n14
dismantling, 173–9
generation of, 44, 47–9, 69, 84–5, 117–8,
    161–2, 218
internal/external divisions of, 82, 115–6,
    144, 206, 213–4
naming, 47–48, 151
Palota Konga, 110, 162, 170–1, 185
Parkin, D., 199
paru (spells), 124n2, 169, 184–5
passae (haus tambaran), 38, 41–2, 121, 137,
    172
paternity, 116–8, 143, 146–7, 150
paths, 110–113
patrilineage, 45–51, *see also* lineality
Patrol Report, 14–15
patuki, 76–7, 169, 175, 184, 217–8
peace makers, 44, 93, *see also* gorogor
people as contained, 30, 99, 115–6, 147, 156,
    206–8
perception, Chapter 7
    and hearing, 203 –205
    and vision, 200–204
performance, 151–4, 204–5
    and representation, 200
    of place, 176–183, 185, 204, 208
    vs. performative, 25, 200
perfume 177–8, *see also* fragrance
person
    boundaries of, 211–3
    production of, 17–18, 29–31, 53, 116–7,
        185, 216
    specification of, 145, 172, 194, 211
    value of, 17–18
personhood, 28, 53, 140, 146–8, 151
perspective, 53, 145, 155–6, 200–1
Peter Nombo, 6, 145, 155–6
phenomenology, 202, *see also* Merleau–Ponty
pigs, 10, 113
    raw/cooked in exchange, 47, 67, 129, 134,
        143, 157n14, 167–8
Pinabin Sisau, 127

Piro, 31n5, 207–8, 211
place, 29–31, 205–6, 211–4
    and bones, 182–3
    and identity, 172–3
    and spirits, 182–3, 185–6
    and women, 149
    emergence of, xviii, 31, 31n5, 40, 48, 122,
        199
    names of, 183–6
    and history, 208, 214
placenta, 131
plantations, 3, 13, 16
poison (*mernung*), 45, 188–9
pollution/dirt (*samu*), 131, 134, 138, 188
pomo myth, 79–85, 131, 184
Porer Nombo, 36, 44, 95, 162, 165
post-colonial administration, 5, 15, 34
post-partum restrictions, 132
power, xviii, 19n11, 70, 99, 122, 137–8, 154,
    193–4, 217–8
    and bones, 173, 187–8
    and names, 45, 77, 184
    and places, 22, 122, 185–6
    and spirits, 95, 99–100, 116, 175, 185, *see
        also* garden, knowledge
pre-colonial, 4
present (*kalawung*), 129, 134, 167
procreation, 85, 145–9, 189

R
Radcliffe-Brown, A.R., 73, 94, 127–8, 143–5
recognition, 26, 30, 66, 70–71, 116, 133–4,
    146–8, 151–2, 201–5, *see also* visibility,
    emergence
religious/secular, 95, 101–2
regeneration, 30, 117–8
Regiana bird of paradise, 191
Reite, 6–8, 33–41, palem, 43–44, 45, yating,
    38, community, 9–10, 44
representation, 86, 194, 206, 208
    and landscape, 195–208
Ripia palem/yating, 34
Ririnbung, 8, 38
ritual, 101, making palem, 168–83
ritual offices, 44–5
Road Belong Cargo, 26–27, 78, *see also*
    Lawrence, P.

S

sago, 9

Saidor, 1, 3–6, 13–16

Sarangama, 14–15, 34, 54nn6–9, 162, 170–2

sare'keiting (decorated dancing and singing),
140, 152–4, 175–86, 204–6, *see also*
performance, dancing

Saruk, 8, 34, 38–39, 42, 47–8, 190n2

Schneider, D., 23, 85

secrecy/secret knowledge, 14, 70, 96, 159

security circle (Lawrence), 27, 40, 50, 117

Seng River, 7–8, 41

senses, 202, *see also* hearing, vision

separate dwellings (men and women), 38,
41–42

separation, 66, 75–76, 83–85, 144–5, 212

   of gender, 42, 83–84, 218

   in marriage and exchange, 67–68, 84–5, 150

   of places, 118, 161, 172

   as generation, 184–6

Serieng, 8, 39, 186

sex, 88n3

   abstinence from, 65–66, 138, 168

   and gender, 60–61, 82–4, 87n1

   and procreation, 95–97

   and terminology, 58–59, 62–66, 68, 70,
72–5, 194, *see also* incest, gender

sexual division of labour, 61

shoot/growth, 38, 105–7, 180, *see also*
growth, *ting*

sibling

   elder/ younger sibling, 59–61, 80–82,
130–1, 156n4, 190n6

   marriage, 74

   order and hierarchy, 130–133, 156n4

   and palem, 43–4

   relations between, 60–62

sickness, 97, 106, 114, 132, 176, 179

singsing, 151, 175–82

singularity/multiplicity

   of bodies/persons, 28, 172–3, 193–4

   of places, 188–9

Siriman Kumbukau (Kiap), 18n3, 93, 119,
124, 156n4, 180–1

sister's child, role in funeral, 187

skin, 74, 80–81, 108, 111, 133–138, 165–6,
172, 208, 214

   dye for, 133–5, 137–8

social/biological dichotomy, *see*
biological/social dichotomy

social organisation, 33–53

society, 26–29, 49

Songhay (West African people – sound/sor-
cery), 201–3

Sorang, 8, 119, 135, 171, 190

sorcery, 15, 18n8, 44–45, 88n4, 187–9

sound

   in perception, 201–5

   of *kaapu*, 180, 183

soundscape (Feld), 204

spells (*paru*), 124n2, 169, 184–5, *see also* names

spirits, 91, 93–8, 100, 110–17, 157n22, 168,
184–6, 192n21, 194, *see also* kaapu,
tambaran

   dwelling places of (*mundutor*), 17, 36, 40,
54n14, 168–73, 175, 177, 179

   voices of, 95–8, 151–4, 175–83,
191nn13–14

   composition of, 180–3

stars, 106

steel tools, 12, 16, 193

Stoller, P., 201–4

Strathern, A., 51–2, 149

Strathern, M., 27–8, 52–3, 60, 117–8, 144,
147, 155–6, 207, 213–6

structural functionalism, 27–28, 51

subsistence, 16–17, 31, 116

substance, 28–31, 46, 71, 87, 99, 114–8,
212–3

   and payments, 127–8, 146–50, 155

   continuity of, 117–8, 172–3

T

taboos

   on food, 97, 104–7, 111, 129, 133

   on water (*kundeing*), 114, 137, 188–9,
193–4

   on sexual contact *see* sex, initiation

tambaran of childbirth (women's), 95–7

tambaran of the sea, 139–40

tambaran of the water (men's), 14, 116,
 157n21, 159, 163–9, 190n3,
 192nn19–21
 and growth, 93–5, 97–8, 122–3, 148, 194
 and singsing, 151–3, 175–85
 as love magic, 151
 feeding of, 175
 in myth, 119–22, *see also* kaapu, spirits,
 ancestor
Tanga, 100
taro, 92–93, 123–4, 161–3, 168–9
 child, 103–4, 109, 113, 165
 harvest, 113–4
 male/female varieties, 104, 125n17, 132
 myths of origin, 107–8, 112–3, 118–22
 proceedure for growing, 101–114, 183–4,
  see also growth, children, garden, harvest
ting (shoot, growth), 38, 104, 106–7, 175–6,
 180
torr posts, 140, 142, 177–9, 182
trade, 4, 12
transformations/severance from past state,
 135, 146–8 *see also* taboo, initiation
tunes (spirit voices), 94, 183–8, *see also* composition, spirits, tambaran, *kaapu*
turum maliemung, 162–3
 as translation of kastom, xviii, 206

U
Umeda (Papua New Guinea people), 203,
 206
umbilical cord, 131
Unilineal descent group model, 27–28
Urangari Kumbukau, 13, 107–8, 156n4, 169

V
view
 as perspective on other's identity, 82–83,
  98–99, 155
 in landscape, 196–200
violence (aspect of marriage/love magic), 22,
 70–71, 84, 123
visibility, (social, as analytic description), 60,
 74, 88n11, 145–7, 151–2, 200–1,
 204–5
vision, 106, 196, 200
 and hearing, 202–205

Vitiaz Straits, 1, 4, 7
Vivieros de Castro, E., 46

W
Wagner, R., 71–4, 91, 106, 128, 145
warriors (*salap-ai*), 44
water, *see* taboo, tambaran
wating, *see* garden
Wau/Bulolo, 13
 wau, as kinship term, *see* mother's brother
wealth (*palieng*), 17–18, 21, 74, 100, 115–6,
 129, 134–6, 148–9, 173, 212–3, *see also*
 bones, palem, payments
weather magic, 103, 106, 114, 125n19,
 187–8,
Webster, S., *see* ethnography
Weiner, J., 76, 78–79, 147–8, 183, 201
Werbner, R., 206
West New Britain, 4, 60
wet/dry contrast, 21, 96, 99, 137, 187–9, 193
Winedum, 162, 165–7, 171
Whitehead, A.N., 25, 218
women
 as objects of men's exchanges, 149–51
 identity and marriage, 150–51
 and place, 149
 raucous play (*rauang*), 96–7
 relation to land, 213
 women's tambaran (*kaapu parieng*), 95–7
 see also, affinity, childbirth, gender, initiation, palem, sex, tambaran, kinship
 terminology
wooden bowl (*utung*), 4, 125n13, 129, 132
work (Nekgini concept), xviii, 24, 30, 64, 95,
 99, 102, 116, 150–1, 155, 186–7, 207
World War II, 12, 17, 40
Worsley P., 76

Y
Yabob, 4
Yali Singina, xvii, 14, 15, 26
Yakai River, 7, 13, 41, 54n6
yam
 growing, 104, 109–10, 124n3, 132
 in myth, 165
Yamui, 132
Yawaspiring palem, 31, 39, 45, 92, 104